GW01606639

A-4 Skyhawk

'Heinemann's Hot Rod'

TA-4Js of VC-8 break for landing at NAS Key West in October 2000. The 'Redtails' were the last of 150 Navy and Marine units to fly the Skyhawk and the only one to take it into the Twenty-first Century.

Author

A-4 Skyhawk

'Heinemann's Hot Rod'

Jim Winchester

Pen & Sword Books Ltd
Barnsley . Yorkshire

Dedicated to

Edward H. Heinemann, Leo Devlin, R.G. Smith, Harry S. Gann and all those at Douglas and McDonnell Douglas who created, nurtured, refined and promoted the Skyhawk, the greatest attack jet ever built.

First published in
Great Britain in 2005
By Pen and Sword Aviation
an imprint of Pen and Sword Books Ltd
47 Church Street
Barnsley
South Yorkshire
S70 2AS
England

ISBN 1 84415 085 2

Typeset in Times New Roman
Printed and bound in Singapore by Kyodo Printing Co. (Singapore) Pte Ltd

Pen & Sword Books Ltd incorporates the imprints of Pen & Sword Aviation, Pen & Sword Maritime, Pen & Sword Military, Wharncliffe Local History, Pen & Sword Select, Pen & Sword Military Classics and Leo Cooper.

For a complete list of Pen & Sword titles please contact
Pen & Sword Books Limited,
47 Church Street, Barnsley, South Yorkshire, S70 2AS, England
E-mail: enquiries@pen-and-sword.co.uk
Website: www.pen-and-sword.co.uk

Contents

Preface

It is now fifty years since the A-4 Skyhawk first flew from Edwards Air Force Base in California. It is not the first combat aircraft to remain in service after fifty years, nor will it be the last. It is, however, one of the most loved by those who flew it in combat and in peace, who trained in it, fought in it, worked on it or who relied on it for accurate and effective close air support. Although, like all production flying machines the result of a collaborative effort, the A-4 is one of the last combat aircraft to be associated with a single designer, Edward H. Heinemann, the creator of many legendary attack aircraft.

The Skyhawk was designed and built by Ed Heinemann and his team with one role in mind, that of tactical nuclear delivery from aircraft carriers. Thankfully, no A-4 was ever called upon to carry out that mission, but the basic airframe was so well designed that it proved adaptable to many other uses, and found favour with air arms around the world. No modern equivalent has yet appeared that offers similar performance and payload while remaining as simple to fly and operate as has 'Heinemann's Hot Rod'. Designed for carriage of a single centreline store, the 'one engine, one man, one way nuclear bomber' was soon tested with and adapted for the new generation of low drag weapons racks and stores, also developed by Heinemann and Douglas. Guided missiles soon followed, as did electronic countermeasures and basic radar. Miniaturization of electronics allowed the compact airframe to later accept multi-mode radar and sophisticated navigation and electronic warfare systems, giving many of the capabilities of the F-16 and other third-generation fighters.

More so than most aircraft the Skyhawk attracted nicknames: 'Scooter', 'Mighty Mite', 'Mighty Midget', 'Tinker Toy' and 'Bantam Bomber' among them. The latter at least was an invention of the Douglas public relations department, as was 'Heinemann's Hot-rod', which appeared in print even before the first flight. Test pilot Bob Rahn said

Many A-4s have had multiple careers. This A-4C served in the ASW fighter role with VA-45 Det 11 on the USS Intrepid *in 1971. It and went on to become A-4SU Super Skyhawk 991 with the Republic of Singapore Air Force.*

this was his personal favourite.

By 1950s' standards the Skyhawk was indeed 'pocket-sized' at a time when fighters and bombers were becoming heavier, more complex and increasingly demanding of maintenance. Heinemann's genius was to insist that every component justify its installation and every pound of its weight. 'Simplicate and add lightness' was the El Segundo mantra in 1952-54 when the Skyhawk took shape.

Heinemann's achievement was to create a cheap, tough aircraft that exceeded the performance targets at less than half the originally specified weight. Even in its basic 'dash-one' version, the Skyhawk could be catapulted from a carrier at more than twice its empty weight. From the A-4A to the A-4M, empty weight increased by 20 per cent, loaded weight by 67 per cent and thrust by 56 per cent. Lightly loaded or stripped of surplus equipment, Skyhawks made excellent fighters on smaller carriers and with smaller air forces, and simulated MiGs in the adversary fighter role when the US military relearned the importance of teaching visual air combat.

Skyhawk production was winding down in 1965 when development of the TA-4 two-seater gave the Skyhawk a whole new lease of life and increased its export potential, as did the installation of the J52 'growth engine'. Escalation of the Vietnam War spurred new variants and modifications for the new era of SAMs. Continued production for the US Navy and Marines through the 1970s and operation of US TA-4s into and beyond the 1990s ensured a supply of spares to support foreign users.

From 1954 to 1979 in what was then a record length production run, a total of 2,960 Skyhawks were built, 2,668 of them for the US Navy and Marine Corps. The relatively few new-build export models were backed up by sales and transfers of many more refurbished aircraft. Approximately 770 A-4s served with non-US air arms, and this book reflects the importance of the A-4 to those nations that have relied on the 'Scooter' for air defence and attack missions. Two nations acquired Skyhawks from Douglas for their own carriers and a third took the A-4 back to sea in the late 1990s. The strong structure needed for shipboard operations has ensured the longevity of many airframes and their continued operation into the twenty-first century. Many of the foreign aircraft have had several careers. To help trace them, chapter four presents the most comprehensive lists of tie-ups between US Navy Bureau Numbers, manufacturers' construction numbers and foreign serials to be published to date. The tables of non-US users represent a great deal of research by the author and many enthusiasts. Nonetheless, the lists for Singapore and Israel, two nations sharing a penchant for secrecy, are incomplete as is that for Indonesia, who acquired most of its A-4s from Israel. It is likely that the full picture will never be known for these air forces, but this book has the most comprehensive accounting of export Skyhawks, their origins and fates yet published.

As the A-4 enters its sixth decade.Skyhawks can still be found flying in ten countries. As of 2004 approximately 165 A-4s were still in military service, with another sixty airworthy or candidates for airworthiness on the civil registers of the USA and France, most of which are earning a living on military support contracts. More civil Skyhawks are to come and there are even prospects of further export sales of surplus aircraft to new military users. As the old slogan goes: A-4s forever!

Jim Winchester,
London, November 2004

Acknowledgements

The author would like to thank the many people and institutions who have helped with this book, either by supplying information on, photographs of or access to, the wonderful A-4 Skyhawk. But first and foremost my thanks go to my editor Peter Coles and also to Dave Windle for his fantastic profile illustrations.

Contributors to this account of the Skyhawk story include: naval aviation specialists Rick Burgess; Rick Morgan and Rosario 'Zip' Rausa; Lieutenant Matt 'Cads' Bartel of the Naval Safety Center; The San Diego Aerospace Museum; the Naval Historical Center; the National Museum of Naval Aviation; Corporal Carl Booty, RNZAF Central Photographic Establishment. José Herculano and all at the Skyhawk Study Group Yahoo! Group; particularly Christian Amado, Fernando Benedetto, John Binford, Ricardo T. Caballero, Tom Debski, Barry Dougherty, Laurie Hillier, José M. Rodriguez and Les Stockley. Many people at the Skyhawk Association, including Bud Southworth, Wynn 'Captain Hook' Foster and Jack 'Youthly Puresome' Woodul. A-4 aviators Mike Carroll, Walt Fink, Bob 'Fraz' Frazier, Gordon 'Gordo' Gray, Bob 'Creeps' Krall, M. 'Pat' Patrick, John Weiss and Randy Wilson. All the 'Redtails' of VC-8 1999-2003, but especially skippers Steve Kornatz and Brad Steele, pilots Allen 'Slinky' Minnick, Tony 'Scarface' Fontana, Oscar 'OJ' Patino, Greg 'Dirt' Detwiler and Sean 'Crash' McDermott and all in the PR shop, particularly James Grecenko. Dennis Pratt, Cliff Gion and Al Minnich and all at BAE Systems, Flight Systems; Larry Payne of Airborne Tactical Advantage Company (ATAC); Larry 'Hoss' Pearson of Advanced Training Systems International (ATSI). Mick Oakey at 'Aeroplane'; Alan Warnes and Dave Allport at 'Air Forces Monthly'; Mike O'Connor (author 'MiG Killers of Yankee Station'), Rich 'Lt Dann' Dann (http://home.houston.rr.com/ltdann), Ian Bott, David Evans, Peter Foster Robert Hewson, Mike Hooks, Frank B. Mormillo, José 'Fuji' Ramos, Graham Robson, Corné Rodenburg (http://home.planet.nl/~roden17); Teddy, Ken and Marc at TRH Pictures (www.trhpictures.co.uk), Gary Verver (www.chinalakealumni.org), Dave W; Simon Watson, The Aviation Book Shop (http://www.aviation-bookshop.com) and Mike Yeo, Horizon Modeltech (www.horizontech.bizland.com) and to any others who I may have forgotten.

The author highly recommends membership of the Skyhawk Association (www.a4skyhawk.org), which is a fraternal organisation open to all who share an interest in the A-4, be they aviators, maintainers or just enthusiasts. Their researches into Skyhawk history have provided invaluable assistance to the author.

Glossary

AAA Anti-Aircraft Artillery
AAM Air-to-Air Missile
AB Air Base
ACM Air Combat Manoeuvring
ADF Air Direction Finder
AFB Air Force Base
ALD Airborne Laser Designator
AMARC Aerospace Maintenance and Regeneration Center
ARBS Angle-Rate Bombing System
ATAC Airborne Tactical Advantage Co.
ATG Air Task Group
ATSI Air Training Services International
ASW Anti-Submarine Warfare
BAF Belgian Air Force
BIS Bureau of Inspection and Survey
BuAer US Navy Bureau of Aeronautics
BuNo Bureau Number
CANA Comando de la Aviación Naval Argentina
CAP Combat Air Patrol
CFE Contractor Furnished Equipment
CINCPAC Commander in Chief of the Pacific Fleet
c/n Construction number
CNO Chief of Naval Operations
CSD Constant Speed Drive
CVA Attack aircraft carrier
CVN Nuclear-powered aircraft carrier
CVG Carrier Air Group
CVS Anti-submarine aircraft carrier
CVW Carrier Air Wing
DACT Dissimilar Air Combat Training
DECM Defensive Electronic Counter measures
ECM Electronic Countermeasures
FAA Fleet Air Arm
FAA Fuerza Aérea Argentina
FAC Forward Air Control(ler)
FAI Federation Aéronautique Internationale
FIP Fleet Indoctrination Program
FRS Fleet Readiness Squadron
GF Growth Factor
GFE Government Furnished Equipment
HMAS Her Majesty's Australian Ship
HMS Her Majesty's Ship
H&MS Headquarters & Maintenance Squadron
HUD Head Up Display
HoTaS Hands on Throttle and Stick
IDF/AF Israel Defence Force/Air Force
IAS Indicated Airspeed
IFF Identification Friend or Foe
INAS Inertial Navigation and Attack System
INS Inertial Navigation System
KAF Kuwait Air Force
kT Kiloton
LABS Low-altitude bombing system
LAS Lockheed Air Service
LMAASA Lockheed Martin Aircraft Argentina SA
LST Laser Spot Tracker
MCAS Marine Corps Air Station
MER Multiple Ejector Rack
MFD Multi-Function Display
NAA National Aeronautic Association
NAS Naval Air Station
NATC Naval Air Test Center
NFWS Naval Fighter Weapons Squadron
NS Naval Station
PTM Peculiar To Malaysia/Persekutan Tanah Melayu
RAAF Royal Australian Air Force
RAG Replacement Air Group
RAN Royal Australian Navy
RCAF Royal Canadian Air Force
RCN Royal Canadian Navy
RHAW Radar homing and warning
RSAF Republic of Singapore Air Force
RWR Radar Warning Receiver
SAFTECH Singapore Armed Forces Technical Institute
SAM Surface-to-Air Missile
SATS Short Airfield for Tactical Support
SEAD Suppression of Enemy Air Defences
TAC Tactical Air Command
TAC(A) Tactical Co-ordinator (Airborne)
TER Triple Ejector Rack
TUDM Tentara Udara Diraja Malaysia
UHF Ultra High Frequency
USAF United States Air Force
USMC United States Marine Corps
USN United States Navy
VA- Attack squadron
VAL Light Attack Aircraft competition
VAQ- Electronic Attack squadron
VC- Composite squadron
VF- Fighter squadron
VFA- Fighter-Attack squadron
VFC- Composite Fighter Squadron
VHF Very High Frequency
VMax Maximum permissable air speed
VPAF Vietnamese People's Air Force
W/o Written off

The prototype Skyhawk basks in the California sunshine. Nearly 3,000 would follow over the next twenty-nine years

Aerospace/TRH Pictures

CHAPTER ONE

Birth of a Bomber

In December 1951 Donald Douglas, founder of the Douglas Aircraft Company, dispatched Ted Conent, his senior vice president from the head office at Santa Monica, to talk with Edward H. Heinemann, chief designer at the company's El Segundo Division, located on the south side of Los Angeles Airport. Conent relayed to Heinemann the concerns of his boss over the increasing size and complexity of naval aircraft, which were contributing to greater costs for the company year on year. These were rising at about five per cent per annum, somewhat greater than the overall inflation rate of the time. Conent believed the company faced a bleak future in the military aviation business if costs could not be controlled. He asked Ed Heinemann to make a study of why costs were escalating so fast and suggest how the problem could be tackled in future designs.

Douglas and Conent had chosen the right man. In the field of naval aviation alone Ed Heinemann was partly or wholly responsible for design of the SBD Dauntless, AD Skyraider, XA2D Skyshark and A3D Skywarrior bombers and the F3D Skyknight, F4D Skyray and F5D Skylancer fighters. For the US Army Air Force he had designed the DB-7 (A-20) Boston and A-26 Invader. The Skyraider and Invader were at that time heavily engaged in combat in Korea, but were really World War 2 aircraft in the age of jets.

The new generation was represented by such aircraft as the long-range semi-strategic A3D Skywarrior, the prototype of which first flew in October 1952. With a loaded weight of 68,000lb (30,644kg), the A3D-1 was to become the heaviest aircraft to be regularly catapulted from aircraft carriers. In 1959, an A3D-1 was catapulted from the USS *Independence* at a weight of 84,000lb (38,102kg), which remains a record to this day. The size of the wartime vintage 'Essex'-class carriers in particular limited the number of these heavy bombers that could be deployed and thus the targets struck in the event of all-out nuclear war with the Soviet Union, which was the driving force behind US military planning at the time.

At the other extreme, the lighter end of the carrier-based attack force was tasked with flying eight to twelve hour missions in the piston-engined AD Skyraider, the prototype of which first flew in 1945. After such tests of endurance 'Able Dog' pilots were sometimes barely able to land aboard the carrier deck or walk across it when they climbed from the cockpit. They often carried an inflatable rubber ring to sit on to relieve the discomfort of long missions. The ADs could carry a nuclear weapon, but could not climb over high mountains when fully loaded and were unlikely to survive concerted defences or get sufficiently far away from the blast of their own bombs to escape damage or destruction.

Increasing complexity of airframes and equipment contributed to spiralling costs over

Edward H. Heinemann poses for the press at the out of the first Skyhawk in early 1954. Company releases were already calling the A4D the 'might midget atom bomber'.

Douglas via 'Aer

and above inflation. One hundred million dollars bought 1,100 fighter aircraft in 1940, but by 1955 it would pay for fewer than 100. In today's money $100 million would be unlikely to get you two whole fighters.

Heinemann gave the task of writing the cost study to his deputy Leo Devlin and his team. Devlin had been Heinemann's chief assistant since the late 1930s, and Heinemann trusted him 'like a brother'. Devlin and colleagues found that the Navy's performance requirements were constantly increasing without necessarily achieving much greater combat effectiveness in the finished product. Analysis of previous designs showed that combat aircraft experienced different 'growth factors' as they were developed. The growth factor was the amount that each extra unit of added equipment increased the overall weight of the aircraft. The

A Douglas drawing of the original A4D design, showing differences in the rear fuselage, wing planform and intake design from the eventual Skyhawk configuration.

Douglas

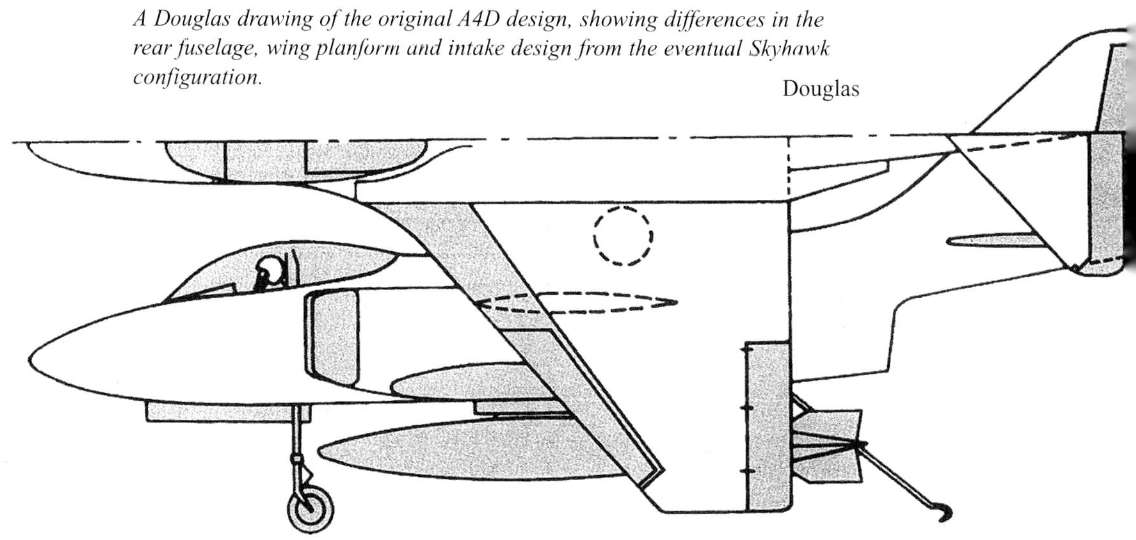

Skyraider was said to have a growth factor (GF) of about 4.3 and the F4D Skyray jet fighter a GF of 10. Thus if the extra structure, military load or equipment add ten per cent to the empty weight, the extra wing area, engine power, fuel and supporting structure required are ten times that extra weight and thus the loaded weight doubles for a given level of performance, range and strength.

Conversely, each pound that could be saved on equipment saved 10 pounds from the loaded weight. The Navy also became aware of a further growth effect on aircraft after they entered service and specified that new designs would still be able to meet their performance specifications at (typically) 110 per cent initial gross take-off weight and 125 per cent initial carrier landing weight.

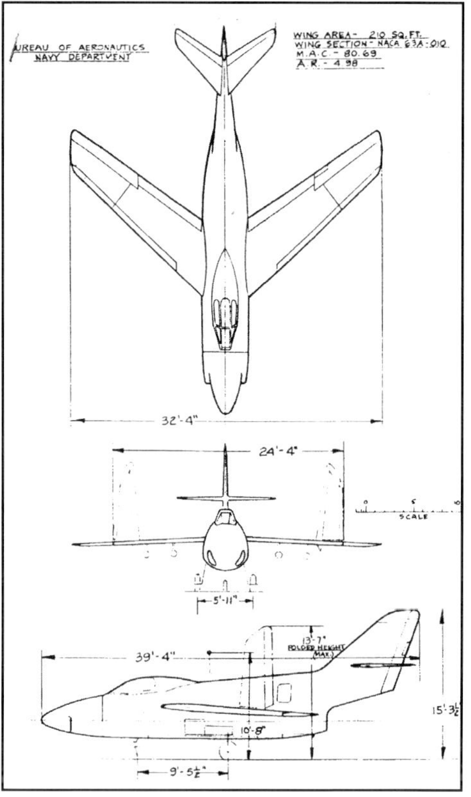

This drawing shows some earlier (1948) Heinemann/Douglas thoughts regarding a light naval bomber. Heinemann literally went back to the drawing board for the Skyhawk.
Douglas via US Navy Historical Center

Armed with these figures, in January 1952 Heinemann went to Washington to meet with Rear Admiral Thomas Combs, the chief of the Navy's Bureau of Aeronautics (BuAer) to discuss his ideas for simple, lightweight, cheaper combat aircraft. Combs was unable to make it to the meeting, but Rear Admiral Apollo Soucek took his place. A pre-war altitude record holder, Soucek had led Task Force 77 in Korea and was soon to become head of BuAer. Heinemann explained his concept of an interceptor fighter built to reduce its potential growth factor, but Soucek wanted to know if the same principles could be applied to an attack aircraft able to carry a 2,000-lb (907-kg) payload, in other words an atomic bomb. Ideally the new aircraft would have a combat radius of 300 nautical miles (557km), a maximum speed of 500kts (928km/h) and a maximum permissible weight of 30,000lb (13,608kg). Heinemann claimed he could exceed the required speed by 90 knots (168km/h) and bring the weight down to half as much as that specified. In a private meeting Soucek and Combs insisted on a maximum unit cost below one million dollars. The Navy's procurement budget was under pressure, not least from the Air Force, who saw the nuclear delivery role as the prerogative of their heavy bombers.

Reviewing Heinemann's proposal, the BuAer staff was sceptical that such a small aircraft could achieve the Navy's missions. One member said that Heinemann's proposed aircraft 'wouldn't have the range to carry a bomb load from here across the state of Maryland'. Admiral Soucek asked for a working concept. Heinemann went back

A cutaway sketch view of the early A4D-1 Skyhawk, with a scrap view showing the instrumentation probe fitted to several of the first aircraft. The navigation package in the nose is well illustrated.

Douglas via 'Aeroplane'

to California, locked himself in his office, took the phone off the hook and stayed there until he had completed a preliminary design analysis with which he was satisfied. The next day he gave a print of his layout to all his senior design staff and gave a brief speech. 'I think this can be done. It will take a tough SOB to do it, and before you say it, I am he. I would like to have you all join my team. Anyone who doesn't want to – there is the door.' Nobody left and the next day senior layout draughtsman Bob Smith delivered a refined three-view drawing, which was soon on the BuAer table in Washington.

Agreeing in principle that such a lightweight jet attacker could be built, the Navy issued a revised set of specifications. The new specified empty weight was 8,136lb (3,690kg), and the maximum gross weight was to be no more than 15,000lb (27,825kg) including double the previous bomb load, and the range was to be100 miles (160km) greater. Heinemann, and project engineer Ben Collins, went back to the design and revised it, again calculating the weight of each individual system and major component as well as the airframe structure itself. The breakdown by components appeared in a document dated 19 June 1952. This is believed to reflect the Navy's estimate at that time, while Heinemann strove to reduce empty weight even further. The XA4D-1 actually weighed in at 7,896lb, a saving of 273lb over the Navy's bottom figure.

On the copy of this document seen by the author, someone has appended the comment 'a great beginning for a great Navy Airplane!'

Keeping to the principles of the Growth Factor, the weight of every component had to be estimated and justified before it could be included. The weight saving measures are discussed in more detail later in the chapter, but one of the simplest and most important was to keep the wingspan within the dimensions of the standard carrier elevator and thus eliminate the wing fold, thus saving about 200lb (91kg) and reducing maintenance needs. Wing folding added a complex and heavy fail-safe mechanism to each wing and required a stronger and heavier wing structure to make up for the weak point of the fold. One of the few previous US carrier aircraft since the biplane era not to have wing folding had been Heinemann's own SBD Dauntless.

After studying five major configurations and a variety of detail variations, including swept, tapered wings, aft-mounted intakes and a T-tail, the design team settled on the delta wing with mid-set tailplane configuration we know today. Company design artist R.G. Smith produced engineering sketches from which clay models were fashioned, followed by a one-quarter scale polished wooden model and several one-tenth scale machined steel models that were tested in wind tunnels at Pasadena's California Institute of Technology and Cornell University in New York.

In January 1952, the Navy ordered construction of a full-scale mock-up of Heinemann's jet attacker design. This was quickly assembled at El Segundo and painted in the then-standard overall dark blue colour scheme with white markings. The mock-up initially featured an undercut rear fuselage like that of the Grumman F9F Panther. As was the practice of the day, it was inspected by a Mock-up Review Board who met in February 1952. After insisting on a few minor changes, they pronounced themselves satisfied, and on 21 June 1952 a contract for two XA4D-1 prototypes was signed. The

The prototype XA4D-1, depicted here in original configuration with nose instrumentation probe, original rudder, windscreen and tailpipe design.

The XA4D-1 is seen pre-first flight alongside its big brother, an A3D-1 Skywarrior in front of the old Imperial Air Terminal at Los Angeles Airport. Even at this time, before the XA4D-1 had flown, the Skyhawk was known as 'Heinemann's Hot-rod'.

Douglas via 'Aeroplane'

initial contract amounted to \$8,680,000, covering one flyable aircraft and a static test example. There was still scepticism from some quarters within the Navy that Heinemann's claims could be met, but otherwise, the bureaucrats were bypassed and the contract was issued without competition, a process that would be unthinkable today.

By September 1952 the Navy was convinced that the design was a winner and ordered Douglas to gear-up for production without waiting for the results of flight tests which were not due to begin for nearly two years. The mock-up was inspected again in October, the design was frozen and tooling was set up to begin production. The order was increased to nine and then to nineteen A4D-1s (sometimes but rarely called YA4D-1s) at about this time.

At this point, a note about the designation system then in use by the US Navy may be in order. The XA4D-1 was the fourth attack design by Douglas to reach the hardware stage, following the AD Skyraider, the XA2D Skyshark and the A3D Skywarrior. X stood for experimental, (Y stood for pre-production test) and –1 indicated the first variant. In September 1962 the three US services were ordered to rationalize the system, and surviving A4D-1s became A-4As, the A4D-2 became the A-4B, the A4D-2N the A-4C, and the new A4D-5 was renamed the A-4E.

In the summer of 1952 a group from El Segundo was dispatched to Korea to observe the combat conditions then being faced by Naval and Marine aviators, particularly in the attack and close-support roles. The group included engineers Leo Devlin, Harry Nichols and Len Quick, and Commander John Brown, the Navy's A4D project chief. Visiting Navy aircraft carriers and Marine shore bases, they saw for themselves the problems of repairing, rearming, refuelling and flying combat aircraft in tough operational conditions and in all weathers. Ed Heinemann had been convinced of the usefulness of such 'field trips' during World War 2 when he made visits to carriers in the Pacific to observe the Dauntless and other naval aircraft in combat. Feedback he received from aviators and sailors influenced the design of the Skyraider, which in turn was the main attack aircraft in USN and USMC service when the El Segundo group arrived in Korea. The group returned with 'a hatful of ideas', which fed into the design of the A4D.

Weight estimate for XA4D-1 Skyhawk

System or part	Weight lb (kg)	Comments
Instruments	76 (34.5)	
Hydraulics	100 (45.4)	based on system in XF4D Skyray
Surface controls	260 (117.9)	
Armament	66 (29.9)	Related systems and structures only
Crew Equipment	186 (84.4)	Personnel furnishings (ejection seat), air conditioning etc
Arresting gear	64 (29.0)	
Electrical	220 (99.8)	
Electronics	135 (61.2)	115lb (52kg) GFE, 20lb (9kg) CFE*
Emergency equipment	0	No fire detection or fuel purging in XA4D-1
Equipment subtotal	1,117 (506.7)	
Powerplant	3,312 (1502.3)	Including J65 engine (2,690lb/1220kg), ducts, tailpipe, fuel system, starter, lubrication
Wing	1,300 (589.7)	Including 50lb (22.7kg) for slats
Horizontal tail	340 (154.2)	Rated at Vmax 595kts at sea level
Body [fuselage]	1,190 (539.8)	Including 40lb (18.16 kg) for speed brakes
Landing gear	910 (412.8)	For a gross weight of 11,350lb (5150kg)
Structural sub-total	3,740 (1696.5)	
Empty weight	8,169 (3705.5)	
Pilot and parachute	210 (95.3)	
Fuel	4,740 (2150.1)	
Oil	48 (21.8)	Including 25lb (11.35 kg) trapped fuel and oil in system
Store	1,106 (501.7)	Mk 12 nuclear weapon
Oxygen	11 (5.0)	
Parakit	30 (13.6)	
Useful Load	6,145 (2787)	
Normal gross weight	14,314 (6493)	

*GFE = government furnished equipment
CFE= contractor furnished equipment

From November 1952 to January 1953 in El Segundo Building Number One, formerly the Douglas Experimental Department, tooling for the A4D was created from thousands of pounds of steel pipe and plates clamped together, which was then welded together into precisely aligned jigs. As was fashionable in the 1950s, Douglas planned to accelerate production by using some of the prototype tooling to produce the production aircraft. Unfortunately, one piece of this 'hard tooling' used to produce the continuous one-piece wing spars needed to be 'debugged'. Difficulties were also found in drilling close-tolerance holes in the new high-strength aluminium skins and in getting a perfect seal for the wing tank. All these problems set the programme back by fifteen weeks.

During February 1953 Naval and Marine pilots were invited to participate in the design process. Several hundred pilots inspected the mock-up and gave their opinions, particularly on the cockpit design. A Douglas publicist later wrote that 'these observers pretty well agreed that the Skyhawk looked right just the way she was'. Despite this, it must be said, the A4D-1's instrument layout was to attract criticism in service and was completely revised for subsequent models. The philosophy behind the overall cockpit design was to make the pilot feel that it was 'an extension of himself' although the tiny space was to take many pilots some time to get used to.

During the spring, summer and autumn of 1953 the various engineering groups created a blizzard of drawings covering the electrical, hydraulic, air conditioning, electronic, armament and ground support systems and the powerplant installation. These drawings were translated into orders for raw materials which were shaped by the production departments into components that came together as sub-assemblies and then were finally put together on the factory floor to create complete airframes.

The XA4D-1 is seen as it is rolled out of El Segundo's old Experimental Shop, where it was essentially built by hand. Note the varied finish of many components at this time. Douglas via 'Aeroplane'

The first of the Skyhawks is seen at its roll-out in February 1954. Note the white-painted undersides and the paper sheet concealing the Bureau Number.

Douglas via TRH Pictures

The second aircraft on the line was the static test example, which was towed to the company test laboratory and put into a 'torture rack' where it was subjected to all sorts of twisting, vibrating, bouncing and tearing. It was suspended in a cradle at a typical approach angle with the wheels spun by small air motors and repeatedly dropped to simulate the stresses of carrier landings. At this time it lacked the nose compartment, rudder, wingtips, airbrakes and engine, and had to be filled with ballast to approximate real landing weights. Instruments measured stresses and strains and any parts that failed before their estimated design strength literally went back to the drawing board. Eventually the static-test airframe, which never received a Bureau of Aeronautics serial, or Bureau Number (BuNo), was tested to destruction.

The first XA4D-1 was rolled out at El Segundo in February 1954, unpainted except for white undersides, national insignia and 'Navy' titles. For some long-forgotten reason, the Bureau Number (137812) was concealed by a taped-on sheet of brown paper. The newly-installed Curtiss-Wright J65 engine was put through many hours of ground running in Douglas' new concrete engine test cell. All pre-flight trials went satisfactorily, with no major modifications required. By this time the delays in construction were beginning to be made up, and the remaining eight aircraft of the first batch were in the final assembly stage.

The XA4D-1 was unveiled to the press at El Segundo on 6 June 1954, with the name Skyhawk, chosen in line with previous successful company products (including the Skyraider, Skyknight and Skywarrior) publicly announced. Already the company press machine was promoting the A4D as the 'Mighty Midget'. Ed Heinemann called the new bomber a 'major step in designing an airplane on a completely functional basis, making each requirement stand on its own two feet rather than by doing things because they have

Bob Rahn lifts the XA4D-1 off the surface of Muroc Dry Lake on its official first flight, 22 June 1954.
Douglas via Mike Hooks

been done that way in the past'.

With ground trials complete, the XA4D was loaded on a flatbed truck and driven the seventy miles from El Segundo to Edwards Air Force Base in the Mojave Desert. The pilot chosen to lead the XA4D flight test programme was Douglas chief test pilot Robert O. Rahn. Bob Rahn had flown Spitfires with the USAAF in the Mediterranean and then became an Air Force test pilot. Joining Douglas in 1945, Rahn tested the Skyraider, Skyray and Skylancer and set a world low-altitude speed record over a 100-mile (160-km) course in the Skyray in October 1953.

First flight

A series of taxi tests on the dry lake bed preceded the official first flight, and on one of them, date unknown, the XA4D-1 was accelerated to 140 knots (259km/h) and lifted a few feet above the ground. Bob Rahn held it there for about a mile, tentatively feeling out the control responses, and ensuring the slats stayed out in their normal low-speed position. As he reduced thrust for the landing, a mild crosswind caught the tiny jet, lifting the right wing. The Skyhawk carried on with one wheel on the ground and the other in the air. Using full right stick to correct the drift, Rahn trapped his leg against the console, but by using rudder and harder stick pressure he brought the wing and wheel down.

The eighth Skyhawk wore an instrumentation probe, at least for some of its test flying. Note that it has the production windscreen and 'sugar scoop' tail fairing. Douglas

The day for the actual first flight came on 22 June 1954, just four weeks behind schedule, and two years and one day after the prototype contract was signed. Take-off was made on the 13,000-ft (3962m) lakebed runway at 125kts (232km/h), requiring only a little up elevator to get airborne. Constant tailplane adjustment was needed to keep the aircraft in trim. The landing gear and flaps were raised at 175 knots (324km/h) and the aircraft climbed to 15,000ft (4572m) for a series of tests. The landing gear, speedbrakes and flaps were cycled and then straight and level flight was tried at a variety of power settings. A few turns were made, then some low-speed handling checks before the XA4D let down and returned to the pattern at Edwards, landing at 150kts (278km/h) after a total of forty-five minutes flight time.

A slight oscillation from the rear fuselage had been noticed during the straight and level portion, but this was the only fault in an otherwise flawless first flight. The potential benefits of a higher thrust powerplant were expressed by Bob Rahn at a post-first flight party at Palmdale that evening. Fortified by several martinis Rahn proclaimed 'wash we need ish more thrush!' The Curtiss-Wright J65 fitted to the XA4D provided only 7,000lb (31.14kN) thrust, but the version furnished for production A4D-1s partially granted Rahn's wish by giving a further 500lb (2.22kN).

On the third flight of the XA4D-1, at about 300 knots (557km/h) an irregular twisting motion of the tail section was experienced. The simple expedient of tightening the attachment bolts for the rear fuselage fixed this problem. In some flight regimes a buffet was felt at the base of the tail. After five different fairings were tested, a simple inverted 'sugar scoop' fairing was found to cure the problem and was fitted to all subsequent Skyhawks. The second aircraft flew exactly on schedule on 14 August and the third – built almost entirely on production tooling – was flown on 23 December, two weeks ahead of schedule.

The flight test programme proceeded with few hitches until a routine test flight in one of the early aircraft in April 1955 when a particular combination of speed, altitude and proximity to a cumulus cloud led to a serious oscillation of the airframe. At 10,000 ft (3,048 m) and 450kts (835km/h) or Mach 0.8, a flutter of up to six degrees left and right at a frequency of twelve oscillations per second occurred in the rudder. The fin tip itself wavered through a range of 12 inches (30cm) and Bob Rahn thought the aircraft was going to come apart. To investigate this phenomenon further, the aircraft was given a telemetry unit to transmit real-time data to the ground and a device known as a sloppy hydraulic dashpot was installed to lessen the chance of an oscillation causing structural failure. To cure this rudder 'buzz,' six different new rudder configurations were tried. These included: rows of one-inch holes at 50 per cent chord; increased fin tip chord; a blunt trailing edge; mass overbalances; leading-edge balance weights and bulb weights at different locations. Trailing-edge bulb weights were the most effective, but they increased the moment (force) needed to deflect the rudder. To adopt this solution would have required power operation of the rudder and thus increased the overall aircraft weight and complexity. While these various fixes were tested, a back-up 'tadpole' rudder was built. This was not - as is commonly stated - the original rudder with the outer skins

The second airworthy Skyhawk is seen nearing completion. A static test airframe followed the XA4D-1 and was eventually tested to destruction.

'Aeroplane'

removed, but a sheet of 0.40in (10.2mm) sheet sandwiched between nine chordwise tapered ribs spaced 8 inches (203mm) apart. This basic arrangement had already appeared on the North American FJ3 Fury and F-100 Super Sabre. The new rudder successfully damped the vibration but was not approved until A4D-2 production began. All subsequent Skyhawks were to sport this rudder, which was essentially a 'temporary' solution that was never replaced with a 'proper' design, something that Heinemann regretted never doing.

The record-breaking A4D-1 '820' is seen on a littered Edwards AFB ramp after an Open House.
Douglas via 'Aeroplane'

Another problem discovered during testing was that pulling high *g*-forces at transonic speeds at high altitude caused random wing drop and buffeting. This was regarded as serious because, although it would not affect the ability to carry out its basic attack mission, it would greatly impair the A4D's ability to evade interception. The cure was again a simple one. Rows of vortex generators, which were simply L-shaped metal strips, were fitted along the leading edge of the wings and at the wing to fuselage junction forward of the line of the ailerons. Large wing fences were also tested but, like the tail fairing and tadpole rudder, the 'quick and dirty' solution was chosen and remained throughout the production run, although the number and pattern of vortex generators changed from the second production model (the A4D-2) onwards.

It was during the exploration of the wing drop phenomenon that the only accident occurred during the initial test programme. The fourth aircraft (137815) was lost, together with pilot Jim Verdin on a routine test flight without a chase plane on 13 January 1955. It appears that the hydraulic system failed while the A4D was flying in a wing down condition, causing high amplitude aileron flutter and a rapid loss of control. The manual stick force needed to recover was beyond the strength of any pilot and would have been increased by fuel flowing into the lower wing due to gravity. Verdin was knocked unconscious as he ejected and was unable to manually separate himself from his seat. The Skyhawk crashed in the desert and was not found until late the following day.

As a result of this accident, a dual-source hydraulic system was introduced on the production line (but did not appear until the A4D-2 model), and baffles were fitted into the wing tanks to prevent fuel sloshing from one wing to the other in flight.

XA4D-1 described

Having related the initial development and early testing of the Skyhawk, a description of the features of the XA4D-1 and other early Skyhawks is in order. Although the A4D's general appearance was quite conventional, this masked many innovative design features that embodied Heinemann's 'simplicate and add lightness' philosophy.

On the XA4D-1 as it initially appeared, a long instrumentation probe was faired into the otherwise blunt nosecone, giving a suggestion of speed that the A4D's appearance otherwise lacked. The A4D was well proportioned, certainly, but hardly sleek, especially with its stalky undercarriage and lumpish main landing gear doors. The intakes were simple half-round shapes mounted midway up the fuselage behind the cockpit. The fuselage tapered towards a simple short exhaust at the base of the tail. The fin was connected to the upper fuselage by a long fillet, giving more than adequate keel area for stability. The cropped delta wing featured large ailerons as well as split flaps on the underside of the inboard trailing edge. The leading edge sported long-span leading edge slats. The slats were aerodynamically operated, in other words they were pushed into the retracted position when there was sufficient airflow over the leading edges and they extended at high angles of attack and for landing and take-off, thus increasing the stalling speed.

The upper wing skin was 0.064in (1.62mm) thick and cut from a single sheet 28ft (12.7m) long by 186in (4.72m) wide and at the time was the largest thin-gauge sheet ever rolled. There were 55 oval inspection holes in the upper wing surface. Covered by fastened plates, in normal operational service these are rarely opened.

The internal structure of the wing was a three-spar box, which doubled as the main fuel tank, with a capacity of 560 US gallons (1992 litres). Another self-sealing fuel tank with a capacity of 240 gallons (854 litres) was installed behind the rear cockpit bulkhead. This gave a total internal fuel capacity of 800 US gallons (2846 litres).

Weapons stations amounted to a single centreline rack with a carrying ability of 3,575lb (1622kg) and two wing pylons, each rated at 1,200lb (544kg). For the strike role, the Skyhawk would have carried the nuclear store on the centreline and

On 13 September 1955 Lieutenant Gordon Gray made the first carrier landings by the Skyhawk on the USS Ticonderoga. The aircraft was *137816, assigned to the Naval Air Test Center.*
US Navy via 'Aeroplane'

'Gordo' Gray is seen with the record-breaking YA4D-1 '820'. Note the later three-part windscreen. The aircraft also had the ribbed rudder fitted. US Navy via 'Aeroplane'

two 150 US-gallon fuel tanks under the wings. For any sort of war mission, either wing or centreline tanks were necessary. The A4D-5 (A-4E) introduced two extra pylons, which were later retrofitted to some earlier export models.

One unusual feature of the XA4D was a set of wedges to hold the pilot in place so that he moved in phase with the rolling plane of the aircraft without bumping off the sides. These were soon found to be unnecessary and omitted from subsequent aircraft. Although the cockpit was remarkably compact, it was able to accommodate a range of pilot sizes due to its electrically-adjustable seat (operated by a switch on the left console) and fore-and-aft adjustable rudder pedals (operated by foot pressure on the tops of the pedals). Using the only biometric data on aircrew available, an Army Air Force study from 1946, Douglas engineers designed the cockpit around the average aviator. Unfortunately, by the time the A4D-1 entered service in 1956, new studies proved that the average naval aviator was about 2in (5.8cm) taller than the 1946 figure, making the cockpit snug to say the least.

Weight saving

During the design process, every part of the airframe and its ancillary equipment was seen as worthy of redesign for simplicity and weight reduction. This included the ejection seat, the navigation equipment, the bomb racks and even the pilot's harness. When systems engineers presented an overweight system, Heinemann sent it back for redesign until it was within his self-imposed limits.

Typical was the design of the pilot's ESCAPAC-1 ejector seat, which was begun from

The second Skyhawk, seen here in September 1963, was one of several of different models tested with tailpipe shields and extensions under Project DIRTY, which involved measurements of infra-red signature by a specially equipped T-39. The connection between these studies and the later use of extended tailpipes as used by Israeli Skyhawks is unknown.

NAF China Lake via Gary Verver

unnecessary features such as footrests dispensed with. Lightness helped improve the seat's performance, although early models were not 'zero-zero' capable. The new Douglas seat had only 80 parts and weighed only 40lb (18kg). A contemporary North American Aviation seat had 240 parts and weighed 98lb (44.5kg).

The communication and navigation equipment normally specified for a low-level attack aircraft consisted of four large black boxes with a combined weight of 133lb (60.3kg) with 25lb (11.3kg) of brackets and cables. Heinemann had free reign to come up with something lighter and cheaper and designed an integrated unit, which fitted in a drum mounted on the forward cockpit bulkhead inside the nose cone. A single power supply replaced the four units in the old system and the whole unit was pressurised with nitrogen. The new unit weighed 105lb (47.6kg), a saving of 48lb (21.8kg). There were only 5lb (2.3kg) of brackets and cables because the equipment was not spread about the airframe.

The first nineteen aircraft had a lightweight one-piece curved Plexiglas windscreen, but this caused distortion and was vulnerable to bird strike. A more conventional three-part unit with curved side panels and a flat armoured glass centre pane was tested in August 1955 and became standard.

The A4D-1 was not designed as a multi-role aircraft, simply as a daylight nuclear attack bomber, so lacked air-to-air or air-to-ground radar. Other equipment taken for granted today such as electronic counter-measures (ECM), inertial navigation system (INS) or precision approach and landing gear was not specified and not supplied. The A4D-1 also lacked air-refuelling capability, which was still in its relative infancy in the Navy at the time.

The nose and main undercarriage units retracted forward into fairings near the wing roots. This saved weight by eliminating the need for air bottles to force the gear down in the event of hydraulic failure. Releasing the uplocks by pulling the emergency T-handle allowed the gear to fall free and be pushed into the locked position by air pressure.

One of the main methods of saving weight was to eliminate the need for wing folding by keeping the wingspan within the limits imposed by the size of aircraft carrier elevators. By adopting a cropped delta wing with a tailplane, the span could be kept low while keeping a worthwhile surface area. This had the side benefit of making the A-4 very stable at low level, although high-altitude speed suffered, mainly because of the thickness of the wing. At 27ft 6in (8.38m), the A-4's wing was 6in (15cm) shorter than that of the Sopwith Camel biplane of World War 1. The wing area of the Skyhawk was slightly greater at 260 square feet (24.2m^2) versus the Camel's 231 square feet (21.5m^2).

One of the few previous US carrier aircraft designs not to have wing folding was Heinemann's own SBD Dauntless. Wing folding added a complex and heavy fail-safe mechanism to each wing and required a stronger and heavier structure to make up for the weak point of the fold. About 200lb (91kg) was saved by omitting wing folding.

The Engine

Ed Heinemann once said that his philosophy for his lightweight aircraft projects was to take the best engine he could get, put a wing under it and fit a saddle on top. The Pentagon's budget for the aircraft limited the unit cost of each A4D to $1 million, however, which narrowed the choice to one engine, the Wright J65, a licence-built version of the British Armstrong Siddeley Sapphire two-spool turbojet. In British use (mainly on some versions of the Hawker Hunter), the Sapphire gave a healthy 8,300lb (38.5 kN) thrust, but the Pentagon decreed that the A4D should only use J65s from existing (USAF) inventory. In most cases this meant reconditioned engines from F-84F Thunderstreaks. Initially Douglas was told to expect 8,000lb (37 kN) thrust, the engines as delivered gave only a little over 7,000lb (32.5 kN). Once the engine parameters were known (or presumed), the airframe size could be calculated. It was said that to use an engine such as the Pratt & Whitney J57 of 11,600lb (53.8kN) thrust would have pushed the weight to 30,000lb (13,608kg) due to the Growth Factor, and that would have increased the unit cost to over $2 million.

This A4D-2N was used for trials of the Mk 4 HIPEG (High Performance External Gun) podded cannon. It still flies today, as A-4SU '939' with the Republic of Singapore Air Force at its training outpost in Cazaux, France. US Navy

Looking much like the XA4D-1, the first A4D-2 (A-4B) flew in March 1956 and initially featured the smooth-surfaced rudder.

TRH Pictures

In 1953 Heinemann had hoped to have a licence-produced Rolls-Royce Avon as a fall back, but the collaboration between Rolls-Royce and Westinghouse only produced the XJ54, essentially a six-tenths scale Avon which put out only 6,000lb (27.8 kN) thrust. This was abandoned when its intended mount, the Sea Dart seaplane fighter was cancelled. The Westinghouse XJ40 intended for the A3D proved a massive disappointment, producing only 7,000lb (32.5 kN) thrust. Heinemann having wisely chosen podded engines, the A3D design could be saved without massive structural changes by substituting the J57 in new larger nacelles. Not surprisingly, having crippled a generation of Navy fighters, Westinghouse soon went back to making refrigerators.

Early engine problems

The J65s fitted to the early Skyhawks suffered from a couple of serious problems. The main bearings of many engines, both new and reconditioned, would fail on start-up. This was traced to oil starvation and could be cured by turning the engine by hand, ensuring all bearings were pre-oiled. A similar procedure was used with radial piston engines in order to lubricate the top cylinders, but was not a usual practice with jets. Many inflight failures, which of course were much more serious, were occurring between 20 and 100 hours of flight. VA-44, the East Coast Replacement Air Group (RAG), suffered at least nine catastrophic engine failures that resulted in the loss of an A4D-1 or A4D-2 during a period of only three months in late 1958 and early 1959. Only when one aircraft was ditched in the St John's River near Jacksonville and recovered largely intact was the cause of the engine failures traced to the high-pressure spline that connected the fuel pump to the accessory gear drive. This was mounted on only four bolts and when any one of these loosened the spline went out of alignment. At the high RPMs involved, the spline was ground down almost instantly, shutting off fuel to the engine and resulting in a flameout with no warning. An inspection of the sixty or so Skyhawks on VA-44's ramp at Jacksonville found that about twenty of them were on the brink of failure. The problem was easily corrected by simple modifications, this saved many aircraft and lives over the career of the first generation Skyhawks.

Even with the relatively low powered J65, the A4D was able to demonstrate supersonic flight up to Mach 1.25 in a dive. Like all good designers, Heinemann had one eye on a 'growth engine' for the A-4 that would be able to handle the inevitable increase in weight and demands for better performance. This was the Pratt & Whitney J52, a turbojet originally designed for the Air Force's Hound Dog stand-off missile. Limits in funding meant that it would not appear in a Skyhawk until 1961, on the prototype A4D-5, later to become the A-4E.

In those early Cold War days of extreme nuclear security and secrecy, even the aircraft designers were often given little official information about the weapons their products

Headed by engineers with a J65 engine, A4D-2s march down the El Segundo line. In total 342 Skyhawks were built here before production moved to Long Beach. US Navy

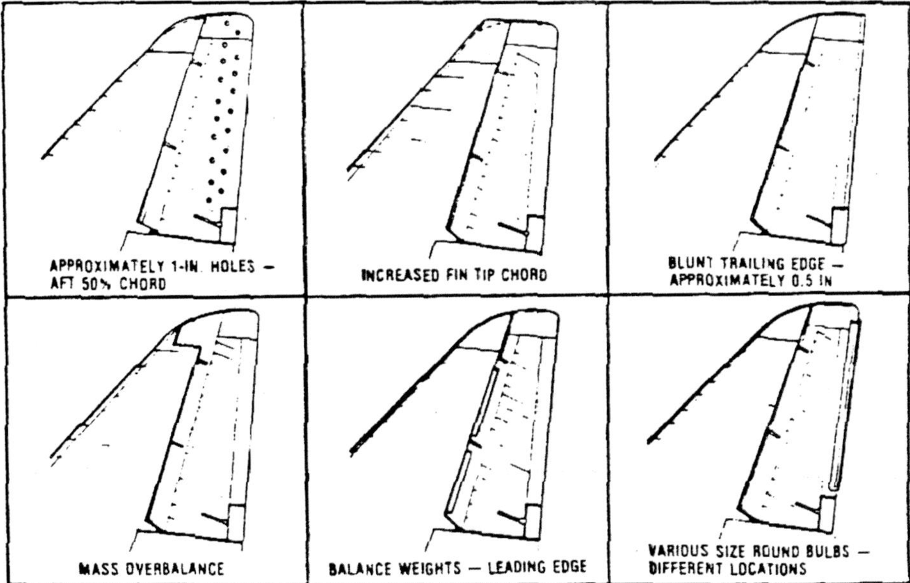

Six of the different rudder configurations tested before the 'inside out' ribbed design (not shown here) was adopted. Douglas

were intended to carry. The figure for weapon weight given in the Navy's requirement reproduced above suggests a MK 12 implosion-type bomb, which was 22in (56cm) in diameter and 155in (394cm) long. This was designed in 1951 and entered the inventory in 1955. In 1950 however, Douglas had been given the contract to build the cases for the larger Mk 7 because the intended contractor (Bendix) had not yet completed its factory in Oklahoma, so Heinemann was no doubt aware of the dimensions and weights of the Mk 7 at an early stage. The physical characteristics of the Mk 7 were critical to the eventual configuration of the Skyhawk. The Mk 7 weighed 1,645lb (747kg) to 1,700lb (772kg), depending on whether the nuclear core was fitted. The body diameter was 30.5in (77.5cm) and the length was 183in (4.65m). More importantly from an aircraft designer's point of view, the Mk 7 had large three large stabilizing fins arranged in a 'Y' configuration.

Long legs

The length of the undercarriage legs was increased by 6in (15cm) during the design phase to ensure adequate ground clearance for the Mk 7. By the time it was introduced to service, the Mk 7 had a retractable lower fin that allowed the Skyhawk (and other platforms such as the F-84) to rotate for take-off. As Skyhawk pilot Bob Frazier recalls, the Mk 7 was 'a big old bomb that could only fit on an A-4 if the tail fin was retracted. After take-off we would have to extend the tailfin and if that didn't work, we came home. Conversely, if you couldn't retract the fin, it was an emergency landing with all [crash-rescue] equipment because you were going to grind the thing off on roll-out'.

The height and spacing of the undercarriage legs affected the turnover and tipback angles of the Skyhawk. As any model maker knows, the A-4 airframe is basically tail heavy and will fall on its tailpipe without additional forward ballast. To prevent tipback,

Test work continued using early Skyhawks through the 1960s. A probe-equipped fuel tank replaced this A-4B's fixed probe in 1969 because the fixed probe affected the seeker for the Shrike missile. Development of the 'cranked' refuelling probe solved this problem. *NWC* China Lake via Gary Verver

the Navy specified that a line between the main wheel and the aircraft centre of gravity had to be at least fifteen degrees. Less obviously, a tricycle-undercarriaged jet can turn over onto its nose and wingtip in certain circumstances, something that happened to Skyhawks on occasion.

The long legs were to give land-based Skyhawk pilots many exciting crosswind landings for the next half century due to its resistance to weathercock into the wind and its tendency to skate on wet runways. Beginning with export models for New Zealand, a braking parachute helped cure this tendency, as did the wing spoilers fitted to most models built or refurbished for export.

Testing continues

The first twelve aircraft were assigned a variety of test tasks by the Douglas Test Group in conjunction with the Navy before the Skyhawk could be accepted for Fleet service. Commander J. Taylor was the first US Navy pilot to fly the Skyhawk, on 29 September 1954. Different A4D-1s were allocated to carrier suitability, weapons test, aerial refuelling and general handling trials. Over 1,540 flights were undertaken by the Douglas Test Team pilots alone during this phase.

Part of the Douglas philosophy was to build enough aircraft for early testing in order to find all the design 'bugs' rapidly. The low unit cost of the A4D-1 allowed for a total of twenty aircraft to be assigned to testing different aspects of the Skyhawk's mission by the Douglas Test Division and the Naval Air Test Center. Once the Skyhawk had been cleared for service, the aircraft of the initial batch, sometimes called YA4D-1s, were used for various tasks – to clear new weapons, try out new equipment and aerodynamic refinements and in missions related to atomic bomb tests. Some were later issued to training and reserve units. Known details of the first twenty Skyhawks are presented in an accompanying table.

Initial carrier qualification of the Skyhawk began on 13 September 1955. Lieutenant

This view of an anonymous early A4D-1 shows the cleanliness and simplicity of the basic Skyhawk airframe design.

Douglas via 'Aeroplane'

Gordon 'Gordo' Gray took 137822 aboard USS *Ticonderoga* for a series of touch-and-go and arrested landings and catapult take-offs. Gray made six touch-and-go and two full-stop landings. The official Defense Department press release credits Marine Major James Feliton with the first full-stop landing, but almost fifty years later it is impossible to be absolutely certain who was first to bring the Skyhawk aboard. Gray recalls that Feliton and some other A4D pilots were aboard during that day, but says no one can say for sure who was actually first. That very same day the first production F4D-1 Skyray was brought aboard 'Tico', and the McDonnell F3H-2N Demon began its carrier trials later the same week. These were busy times for naval aviation, and for Douglas in particular who had three major programmes (Skyray, Skywarrior and Skyhawk) all at a similar stage of development.

Speed record

In 1955 it was decided that Douglas should mount a bid on the 500-kilometre closed-circuit speed record. The Douglas-Navy test team had already broken two speed records during testing of the F4D Skyray in 1953 and the low-level 500-km circuit record, then held by the Air Force, seemed the most appropriate one for the A4D to attempt. The chosen airframe was BuNo 137820, the ninth Skyhawk built and which was fitted with an instrumentation probe on the nose and wired to record various performance parameters.

In October a 100-km (161-km) long test circuit was marked on the Rosamond Dry Lake near Palmdale with a series of twelve pylons erected and fitted with mirrors to help the pilot visually acquire the turn points. Douglas Test Team personnel set off smoke grenades to aid pylon recognition by the speeding pilot. To make doubly sure, a pile of tyres was set alight at the main pylon, generating an unmistakable column of black smoke.

Preliminary flights began on 13 October. On one low-level run flown by Bob Rahn, an unofficial straight-line speed of 703mph (1131km/h) was recorded, but in the process the top part of the rudder came away. It was decided to switch rudders for one of the 'tadpole' type, which had already been selected for the A4D-2. Skyhawk '820' was also fitted with the later-type windscreen with a flat central panel and the sugar scoop tail fitting. The original J65-W-2 engine was used rather than the slightly higher-thrust W-16 version. The airframe was highly polished for the attempt and wore only the basic markings of national insignia and 'Navy' titles.

On 15 October 1955, everything was in place for the record attempt proper. Navy Lieutenant Gordon 'Gordo' Gray was the junior of two pilots assigned to the A4D programme from the Naval Air Test Center at Patuxent River for the official naval acceptance and approval tests. To this day he does not know why he was chosen to be the one to make the record flight. Although an experienced pilot, he had only about eighteen hours in the A4D by this date.

Gray took off from nearby Edwards Air Force Base just after sunrise in order to take advantage of the cooler temperatures that would improve engine performance and reduce turbulence at low level. The Federation Aéronautique Internationale (FAI) and the National Aeronautic Association (NAA) specified that this record be awarded for a flight of 500km (310.68 miles) distance at an altitude no greater than 100 metres (328 feet) above ground level. In fact, most of the flight was made at 100-150ft (30-50m) above the desert floor in order to ensure the height limit was not busted.

With smoke billowing from the turn points and the mirrored pylons flashing in the early morning sun, Gray lowered Skyhawk 820 towards the Joshua trees and sagebrush on the desert floor and accelerated towards the starting point. As he passed the first marker the clocks were started and the little silver jet raced towards the first turn and pulled into a thirty-degree bank. By the third corner the A4D was up to its highest average speed and banking at seventy degrees in order to stay on course. After five circuits of the course in 26.8 minutes and a total flying time of less than 45 minutes, it was all over. The A4D returned to land at Edwards and the scientists made their calculations – the 500km distance had been flown at an average speed of 695.163mph (118.517km/h) and the record belonged to Gray, Douglas and the Navy. Previously held

Used for electronic tests, this YA4D-1 (137824) is seen with a Douglas Navpac navigation pod fitted on the centreline.

McDonnell Douglas via Mike Hooks

The big and the small of 1950s nuclear weapons delivery. Tagging along with this B-52B is an A4D-1 of the Naval Air Special Weapons Facility at Albuquerque, New Mexico.

Douglas via TRH Pictures

by an Air Force F-86H Sabre, this marked the first time the record was held by an attack aircraft.

Skyhawk 820 was returned to test duties and the smooth rudder was re-installed. After service with several test units, including the Naval Aircraft Torpedo Unit, the record-breaking A4D-1 was retired to the Navy's desert storage centre at Litchfield Park, Arizona. In 1969 it was stricken from the inventory, which probably means that it passed to one of the scrapyards near the base and eventually to the smelter.

The First Twenty Skyhawks

BuNo	First flight	Test role	Retired	Fate/notes
137812	22 Jun 54	Flight tests	Jan 60	Last noted 1962
137813	14 Aug 54	Flight tests, weapons	Oct 69	Displayed Pensacola
137814	23 Dec 54	Flight tests, refuelling	Jun 63	Displayed China Lake
137815		Flight tests	n/a	Crashed 13 Jan 55
137816		Carrier suitability	Sep 56	Accident 7 Sep 56
137817		Nuclear weapons separation	Jan 68	Damaged Jan 68
137818		Weapons, HIPEG cannon	Oct 63	Stored China Lake
137819			Feb 63	Damaged Jan 63
137820	May 55	500 km speed record	Apr 69	Damaged Oct 68
137821		Flight tests, refuelling	Aug 68	
137822		Carrier suitability	Feb 64	
137823		Service test	Dec 68	
137824		Electronic tests	Jan 61	
137825		Service test	May 69	
137826		Issued to VA-125	Oct 68	Displayed Paso Robles CA
137827		Nuclear weapons	Oct 68	
137828			n/a	W/o Apr 68
137829		Weapons	Oct 68	Displayed USS *Hornet*
137830		Nuclear weapons	Mar 63	
137831		Nuclear weapons	?	Displayed Orlando

Lieutenant Gray considered himself a fighter pilot rather than an 'attack puke' (to use a later parlance) and went on to fly the F8U (F-8) Crusader in the Fleet after his tour at the NATC was over, and did not fly the Skyhawk again after that time.

In mid 1955, six aircraft of the first twelve were selected and ferried to NAS Patuxent River, Maryland in mid 1955 to undergo Bureau of Inspection and Survey (BIS) trials, and all passed with flying colours. At about this time, the Navy made the first large production orders, which were eventually to total 165 A4D-1s.

Navy evaluation

In October 1955 a fuller Navy evaluation began including tests with various tanks, bombs and other stores. The new dual hydraulic system was being readied for testing at this time. To qualify the A4D for its intended role of nuclear strike, the Naval Air Special Weapons Facility (NASWF) conducted weapons separation trials at China Lake, California between March and July 1956. The Skyhawk was cleared for carriage and release of the Mk 7, Mk 12 and Mk 91 nuclear weapons.

The next stage was the Fleet Indoctrination Program (FIP), conducted at Quonset Point, Rhode Island. Pilots of fleet squadron VA-72 flew the six aircraft for up to eighteen hours a day, achieving the best daily availability rate of any design tested under the FIP system to that time. More than 600 hours were flown on FIP, which was completed ahead of schedule in September 1956.

Fleet squadron VA-72 at Quonset Point, Rhode Island took over several of the FIP aircraft permanently in August 1956 and accepted the first factory-to-fleet delivery in October when BuNo 139935, the thirty-seventh A4D-1, was flown by Lieutenant O.J. Durey from El Segundo to Quonset. From then on the squadrons sent their pilots out to the factory to pick up individual aircraft, although on occasions bulk deliveries were made.

The skipper of VA-72 was Commander Bob Hunt, one of the most experienced

Ed Heinemann's designs filled many carrier decks in the 1960s. Here an A4D-2 of VA-86 'Sidewinders' prepares to launch from Independence *during a Mediterranean cruise in July 1962, following a Marine F4D-1 Skyray and an A3D-2 Skywarrior. All were part of CVG-3.*

USN via 'Aeroplane'

nuclear attack aviators at that time, having led a detachment of Mk 7-equipped F2H-2B Banshees aboard the USS *Franklin D Roosevelt* on a 1952 Mediterranean cruise. The 'Hawks' themselves were previously fighter squadron VF-72, equipped with Grumman F9F Panthers. VA-72 had used a hawk as its squadron insignia for several years and was unofficially known as the 'Skyhawks'. Not long after the A4D-1 entered service with the squadron, Douglas told them to give up the name as it was their copyright. After some correspondence, the squadron relented and became the 'Blue Hawks' instead. A few years later in a twist of corporate logic, Douglas essentially ignored the Cessna Aircraft Company's use of the name for its best-selling Model 172 light aircraft, leading to occasional confusion over the years.

Pacific Fleet squadron VA-93 'Blue Blazers' at Alameda, California became the second Navy Skyhawk squadron in November 1956, transitioning from the F9F-8 Cougar. The squadron began its first cruise in September 1957, aboard the USS *Ticonderoga*. VMA-224 'Bengals' were the first Marine outfit and was equipped with its full complement of fourteen A4D-1s by the end of 1956.

Surprisingly, the fleet training units then known as Replacement Air Groups (RAGs) did not form with Skyhawks until 1958 when VA-44 'Hornets' at Jacksonville, Florida and VA-125 'Rawhides' at Moffett Field, California stood up. This would be because the initial cadre of VA-72 and -93 were experienced jet carrier aviators and the need for specific type training was regarded as less important than it became later. VA-44 received it's A4D-1s in February and officially became the RAG in June. The A4D-2 arrived in September. The first two-seat Skyhawks did not appear at VA-44 until August 1966, so for many years every pilot's first Skyhawk flight was a solo one.

VA-125, the West Coast RAG received its first A4D-1s in June 1958. The squadron

Deck crew start the engines on A4D-1s of VA-34 aboard Saratoga. *The 'Blue Blasters' made their first Skyhawk cruise from January to October 1958, conducting cross-deck operations with HMS* Ark Royal *and supporting Marine landings in Lebanon.*
US Navy via 'Aeroplane'

A4D-2s of VMA-533 'Night Hawks' demonstrate their air refuelling capability with a GV-1 (later KC-130F) Hercules. The combination of these two classic aircraft types allowed the Marines to deploy airpower much faster and more efficiently to the world's trouble spots. US Navy

moved inland to NAS Lemoore near Fresno in 1961 and has been there ever since. As VFA 125 they are the West Coast Fleet Readiness Squadron (FRS), today's equivalent of the RAG, for the F/A-18 Hornet. In the much larger naval aviation community of the 1960s, when there were many more bases and different aircraft types, a common refrain by 'nugget' pilots when they received their first orders just out of Training Command was 'what's an A-4 and where the hell's Lemoore?'

The mission of the Skyhawk RAGs was officially described as 'pilot and enlisted personnel indoctrination and training in fleet attack aircraft before combat carrier squadron assignment'. Over the course of VA-125's Skyhawk tenure the unit operated all US models of the A-4 and trained over 2,000 fleet pilots and several thousand maintenance personnel. TA-4Fs arrived in May 1966, making the Rawhides the first users of the 'T-bird' Skyhawk. The RAGs also trained foreign pilots, with Australia's and Singapore's A-4 pilots and groundcrews training at Lemoore. New Zealand personnel trained with VA-44 at Jacksonville after VA-125 began transition to the A-7 Corsair II in 1969.

The RAGs trained pilots to the point of being operationally ready, including (for US pilots) in the nuclear role. Students trained with practice nuclear 'shapes', which were the same size, shape and weight as the real thing, although they contained no nuclear materials.

One unusual task carried out by VA-44 in 1960 was the testing of spray equipment, ostensibly for mosquito control. The NAS Jacksonville Disease Vector Control Center sponsored the trials to test the effectiveness of jet-powered aircraft for spraying insecticide in combat areas where piston-engined aircraft would be too vulnerable. The Skyhawk could put out 300 gallons of spray per minute at 500mph and 150ft altitude from an 85-gallon tank. This was 'the first known use of jets in the war against insects' according to local entomologist David Hayden. Although it was seen as too expensive for civilian use, the technique was thought to have use in support of tactical military operations. If insecticide could be dispersed by Skyhawks or other jets, so of course could nerve agents or other chemical weapons, and this may have been the real intended purpose behind the trials.

Production gears up

At El Segundo, space was becoming critical. Heinemann's 1,500-person engineering team had moved into a new facility in July 1954, having replaced a former car factory used by Douglas since 1935, but all the factory space was taken up with production of the A3D, F4D and the last of the AD Skyraiders. Some unused acreage was found at the south end of the plant and a steel-framed building was erected in short order for the A4D production line.

When production got fully underway at El Segundo, new A4D-1s were rolling off the line and across to the paint shop every eighteen hours. After painting in the new gull grey and white colours, the 20-mm cannons were boresighted and fired into a bunker. The next step was to tow the aircraft down Douglas Street and across Imperial Boulevard to the company's flight line at Mines Field, more commonly known by then as Los Angeles International Airport. All Douglas's El Segundo and Santa Monica production aircraft had been test flown from Mines Field, but by 1957 increasing development around the airport saw the flight test operation move to Palmdale in the High Desert for noise and safety reasons.

Even before the A4D-1 was delivered to fleet units, an improved version was ordered as the A4D-2. The state of the art in aerial refuelling had progressed, and a fixed probe and a pressure refuelling system were installed. The landing gear was strengthened and an improved air-to-ground weapons delivery system was fitted. All A4D-2s had the 'tadpole rudder' The A4D-2, (A-4B after 1962) could carry the new Douglas-designed D-704 'buddy pack' refuelling pod, which allowed the Skyhawk to act as a tanker to top up other aircraft, mainly after launch or before landing. The first A4D-2 flew on 26

VMA-224 'Bengals' was the first Marine Corps Skyhawk squadron. This very clean A4D-1 was photographed in May 1957. Its cockpit section is preserved at Topeka, Kansas.

Douglas via TRH Pictures

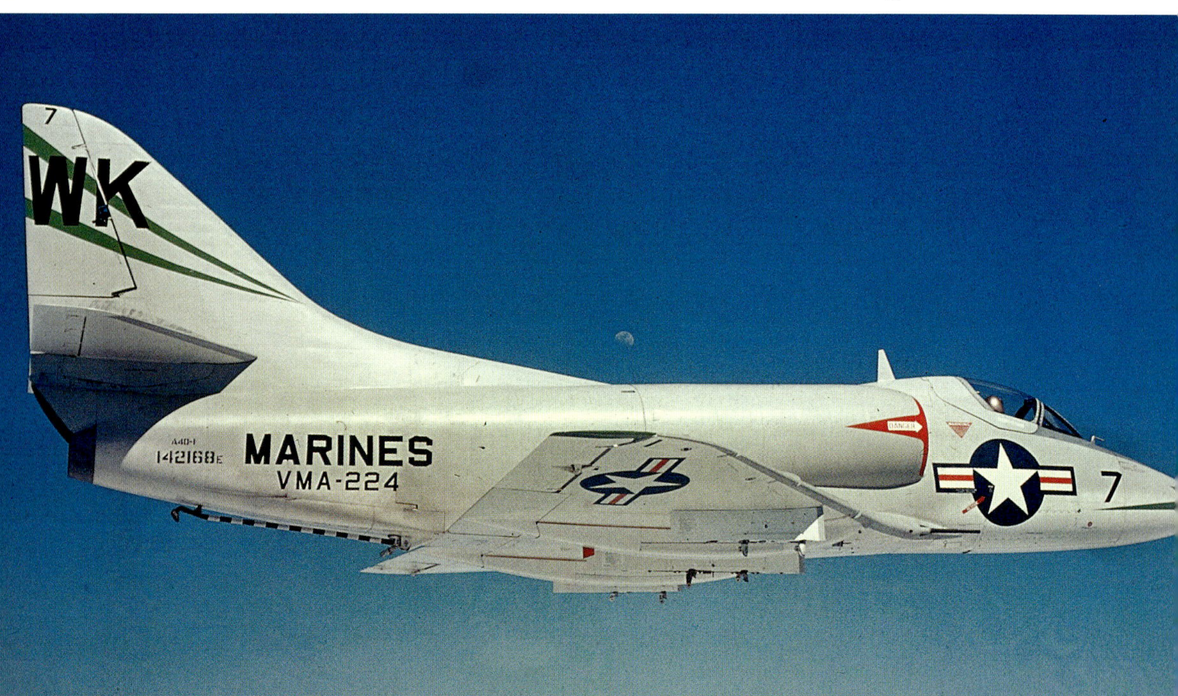

An A4D-1 of East Coast Replacement Air Group (RAG) VA-44, based at Jacksonville, Florida in 1958/59. The weapon depicted is a Mk 7 nuclear bomb.

March 1956 in the hands of Drury 'Dru' Wood. Deliveries of the first batch of sixty A4D-2s began in September 1957. VMA-211 received the first of these aircraft that month, but had to wait until early the following year for supply of the refuelling probes.

As an aside, the first -2 model officially handed over was BuNo 142102. It was sold to the Argentine Air Force nine years later and shot down by cannon fire from HMS *Fearless* over Falkland Sound in May 1982. More details of the A4D-2/A-4B and later versions follow in chapter two.

A mid-1970 tabulation of the cost per airframe and per pound of empty weight of the early Skyhawks showed the benefits of mass production and Ed Heinemann's rigorous control of weight and complexity. Whereas the hand-built XA4D-1 and static test example cost $4.34 million apiece, or $763 per pound, and the following nine aircraft $3.19 million ($520/lb) each, the last production batch of 94 A4D-1s ordered in September 1957 came in at $336,000 ($56/lb) and the second batch of A4D-2s (280 ordered in December 1958) were only $296,000 each, or only $45/lb. Over the first 500 Skyhawks, the average was $680,000 per airframe, excluding government-furnished equipment (GFE) such as the 'recycled' J65 engines. Production F/A-18C Hornets cost around $400/lb in today's money. The requirement to bring the A4D in at an exceptional performance and low weight at a unit cost of less than $1 million was well and truly met in the face of those who scoffed at Ed Heinemann in 1952.

Although the Navy got a bargain with the A4D-1, getting 146 full production standard jet attack bombers for $71 million, the funding to support them was less secure. By January 1958 the Commander in Chief of the Pacific Fleet (CINCPAC) had registered his dissatisfaction with the availability of the Skyhawk because of spare parts shortages. The previous year had seen a serious 'money crunch' in naval aviation. This saw cancellation of the A4D-3, an improved version with the J52 'growth engine', six months after a contract had been signed. More importantly for current Skyhawk operations, the funding for purchase of spares and support equipment was lacking in the spring of 1957, and frozen completely in the summer. Money was released in September but contract negotiations lasted until November. This 'purchase holiday' forced the Navy's logistics

The Skyhawk wing was built essentially as a one-piece unit,and was sealed to form the main fuel tank. Some of the first A4D-1 wingsets are seen on the El Segundo production line.
Douglas via 'Aeroplane'

organisation to borrow parts from the Douglas production line to satisfy operational needs. A contemporary memo to the Chief of Naval Operations (CNO) acknowledged that this was 'limited, unpredictable and must be repaid in kind ultimately'. This 'awkward period' was expected to last up to a year and would also affect production of

Cost and weight of early Skyhawks

Model	Delivered	No.	Empty weight	Cost ($ million) Total	per aircraft	per lb ($)
XA4D-1	06/54	1*	5,620 lb	8.68	4.34	763
A4D-1	11/55	9	6,150 lb	28.70	3.19	520
A4D-1	05/56	10	6,145 lb	8.58	0.858	140
A4D-1	02/57	52	5,975 lb	39.40	0.757	127
A4D-1	09/57	94	6,000 lb	31.60	0.336	56
A4D-2	01/58	68	6,660 lb	33.40	0.490	74
A4D-2	12/58	280	6,600 lb	83.00	0.296	45

*Plus static test example

The last A-4Ms cost approximately $5 Million apiece or $478 per pound the A4D-2, deliveries of which began in September 1957. Spare parts commonality between the A4D-1 and -2 was about seventy-two per cent.

Rear Admiral Soucek, regarded by many as the godfather of the Skyhawk, was not to see it enter Navy service, for he died on 22 July 1955. The US Navy's main East Coast jet base, Naval Air Station Oceana, Virginia, was named 'Apollo Soucek Field', in his honour. As for the first of all the Skyhawks, BuNo 137812, it appears to have had a shorter flying career than most of its contemporaries, several of which were still going in 1969. The last reported sighting of '812 was in late 1962 at the Long Beach plant where it was in use as an engineering mock-up for the features of later versions. After this it seems to have simply faded away. It may be that by then, possibly encumbered with new intakes, a new nose and cockpit, an avionics hump, a ribbed rudder, a refuelling probe and other parts that did and didn't make it onto the later Skyhawks, it was no longer recognizable as the first of the breed. Its significance forgotten, perhaps it fell victim to a clean-up at the plant and was scrapped, but without confirmation of this or a later sighting, the fate of the first of nearly 3,000 Skyhawks will have to remain a mystery.

Further down the line, wings were added to forward fuselages (top right) and rear fuselages attached (centre) before final fitting out (left). Douglas

The 2,500th Skyhawk, an A-4M for the Marines was delivered in 1971. Skyhawk production, mainly Ms and export models for Israel and Kuwait continued until 1979.

McDonnell Douglas/TRH Pictures

CHAPTER TWO

Further Developments

As soon as it appeared, Ed Heinemann and his team were drawing up ways of improving the Skyhawk. Many of these would come to fruition and others would not, but the continued development, indeed reinvention, of the A-4 would ensure the greatest production and service longevity of any American naval aircraft.

By the time the A4D-1 was ready to enter service, the role of the Skyhawk was undergoing a subtle shift. Built around the idea of delivering a single weapon faster than its predecessors over a relatively short distance, the development of new aerodynamic weapons shapes and associated bomb racks saw the A-4 begin to develop into the light attacker role that was to make it famous.

Ed Heinemann himself was behind one of the most important developments in weapons that allowed the Skyhawk and other tactical aircraft to greatly increase and expand their tactical capabilities. The Aero-1A family of external stores was developed by Ed Heinemann from 1949 as a way of improving the performance of the underpowered F3D Skyknight night-fighter. Using a fineness ratio (ratio of length to diameter) of 8:2.1, Heinemann created a series of drop tanks, weapons racks, and most importantly, bombs. The use of these Mark 80-series low-drag bombs, combined with triple and multiple ejector bomb-racks in particular allowed the A-4 (and other attack aircraft) to more than double their bomb load compared to carriage on single pylons of the bulky, high-drag bombs of World War 2 vintage then still in use.

As mentioned in the previous chapter, the A4D-1 was quickly followed by the A4D-2. At relatively little cost (about $40,000 extra per production aircraft), Ed Heinemann's team was able to refine the Skyhawk and greatly expand both its conventional and nuclear attack capabilities.

Most importantly, a fixed refuelling probe was added along the left side of the A4D-2's forward fuselage and plumbed into the wing tank. This simple device, which required no switches to operate or other cockpit changes other than a fuel flow gauge allowed the Skyhawk and pilot to stay aloft as long as he could remain awake or until the oil ran out, assuming there was tanker gas available. In practice, the coincident arrival of the Heinemann-designed D-704 refuelling package or 'buddy pod' allowed one Skyhawk or other tactical aircraft to top up the A4D-2 and extend its endurance from ninety minutes or two hours to up to four and a half hours. The introduction of 300-gallon (1067-litre) external tanks, double the volume of the original A4D tanks, also helped increase range, loiter time and safety margins when operating at sea.

The A4D-1 and -2 in turn were followed by numerous improved models for US and foreign service. The Skyhawk was in fact built in more different major versions than just about any other western jet combat aircraft. There were six single-seat models for the US

Navy and Marine Corps and four two-seat versions. There were fourteen export variants including rebuilt and redesignated aircraft.

Some things remained consistent throughout production. The wing area on all Skyhawk models was 260 sqft (24.15m^2), and the wing span was 27ft 6in (8.38m). Height was 14ft 11in (4.54m) except on those fitted with the ALR-45 'hot dog' tail antenna, which were 15ft 3in (4.69m) tall. All export versions except the Argentine A-4B, P and Q and the Australian A-4G had braking parachutes. The A-4M and 'Blue Angels' A-4F also had brake chutes.

Every A-4, whether carrier or land-based except (initially) the prototype, had an arrester hook. It has been said that Argentine Air Force A-4Ps did not have hooks to placate the Navy, but this is not supported by photographic evidence. Wing spoilers and nosewheel steering were fitted from the A-4F onwards, and retrofitted to almost all the older export models and some US A-4Es.

The A-4E and F and related models had a simple radar, good only for terrain avoidance and navigation. The longevity of the A-4 design and the increasing miniaturization of electronics allowed sophisticated modern radars with air-to-air and air-to-ground capability to be fitted to some upgraded export versions without altering the nose profile.

A detailed breakdown of the different variants and their salient features begins with the initial model, upon which more and more was added; more electronics, more equipment, more weapons and, most importantly, more thrust.

XA4D-1

The first two Skyhawks were virtually hand built, and flew at Edwards AFB on 22 June and 14 August 1954, respectively. A long instrumentation probe protruded from the nose of the first aircraft, which initially had a short tail pipe, a single-surface rudder and no arrester hook or weapons pylons. The XA4D-1s had no cannon.

XA4D-1 Bureau number: 137812
Construction number (c/n): 10709

The XA4D-1 is seen in its initial configuration. Note the lack of an arrester hook or cannon.
Douglas via 'Aeroplane'

A4D-1 (A-4A)

The first nine A4D-1s were known as YA4D-1s for testing purposes, although this designation was not widely used, and the distinction between the first nine and the following ten is blurred. Many features of later A-4s were trialled on the early A4D-1s, which were generally in unpainted metal finish. These included the sugar scoop tail fairing, the ribbed rudder and the tail hook. The first nineteen A4D-1s had a one-piece curved windscreen. From then on the three-piece windscreen with oval centre panel was used. Cannon armament (two 20-mm Colt Mk 12s) appeared on some of these early aircraft but not on others.

Service deliveries began with the twentieth aircraft built, although most early aircraft remained at Palmdale for modification before being issued to fleet and Corps units. The thirty-seventh A4D-1 was the first delivered directly from the factory to the fleet, to VA-72 in October 1956. The twentieth and subsequent aircraft had a liquid versus a gaseous oxygen system, the three-piece windscreen and other changes.

A TA-4A based at NAS Olathe, Kansas. Reserve units VA-881 and VA-882 pooled aircraft at this base.
Author's collection

A total of 165 A4D-1s was produced. After October 1962 they became A-4As. For administrative purposes, mainly to reduce the apparent number of attack aircraft in the inventory so the Navy could seek appropriations for more, the designation TA-4A was promulgated in June 1968 for the non combat-suitable A-4A models which were by then mainly being used as trainers. No physical changes were made to the aircraft.

A4D-1s were later to be armed with a wide range of conventional bombs, rockets and missiles but as designed and employed, their capability was essentially limited to nuclear stores. This included the Mk 7 with a variable yield of between 8 kilotons (kT) and 61 kT, the Mk 8 (25-30 kT) and the Mk 12 of 12-14 kT.

A4D-1 (A-4A) BuNos:

137813 – 137831 (19)	c/ns 10710-10728
139919 – 139970 (52)	c/ns 11284-11335
142142 – 142235 (94)	c/ns 11396-11489
Total 165	

A4D-2 (A-4B)

The A4D-2 introduced the externally-ribbed 'tadpole' rudder into production. The landing gear, nose structure keel and horizontal stabilizer were strengthened mainly to

One of the lesser-known Skyhawk units was the National Parachute Test Range at El Centro, who operated this A-4B circa 1968. Later they were renamed the Aerospace Recovery Facility and moved to China Lake.
Author's collection

withstand catapult launches at increased gross weights. Douglas said the new model had twenty-eight per cent new structure compared to the A4D-1. The stabilizer actuator assembly was strengthened and the degree of trim was reduced. The loss of one of the YA4D-1s caused by hydraulic failure brought about the introduction of a dual non-reversible hydraulic system.

The most noticeable and most important development for the Skyhawk's future was the addition of a fixed refuelling probe running from the starboard wing root along the side of the nose. Buddy refuelling capability with the D-704 store also first appeared on the 'Bravo'. The A4D-2s had the J65-W-16A turbojet of 7,200lb (34.2kN) thrust.

As well as nuclear weapons, conventional low-drag bombs from 250lb (113kg) to 2,000lb (907kg) could be carried on the new triple ejector racks (TERs) and multiple ejector racks (MERs) or directly on the three weapons pylons.

A total of 542 A4D-2s were built, and the variant was designated A-4B after 1962. In the same fashion as the TA-4A, many A-4Bs became TA-4Bs and utilized for training. Argentina and Singapore took large numbers of refurbished A-4Bs.

A4D-2 (A-4B) BuNos:

142082 – 142141	(60)	c/ns 11336-11335
142416 – 142423	(8)	c/ns 11601-11608
142674 – 142953	(280)	c/ns 11736-12015
144868 – 145061	(194)	c/ns 12114-12307

Total 542

A4D-2N (A-4C)

The A4D-2N (N standing for night) introduced radar in the form of an AN/APG-53A set for terrain clearance. This necessitated that the nose be lengthened by 9in (23cm). Fifteen per cent of the structure was new compared to the A4D-2. Other avionics improvements included a low-altitude bombing system (LABS) and a new autopilot. The introduction of these 'all weather' avionics marked a shift away from high-level nuclear strike missions to the low-level conventional attack mission which was to become the Skyhawk's forte.

The A4D-2N (A-4C from 1962) was the most numerous version of the Skyhawk, with

A China Lake A-4C is seen test dropping an AGM-62 Walleye, NWC China Lake via Garry Verver

a total of 638 produced. Many were later refurbished and supplied to foreign customers, such as Singapore and Argentina, and 100 were converted to A-4Ls for the US Naval Reserve (see below). During 1963 the production line was moved from El Segundo plant down the Pacific coast to the Long Beach plant, with final assembly at Palmdale. In total 1,168 Skyhawks were completed at El Segundo.

New to the A-4C was the AGM-12 Bullpup air-to-ground missile, of which a maximum of three could be carried, although a normal load was a pair, alongside a drop tank. More importantly to the pilots, the 'Charlie' introduced a relief tube in the cockpit. One early A-4 aviator recalled why this was one of the most important improvements in the whole Skyhawk series. '[The A-4]A could only stay airborne for about 1.5 to 2.0 hours and most of us could hold our coffee overflow without using the plastic bag supplied. The three hundred gallon tanks and refuelling probe meant double cycles of 3.5 to 4.5 hours and that was beyond the bladder capacity for almost all of us excessive coffee drinkers. It was not uncommon to see a double cycled returning A-4 pilot go straight to the shower rather than to the debrief or the ready room. Been there, done that'.

A4D-2N (A-4C) BuNos	
145062 – 145146 (85)	c/ns 12308-12392
147669 – 147849 (181)	c/ns 12433-12613
148304 – 148317 (14)	c/ns 12614-12627
148435 – 148612 (178)	c/ns 12628-12805
149487 – 149646 (160)	c/ns 12812-12971
150581 – 150600 (20)	c/ns 12992-13011
146460 to 146693 (33)	Cancelled
Total 638	

A pair of VA-144's A-4Cs fly over Mt. Fuji, Japan, either during their 1963 WestPac cruise on Constellation *or their first Vietnam War cruise the following year.* Via Gary Verver

VA-125 at was the main training unit for Pacific Fleet Skyhawk squadrons. A4D-2Ns (A-4Cs) arrived at Moffett Field in 1960, a year before the squadron moved to Lemoore.
Author's collection

A4D-3

The A4D-3 was the variant that Douglas wanted to build with the J52 engine and a new avionics package. A mock-up was built in 1957, so chronologically it preceded the A4D-2N, but was not built for budgetary reasons. The A4D-2N was a compromise version. Four aircraft were contracted and a further six Bureau Numbers allocated for planning purposes. More details of the unbuilt versions follow at the end of this chapter.

A4D-3 BuNos
145147-145156 (10) Cancelled

A4D-4

Proposed in 1958 as a low-altitude nuclear attack version, the A4D-4 would have had an all-new tapered, swept wing with a 10ft (3.2m) greater wingspan. Seven stores pylons would have been needed, and the wing would have incorporated folding for carrier stowage and 'Whitcomb' aerodynamic bodies on the trailing edge near the tips. Funding was not available and no examples were built.

A4D-5 (A-4E)

Incorporating many features proposed for the A4D-3, the A4D-5 (later A-4E) gave the Skyhawk a new lease of life, greatly improving the performance and attack capabilities and paving the way for most export versions and the TA-4 two-seaters.

The boost in performance came from the 9,300lb (43.1kN) thrust Pratt & Whitney J52-P6A turbojet, which gave 800lb (3.5kN) more thrust with 770lb (350kg) lower weight. Fuel consumption was better and the J52 had development potential that the J65 did not. Eventually, the J52 would offer nearly 2,000lb (9.3kN) greater thrust in later versions. New wider intakes separated from the fuselage with a splitter plate were one of the few visual concessions to the new engine.

The structure of the fuselage was beefed up to handle the extra power and the wing structure was revised with a stronger main spar to handle two extra wing pylons, making a total of five. This usually allowed for a pair of 300-gallon (1136 litre) drop tanks to be carried on the inboard pylons (stations 2 and 5) and weapons on the centreline and outboard pylons. Alternatively, the centreline station (station 3) could carry a 400 gallon (1514 litre) tank, leaving the wing pylons free for bombs, rockets or missiles. The nose was lengthened again, by 14 inches (36cm) to incorporate an AN/ASN-19A navigation computer. A Mk 9 toss-bombing system allowed a wider range of weapons delivery options and the low altitude bombing system was the improved AJB-3A. Other new equipment included a new TACAN, Doppler navigation, and a radar altimeter. The windscreen wiper seen on most A-4Bs and Cs was replaced by a rain removal blower system, and a fuel dump mast was added at the rear of the starboard landing gear fairing. In all, the A-4E had twenty-nine per cent new structure.

Only the first eight A4D-5s built were so designated, as the tri-service redesignation system came into effect before deliveries began in January 1963, and the 'Dash Five' became the A-4E.

Apart from the intakes, the early A-4Es looked much like the A-4C. In fact the first two were converted on the production line from A-4C airframes. During production of the 500 A-4Es, a couple of distinctive features appeared, namely a dorsal avionics 'hump' and a 'cranked' refuelling probe.

The avionics hump sat on the fuselage saddle between the rear of the canopy and the base of the fin, and was a solution to the diminishing internal space of the Skyhawk. It contained ALQ-126 defensive electronic countermeasures (DECM) equipment and also held control boxes for the ALR-50 SAM alert and launch warning system. The refuelling probe was redesigned with a prominent kink in it that brought the nozzle slightly outboard of the starboard intake. This reduced the occasional problem of fuel spraying into the intake during aerial refuelling and causing an engine flameout.

In 1971 a batch of sixty A-4Es was transferred from US stocks to Israel and in late 1973 a further forty-eight A-4Es and Fs were shipped and flown out to make up losses experienced in the Yom Kippur War in October. In 1979 fourteen surplus A-4Es were

Built in 1964, this A-4E had made three Vietnam carrier deployments by the time it was pictured here with Hawaii-based VC-1 circa 1977. It flew on with various Navy and Marine squadrons until 1987. It is preserved today at the Pacific Coast Air Museum in Santa Rosa, California.

US Navy

The fourth A4D-5 was used for carrier suitability trials with the Naval Air Test Center at Patuxent River.
TRH Pictures

supplied to Indonesia from the Israeli inventory, followed in 1985 by a further batch of sixteen.

A4D-5 (A-4E) BuNos		
148613 – 148614	(2)	c/ns 12806-12807
149647 – 149666	(20)	c/ns 12972-12991
149959 – 150138	(180)	c/ns 13012-13191
151022 – 151201	(180)	c/ns 13192-13371
151984 – 152100	(117)	c/ns 13372-13488
151202 – 151261	(141)	cancelled
Total 499		

A-4F

The A-4F was an evolved version of the A-4E and incorporated all the improvements that appeared during A-4E production while adding some new ones. The cranked probe and avionics hump were fitted as standard. Many also had ALQ-100 deception jamming equipment, characterized by a small undernose fairing. Lift-dumping spoilers were

Many A-4Es, such as this VC-5 example were retro-fitted with features of the A-4F, such as the avionics hump, bent probe and wing spoilers.
TRH Pictures

In their later service as adversary aircraft the A-4Es and Fs grew even harder to distinguish, as most were modified to a common standard. BuNo 154183 'double nuts' was an F, and marked with a Russian Federation flag when with VA-127 in the 1990s. Graham Robson

created by hinging the section of the wing above the trailing edge flap. Operated together with the flaps, they forced the nose down in the landing roll and helped keep the aircraft tracking straight. Nosewheel steering was introduced for the first time. The standard engine was the J52-P8A of 9,300lb (43.1kN) thrust, although later 100 modification kits were later issued to convert A-4Fs to 'Super Fox' configuration. The Super Fox had the –P408 engine rated at 11,200lb (49.8kN) and this required slightly wider intakes.

Some of the earliest A-4Fs were later converted to Super Fox configuration and supplied to the 'Blue Angels' flight demonstration team. These aircraft differed from standard Fs in having no hump, no guns or weapons equipment and an integral folding boarding ladder in a fairing where the port gun normally was. A braking parachute was mounted under the tail to assist with crosswind landings, which were more common at the sort of civil airports with a single runway that the 'Blue Angels' regularly operated from. The Marines' A-4M was the only other US-operated Skyhawk model to see service with a drag chute. The leading-edge slats were locked shut to prevent asymmetric operation, which could be disastrous during close-formation manoeuvres.

Many late A-4Fs had an ALR-45 radar warning receiver (RWR) antenna in a fin-tip extension. Control boxes for this equipment were added to the hump. In later service in the adversary role, the hump and tail fairing were usually removed to save weight and drag.

A-4F BuNos:

152101 (Converted A-4E)	(1)	c/n 13371
154172 – 154217	(46)	c/ns 13629-13674
154281 – 154286	(5)	Cancelled
154970 – 155069	(100)	c/ns 13786-13885

Total 147

A classic photo of a VA-22 'Fighting Redcocks' A-4F and its home away from home in 1969-70, the USS Bon Homme Richard.

US Navy via TRH Pictures

TA-4F

The first two-seat Skyhawk variant began life as the TA-4E in 1964. After considerable efforts by Douglas, the Defense Department was convinced that a two-seater for use as an advanced trainer and for some combat roles would free up more single-seaters for use in Vietnam. A very realistic wooden mock-up was created using a surplus A-4E airframe and displayed at the 1965 Paris airshow to help drum up export interest. The last two A-4Es were completed as TA-4Es and the first of these flew on 30 June 1965.

Many features of the new A-4F then in development were added such as spoilers and nosewheel steering, and the designation was soon changed to TA-4F to reflect these improvements. To create the TA-4F, the fuselage was stretched by 28in (71cm) and a long canopy was fitted, actuated by a piston between the two Escapac 1C-3 seats. The windscreen had a straight-edged centre panel. Powered by the J52-P8-A engine of 9,300lb (43.1kN) thrust, the TA-4F was fully combat-capable, with five pylons and the same two cannon as single-seaters.

The TA-4F entered service with VA-125 in May 1966. The first combat use was as a fast forward air control (FAC) aircraft with the US Marines in Vietnam.

Many surviving TA-4Fs were later converted to TA-4Js by the deletion of most of the combat equipment, the outboard pylons and one or both of the cannon. Of the 241 TA-4Fs

The 'Blue Angels' demonstration team made many changes to their A-4Fs. The retractable boarding ladder in the port wing root is one that is visible here.

Frank B. Mormillo via 'Aeroplane'

The first two dual-control Skyhawks were converted from A-4Es on the production line and were designated TA-4Es when they first flew in 1965.

McDonnell Douglas

produced, 130 were later reworked as Js.

A-4Es converted to TA-4E:

152102 and 152103 (2)	c/ns 13490-13491

TA-4F BuNos

152846 – 152878 (33)	c/ns 13492-13524
153459 – 153531 (73)	c/ns 13525-13597
153660 – 153690 (31)	c/ns 13598-13628
154287 – 154343 (57)	c/ns 13675-13731
154614 – 154657 (44)	c/ns 13732-13775
155071 (1)	c/n 13887

Total including conversions 241

EA-4F

Four converted TA-4Fs became EA-4Fs to act as threat simulators for naval exercises. As part of their 'electronic adversary' role they could be fitted with AST-4 threat simulation pods and a variety of ECM pods, including ALQ-71, -72, -76 and -167 emitters. As such they could fly flight profiles appropriate to a variety of threats, including sea-skimming cruise missiles. All the EA-4Fs served with electronic adversary squadron VAQ-33 at Key West, alongside specially modified A-3 Skywarriors and an EC-121 Constellation. Two of the four EA-4Fs crashed, one into a mountain in Colorado in 1980, and the other at North Island, California in 1985 following a missed approach.

EA-4Fs (converted from TA-4F)
152852, 152869, 153481, 154655

TA-4J

The TA-4 proved an ideal replacement for the TF-9J Cougar in the advanced training role. After one TA-4F was converted to TA-4J standard with removal of tactical equipment and fitted with the lower-rated P6 engine, an initial batch of forty-eight was

The EA-4F was the rarest US variant with only four created by converting TA-4Fs.They served with electronic attack squadron VAQ-33 at Key West in the electronic warfare training role.
TRH Pictures

ordered for Training Command in a contract worth $26.83 million. The converted aircraft first flew in December 1968 and by mid-1969, all of the first batch were in service with the training squadrons based in the southern USA. In addition to 277 new-build TA-4Js, the majority of TA-4Fs were converted to J standard by deleting missile-launching equipment, radar and two of the five weapons pylons as well as installing the lower-powered J52-P6-A or-B engine. Generally speaking, the two 20-mm Mk 12 cannon were not fitted to the TA-4J and were removed from converted TA-4Fs. A number of aircraft retained the starboard-side gun for use in the advanced strike part of the syllabus.

This TA-4J, converted from a TA-4F wore the full colours of attack squadron VA-192 'World Famous Golden Dragons' who used it as an instrument trainer in 1968. It was lost in a crash near San Clemente Island in 1990 when serving with VC-7.
TRH Pictures

TA-4J BuNos (new build)

155070	(1)	c/n 13886
155072 – 155119	(48)	c/ns 13888-13935
156891 – 156950	(60)	c/ns 13984-14043
158073 – 158147	(75)	c/ns 14110-14184
158453 – 158527	(75)	c/ns 14258-14332
158712 – 158723	(12)	c/ns 14333-14344
159099 – 159104	(6)	c/ns 14405-14410

Total 277

TA-4J BuNos (converted from TA-4F)

152103, 152847, 152848, 152850, 152853, 152854, 152855, 152858, 152859, 152861, 152862, 152863, 152864, 152863, 152864, 152867, 152868, 152870, 152871, 152872, 152875, 152878, 153460, 153461, 153462, 153463, 153465, 153467, 153468, 153469, 153471, 153473, 153474, 153475, 153476, 153477, 153478, 153479, 153482, 153486, 153492, 153495, 153496, 153497, 153498, 153500, 153502, 153504, 153505, 153509, 153512, 153513, 153515, 153516, 153517, 153518, 153521, 153522, 153524, 153525, 153526, 153528, 153530, 153661, 153663, 153664, 153667, 153669, 153670, 153671, 153672, 153674, 153675, 153676, 153677, 153678, 153679, 153680, 153681, 153683, 153685, 153687, 153689, 153690, 154287, 154288, 154289, 154290, 154291, 154292, 154293, 154295, 154296, 154297, 154298, 154300, 154303, 154305, 154310, 154312, 154313, 154314, 154315, 154317, 154318, 154319, 154322, 154323, 154327, 154330, 154332, 154338, 154341, 154342, 154343, 154614, 154615, 154616, 154617, 154618, 154619, 154626, 154631, 154632, 154634, 154635, 154636, 154649, 154650, 154653, 154657

A-4G/TA-4G for Australia

The A-4G for the Royal Australian Navy (RAN) was the first new-build export variant. In late 1965, the Australian government ordered eight A-4G models based on the A-4F, and two TA-4Gs based on the TA-4F airframe for use on the carrier HMAS *Melbourne*.

For a time VT-21 'Fighting Redhawks' adapted the standard red/white Training Command colour scheme on their TA-4Js with red 'tail feathers'. TRH Pictures

A-4Gs visited the United Kingdom in 1977 when HMAS Melbourne *attended the Jubilee Fleet Review. This example also attended the International Air Tattoo at Greenham Common.*

Via Mike Hooks

On 19 July 1967 the first A-4G flew, followed two days later by the first TA-4G. The Australian Skyhawks were stored in the US as they were completed and delivered together on the carrier *Melbourne* in November1967. A second batch of refurbished A-4Fs (eight) and TA-4Fs (two) were ordered in 1971 and modified to G standard.

The Gs differed from the USN's Fs in having AIM-9B Sidewinder capability on all wing pylons, but reduced air-to-ground weapons provisions. Weapons were limited to the Mk 81 and Mk 82 free-fall bombs (although the 750lb M117 bomb was very occasionally used), and 2.75in (70mm) HVAR or Hydra rockets in a seven-shot launcher and 5in (127mm) Zuni rockets in a four-shot pod. Additionally the A-4Gs could tow the DelMar Radop target for ship-to-air gunnery training.

The A-4Gs had no dorsal hump and some slight revisions to the avionics, but essentially were the same as the A-4F. With its different centre of gravity, the TA-4G was not considered able to perform a 'bolter' landing on *Melbourne's* short (690ft/210.3m) flight deck, but was otherwise equipped with all the weapons and avionics of the single-seaters.

Ten of the twenty RAN Skyhawks were lost in service. The survivors were sold to New Zealand in 1984 and upgraded along with the RNZAF's original A-4Ks and TA-4Ks.

A-4G BuNos (new build)
154903-154910 (8) c/ns 13734-13741

TA-4G BuNos (new build)
154911 and 154912 (2) c/ns 13884 and 13885

A-4G BuNos (converted A-4Fs)
155051, 155052, 155055, 155060, 155061, 155062, 155063 and 155064 (8)

TA-4G BuNos (converted TA-4Fs)
154647 and 154648 (2)

One of the TA-4Gs destined for Australia is seen at Long Beach prior to delivery.This aircraft became 880 in RAN service and then TA-4K NZ6255 with the RNZAF.

Douglas via TRH Pictures

A-4H for Israel

Israel's Skyhawks were in action soon after the arrival of the first of forty-eight A-4Hs in December 1967. The A-4H was based on the F airframe and had a braking parachute and a squared-off fin-tip which housed AN/APX-46 Identification Friend or Foe (IFF) equipment. As delivered, they all lacked the dorsal avionics package. By October 1973, many Hs had been 'given the hump', which was filled with the locally-developed WDNS 391 TAAL-Crystal navigation package.

The contract to supply the A-4H was signed in August 1966 and the first aircraft flew on 27 October 1967. In light of combat experience, the IDF/AF soon began to modify these aircraft, plus a further forty-two delivered in 1969 and the 106 A-4E and Fs transferred from the US Navy in October 1973 and shortly thereafter for greater survivability and combat effectiveness. The first modifications begun in 1974 included extending the jetpipe to reduce the heat difference between the efflux and the outside air as a defence against infrared missiles, and installing radar warning equipment. Chaff dispensers were another defensive addition. In 1970, the Israelis began to fit French-made 30-mm DEFA type 552 cannon to their Skyhawks in place of the jamming-prone 20mm Colt Mk 12. The A-4Es were further modified with wing spoilers and brake parachutes. The Es appear to have mainly retained their avionics humps and kept the curved tailfin tip. The equivalent two-seater was the TA-4H, of which 25 were built. This combat-capable version was used as a trainer and at times in action as a bomber.

Two TA-4Hs went to Indonesia as part of the first batch of Skyhawks supplied in 1979.

Israeli A-4H BuNos
155242 – 155289 (48) c/ns 13936-13983
157395 – 157428 (34) c/ns unknown
157918 – 157925 (8) c/ns 14096-14105
Total 90

An A-4H from the second batch delivered to Israel is seen before delivery in the USA. The main visible difference from the A-4E was the square fin tip and blade aerial.

Douglas via TRH Pictures

Israeli TA-4H BuNos	
157429 – 157434 (6)	c/ns 14044-14049
157926 – 157929 (4)	c/ns 14106-14109
159546 – 159556 (11)	c/ns 14423-14433
159795 – 159798 (4)	c/ns 14494-14497
Total 25	

A-4K and TA-4K for New Zealand

New Zealand's A-4K and TA-4K Skyhawks remained essentially the same from delivery in 1970 until 1984, at which time they were extensively modified. The twelve aircraft were basically A-4Fs and TA-4Fs with slightly different radios, an APX-72 IFF antenna in a square fin tip and the addition of a braking parachute. In 1984, New Zealand purchased Australia's ten surviving Skyhawks – eight A-4Gs and two TA-4Gs for A$28.2 million. Minor changes such as changing the radios and adding the brake chute were made quickly, but in 1985 a comprehensive refurbishment programme was started on all the aircraft. This was called Project 'Kahu' (Hawk) and involved a structural upgrade and modernising of the avionics and weapons capability.

As part of this, all the Ks lost their avionics humps (which were in fact empty), and gained a new Litton inertial navigation and attack (INAS) system, a rebuilt cockpit with a Ferranti wide-angle HUD, MFDs, and HoTaS (Hands on Throttle and Stick) controls. Most importantly, a version of the F-16's radar with an extra sea-search mode, designated APG-66(NZ), was installed. The capability to launch AGM-65 Maverick and AIM-9L Sidewinder missiles and laser-guided bombs was added. An ALR-66 radar warning receiver was fitted as were AN/ALE-39 chaff/flare dispensers. The work was carried out by Safe Air Engineering at Woodbourne, and the last of twenty rebuilt aircraft was delivered in 1989.

The A-4Ks equipped No. 75 Squadron at Ohakea. For a brief period, two of the TA-4Ks and one A-4K were on the books of No. 14 Squadron, otherwise equipped with BAC

A line-up of TA-4Hs (with square fin tips) and TA-4Js of the Israel Air Force Flight Training School Advanced Squadron, which pools aircraft with No. 102 Squadron. IDF/AF

The first A-4K (right) and TA-4K for New Zealand await delivery in 1970. They have the original straight probes, silver fern (rather than kiwi) roundels and unswept fin flash.

Douglas via TRH Pictures

Strikemasters. The addition of the A-4Gs allowed the outfitting of No. 2 Squadron, which was based at Ohakea and later at Nowra in Australia where it helped train Australian sailors and aircrews in air defence.

When a lease-purchase deal for embargoed Pakistan Air Force F-16As from the USA was signed in 1997, a proposed 'Kahu II' upgrade was cancelled. This would have seen installation of a new ejection seat and a laser-self designating capability as well as a further structural upgrade. This was cancelled in 1998 following a defence review, and in 2001 the New Zealand government decided to disestablish the RNZAF's air combat force altogether, and the Skyhawks and Aermacchi MB.339 trainers were stored awaiting sale.

A-4K BuNos (new build)
157904 – 157913 (10) c/ns 14084-14093

TA-4K BuNos (new build)
157914 – 157917 (4) c/ns 14102-14105

A-4L for the Reserves

In order to equip two Naval Reserve carrier air wings with aircraft having up-to-date avionics and self-defence equipment, a total of 100 A-4Cs were reworked as A-4Ls, beginning in 1969. The first A-4L upgrade was flown on 21 August 1969. The A-4L had the fuselage avionics hump, nosewheel steering and wing spoilers of the A-4F. All were

'Kahu' modified A-4K NZ6205 is seen near PalmerstonNorth Airport sporting AIM-9L Sidewinders and AGM-65 Mavericks. This overall green scheme was the last worn by RNZAF Skyhawks.

RNZAF Official

fitted with the J65-W-20 of 8,400lb (38.96kN) thrust.

The following A-4Cs were converted to A-4Ls:

145065, 145076, 145077, 145078, 145092, 145101, 145103, 145114, 145117, 145119,145121, 145122, 145128, 145133, 145141, 147669, 147671, 147690, 147703, 147706,147708, 147717, 147723, 147727, 147736, 147750, 147754, 147761, 147768, 147772,147780, 147782, 147787, 147793, 147796, 147798, 147802, 147807, 147815, 147825,147827, 147836, 147843, 148306, 148307, 148316, 148436, 148446, 148453, 148479,148487, 148490, 148498, 148505, 148530, 148538, 148555, 148578, 148581, 148586,148588, 148600, 148602, 148611, 149497, 149500, 149502, 149506, 149508, 149516,149518, 149531, 149532, 149536, 149539, 149540, 149951, 149555, 149556, 149569,149573, 149579, 149583, 149591, 149593, 149595, 149604, 149607, 149608, 149620,149623, 149626, 149630, 149633, 149635, 149640, 149646, 150586, 150593, 150598

The A-4L was modified for the Naval Reserve, but also saw service with Marine Reserve units such as VMA-124. This A-4L was later further converted to a two-seat TA-4PTM for Malaysia.

Author's collection

A-4M for the Marines

The US Navy's 1963 VAL (light attack aircraft) competition to replace the A-4 was won by the Vought A-7 Corsair II. The Marines however wanted a lighter, less complex aircraft able to operate from unprepared strips. The solution was found in the development of the 11,200lb (49.8kN) thrust Pratt & Whitney J52-P408 engine, which offered 20 per cent greater power with very little extra fuel consumption. Development of a P408-engined version for the Marines was authorized in 1969 as the A-4M.

Following conversion of two A-4Fs as test aircraft, the first A-4M proper flew on 10 April 1970 at Palmdale. The first production examples were delivered to VMA-324 at Yuma in February 1971. The A-4M, sometimes called the 'Skyhawk II' had a smokeless burner can, a larger, increased-visibility canopy and new windscreen, a ribbon-type drag chute, a self-starting unit, a more powerful generator and a repositioned IFF antenna atop a squared-off vertical fin. Cannon ammunition capacity was increased from 100 to 200 rounds.

Development continued during A-4M production. In 1974 an Elliot HUD was added and the instrument panel was completely revised. The addition of ALR-45 radar homing and warning (RHAW) gear resulted in a large fintip bullet antenna and small blister antennas beside the nose and on the 'sugar scoop'. During 1977 production, the Hughes Angle Rate Bombing System (ARBS), including a laser spot tracker (LST) which allowed use of laser-guided bombs, was added in a glass dome at the tip of the nose. A secure UHF radio with over 7,000 channels was another part of the package. On the final production aircraft the landing gear was strengthened, and some had bulged main landing-gear doors.

At one point it seems that the late model A-4M was going to be redesignated A-4Y, although this did not come about. Most of the early aircraft were in time upgraded to this later standard, although not all aircraft received the ARBS system. When the A-4M was

A-4Ls of Reserve squadron VA-203 'Blue Dolphins' are seen on a rare carrier deployment, in this case to the USS John F. Kennedy *in August 1971.*

US Navy via TRH Pictures

An early A-4M of VMA-324 launches a Zuni rocket during a training sortie. This aircraft collided with another while air refuelling over the Pacific in May 1986 and was lost.

Harry S. Gann/McDonnell Douglas

The last Skyhawks were delivered with ECM and radar warning equipment not found on the first A-4Ms. This is the final aircraft built, which was delivered in this colour scheme commemorating all the Skyhawk's users and wore it into service with VMA-311, VX-5 and VMA-223.

McDonnell Douglas via Mike Hooks

The A-4M was built exclusively for the Marines, but saw some service with Navy units such as the Fighter Weapons School (Topgun) in the adversary role. This A-4M (160045), later went to Argentina as C-922.
Graham Robson

retired in the 1990s, the ARBS gear was removed from the surplus A-4Ms and fitted to AV-8B Harriers. The last A-4M, which was in fact the last of 2,960 Skyhawks completed, was rolled out in February 1979.

A-4Fs converted to A-4M configuration (2): BuNos 155042 & 155049

A-4M BuNos

158148 – 158196 (49)	c/ns 14185-14233
158412 – 158435 (24)	c/ns 14234-14257
159470 – 159493 (24)	c/ns 14411-14434
159778 – 159790 (13)	c/ns 14477-14489
160022 – 160045 (24)	c/ns 14524-14547
160241 – 160264 (24)	c/ns 14584-14607

Total including conversions 160

A-4N for Israel

Based on the A-4M, the A-4N for Israel incorporated all of the indigenous improvements developed following combat experience in 1971. Most of these, including the Crystal navigation system, 30-mm DEFA cannon, extended tailpipe and locally designed ECM were fitted after delivery. Other features were an Elliot HUD, dual-disc mainwheel brakes and a new weapons delivery computer based on that of the A-7 Corsair II. The N lacked the self-starting capability of the A-4M. From 1972 to 1976, 117 A-4Ns were supplied to Israel.

Although the A-4Ns were delivered with AN/APQ-145 radar, a few appeared after 1982 with the AN/ABS-19 ARBS sensor in a glass nose cone as seen on the A-4M, although without the associated ECM blisters.

IDF/AF A-4s could carry the full range of US 'dumb' bombs, plus the French-made bombs in the Israeli inventory. SUU-30 and Mk.20 Rockeye cluster bombs were widely used, as were napalm and rockets. AIM-9B and D Sidewinders were available by 1973, later supplemented by Shafrir II IR-guided AAMs. AGM-45 Shrike anti-radiation missiles were used effectively against SAM radars.

The A-4N for Israel shared many features with the A-4M but lacked the self-starting capability. This N is believed to have crashed in August 1992. IDF/AF

Precision weapons included the GBU-8 HOBO TV-guided glide bomb, the AGM-62 Walleye and the Gabriel 3 radar-guided ASM. ARBS-equipped A-4Ns could carry Paveway I and II series LGBs. It is believed that 20mm SUU-16 gun pods were used at one time.

A-4N BuNos

158726 – 158743 (18)	c/ns 14345-14362
159035 – 159052 (18)	c/ns 14363-14380
159075 – 159098 (24)	c/ns 14381-14404
159515 – 159545 (31)	c/ns 14411-14465
159799 – 159824 (26)	c/ns 14544-14523

Total 117

A-4KU/TA-4KU for Kuwait and AF-1/AF-1A for Brazil

In 1974, the Kuwaiti Air Force (KAF) ordered thirty-six Skyhawks based on the airframes of the A-4M and OA-4M. Designated A-4KU (thirty) and TA-4KU (six), they all had the self-starter of the A-4M, squared-off fintips, braking parachutes and J52-P-408-A engines. Although both versions had avionics humps,

The TA-4KU for Kuwait was another variant derived from the A-4M. The exhaust for the jet fuel starter is visible above the base of the IFR probe. Unlike the A-4KU, the TA-4KU featured the fintip ALR-45 antenna. McDonnell Douglas via TRH

the Kuwaiti aircraft had less sophisticated ECM gear and fewer weapons options than their USMC counterparts. Only the TA-4KUs had the fintip ALR-45 antenna, with a small additional antenna on top. As related elsewhere, most of the twenty-nine Kuwaiti Skyhawks then in service fought in the 1991 Gulf War, one being lost and several others being stripped for parts to maintain the others.

With US assistance, twenty-three of Kuwait's A-4s, three of them two-seaters, were purchased by Brazil for use by its Naval air arm. The Kuwaiti A-4KUs and TA-4KUs only had an average of about 1,700 flying hours when they arrived in September 1998. In Brazilian service the A-4KUs were redesignated AF-1s and the TA-4KUs, AF-1As. To date the only change has been the colour scheme, although Brazil would like to integrate the locally-made MAA-1 Piranha AAM to replace the AIM-9H Sidewinder and to obtain anti-ship and air-to-ground missiles. Currently they are operated solely in the fighter role.

A-4KU BuNos
160180 – 160209 (30) c/ns 14548-14577

TA-4KU BuNos
160212 – 160215 (6) c/ns 14578-14583

A-4P for Argentina

Argentina was the first export operator of the Skyhawk. Eventually the Fuerza Aérea Argentina (FAA) and Argentine Navy (Comando de la Aviación Naval Argentina – CANA) were to operate 138 Skyhawks of five different models. A further dozen were delivered as spares sources.

The first twenty-five A-4Ps for the FAA were delivered in 1966. A second batch of twenty-five arrived in 1970, like the first being refurbished by Douglas at Tulsa, Oklahoma from surplus US A-4Bs. Compared to the standard B, the P had no loft-bombing capability, but had a saddle-type DFA-73 air direction finding (ADF) aerial blister on the spine, and wing spoilers.

The Wright J-65-16A engines were rebuilt to zero hours. Other new equipment

Twenty of Kuwait's A-4KUs became AF-1s with the Brazilian Navy. Note the exhaust for the jet fuel starter just forward of the roundel and that this particular AF-1 has no cannon fitted.
Corné Rodenburg

included a Bendix CNA-4 navigation system, a VOR antenna on the tail, AN/ARC-27 UHF radio and AN/APX-6B IFF were also added. Many older pieces of US Navy-standard avionics were deleted. The last twenty-five aircraft were fitted with the Ferranti D126R Isis weapons sight system.

Argentina did not order any two-seat Skyhawks, as there simply was no such derivative of the J65-engined version. Despite the official export designation, the A-4P was usually called the A-4B in FAA service. The B/Ps were followed in 1976 by twenty-five A-4Cs, refurbished this time by Lockheed Air Services at Ontario, California. Twenty-six A-4Bs and fifteen A-4Cs were active at the outbreak of the Falklands/Malvinas conflict in April 1982. Most were modified to have five weapons pylons, requiring some external strengthening and the removal of one vortex generator from each wing. Ten A-4Bs and nine A-4Cs were lost in action.

After the war the Bs and Cs were combined into one unit, Grupo 5. In 1989, the cannon on the surviving aircraft was replaced by 30mm DEFA weapons. Other Argentine weapons included 70mm rockets, locally-made BK-BR and FAS 125kg (276lb) and 250kg (551lb) bombs and Rafael Shafrir I AAMs. The last of the first-generation Argentine A-4s was retired in 1999.

A-4Q for Argentina's Navy

The Argentine Navy (Comando de la Aviación Naval Argentina – CANA) version was little different from the Fuerza Aérea Argentina's A-4P and the A-4B from which it stemmed. One difference was that the Q had AIM-9 Sidewinder capability whereas the FAA versions did not. Sixteen A-4Bs were refurbished by Douglas and delivered in 1971. Like the FAA aircraft, they had the saddle type ADF antenna and hoop type antennas on the fin, but used the higher-thrust W-20 model J65. The A-4Qs were operated from the aircraft carrier *Vienticinco de Mayo* (25th of May) until the early 1980s and subsequently from land bases. Six of the sixteen A-4Qs were lost before the Falklands War, another three during it, and at least two afterwards, leaving four complete original and one composite aircraft for preservation when the type was finally retired in 1988.

A-4S for Singapore

The Republic of Singapore Air Force (RSAF) ordered 50 surplus A-4Bs from the USN in 1973 and contracted Lockheed to develop an overhaul and upgrade programme for them. Six A-4S and three TA-4S (see below) conversions were made in the USA and the rest

Seen in 1966 its delivery colour scheme, A-4P C-201 did not take part in the1982 Falklands War, having crashed in July 1977. Douglas

Originally built as A-4B 145053, A-4Q 665 is seen at Tulsa where it was overhauled for the Argentine Navy. It was delivered in 1971 and written off in June 1973. Douglas via Mike Hooks

were completed in Singapore. Three airframes were used for parts, leaving forty-seven delivered to the RSAF. Eight of the US-converted aircraft were initially based at NAS Lemoore to train air and groundcrews.

Over 100 changes were made to the basic A-4B, including a longer nose containing a new communication/navigation package, five weapons pylons, a dorsal ADF (air direction finding) aerial in a saddle fairing, wing spoilers and a braking parachute. The cannons were changed to 30-mm Adens, a cranked refuelling probe was fitted (although some A-4Ss were seen without probes before Singapore acquired KC-135 tankers in the 1990s), and AIM-9 capability was added. Avionics improvements included a new Ferranti lead-computing gunsight and weapons delivery computer, Decca Type 72 Doppler system, new radios, IFF, Tacan and radar altimeter. Four more TA-4S trainers were ordered in 1977.

A further 70 airframes were purchased from US surplus stocks in 1980. A mixture of A-4Bs and Cs, the former were used for spare parts while the latter entered service from 1982 as the A4S-1 (written without the dash in A4) without the Doppler set and with 20mm cannon. Sixteen more A-4Bs were converted to TA4S-1 standard in 1983. The original A-4S/TA-4S was finally retired in 1993, but the S-1s went through a major upgrade to 'Super Skyhawk' standard (see below). No official list of Singapore's Skyhawks has ever been issued and the RSAF serials are non-sequential , but over the years observers have identified 45 different A-4S airframes in service.

TA-4S

The Singaporeans chose a unique method of creating a two-seat trainer version of the A-4. Instead of purchasing TA-4Fs or Js (all of which had the J52 engine) in 1974 they

The A-4Ss were refurbished A-4Bs and Cs. As A-4B 142900, this 143 Squadron A-4S served with VA-95 'Green Lizards' on the Intrepid *and* Shangri-La *in Vietnam.* TRH Pictures

The TA-4S was built from surplus A-4Bs with a unique two-canopy arrangement. Used for initial training in the USA, the first TA-4S (651) was issued to No. 142 Squadron in Singapore. Its nose is preserved at the RSAF Museum. Lockheed Air Services

instructed Lockheed to develop a two-seater from the A-4B airframe. This involved a 28inch (71cm) fuselage extension, giving a length of 40ft 6in (12.34m), just slightly longer than a single-seat A-4E or F. Unlike the later TA-4PTM for Malaysia, this TA-4S conversion involved two separate canopies and windscreens. The rear windscreen was a curved one-piece unit and the rear canopy was later bulged outwards to give better forward visibility to the instructor pilot. Only the canopy frame was the same as the A-4B's. Initially there were three TA-4S models, followed in 1977 by four TA4S-1s. None of these were upgraded to TA-4SUs.

Known A-4S BuNos (all A-4Bs)

142101, 142119, 142125, 142131, 142711, 142746, 142751, 142770, 142771, 142774, 142778, 142800, 142819, 142832, 142840, 142850, 142870, 142876, 142882, 142908, 142942, 144874, 144926, 144956, 144971, 144974, 144980, 145013, 145030, 145038, 145043, 145046, 145056, 145059

Known TA-4S BuNos (all A-4Bs)

144894, 144937, 144979, 145043, 145047.

A-4SU/ TA-4SU 'Super Skyhawk'

By the mid-1980s, the age of the J65 engine in the RSAF's A-4s was contributing to increasing unreliability and numerous inflight failures. The decision was taken to re-engine the A4S-1s and TA4S-1s and then update their avionics. The chosen powerplant was the General Electric F404-GE-100D turbofan as used in the F/A-18 Hornet, albeit without the Hornet's afterburner. The work was carried out by Singapore Aircraft Industries (later Singapore Technologies Aerospace). The first stage upgrade, involving the engine alone, was called A4S-1/F404 and unofficially designated A-4U. The F404 gave the Skyhawk

The A-4SU upgrade gave some very old Skyhawks a massive boost in performance. This former A-4C has had over forty years of service and continues to serve with the RSAF's training detachment at Cazaux, France.
Author's collection

fifteen per cent higher dash speed, forty per cent better acceleration, improved turn performance and increased fuel efficiency, giving significantly better range. Maintainability and reliability improved greatly over the 1940s-vintage J65. Compared to the J52-P408, the lighter F404 gave a higher thrust-to-weight ratio, despite its lesser power (11,200lb/49.82kN versus 10,957lb/48.04kN).

The F404-GE-100D is 89in (2.26m) long, 35in (88.4cm) wide and weighs 1,820lb (826kg) compared to the J52-P408's 119in (3.02m) length and 32 in (81.4cm) diameter and weight of 2,318lb (1,051 kg). The smaller dimensions of the General Electric engine, which was raised higher than the position of the J52 to allow an accessory drive to be mounted underneath, required a gently S-shaped transition duct to connect it to the jet pipe and maintain the original thrust line. An intake/ejector duct for the airframe-mounted accessory drive (AMAD) appeared on the port engine intake. This and some new aerials (including the return of the ADF saddle) were the only visible differences from the A4S-1.

The second stage of the upgrade begun in 1991 resulted in the A-4SU and TA-4SU 'Super Skyhawk' and saw installation of a Ferranti HUD, a Litton LN-93 laser INS, new VHF/UHF radios, a monochrome head-down display and AGM-65 Maverick capability. AIM-9P Sidewinders were also integrated as part of the upgrade. Since 2002 some of the remaining RSAF aircraft have been seen with a chin

This view of a TA-4SU at Cazaux shows the two different canopies, the new duct on the port intake and gun blast shield, which differs in shape from that found on other Skyhawks.
Author

The forward retracting undercarriage of the A-4 is well illustrated in this view of an A-4PTM on a test flight. The bulged canopy and the five-pylon wing can be seen.

Grumman via TRH Pictures

fairing, which probably contains RWR antennas. No official list of Singapore's Skyhawks has ever been issued, but over the years observers have identified fifty-seven upgraded A4S-1/A-4SU and twenty-two TA4S-1/TA-4SU airframes.

BuNos of A-4Bs known converted to A-4SUs
145063, 145071

BuNos of A-4Cs known converted to A-4SUs
145106, 145108, 145110, 147731, 147752, 147779, 147797, 147809, 147821, 147823, 147835, 148304, 148458, 148462, 148464, 148482, 148521, 148526, 148528, 148591, 148603, 148605, 149493, 149498, 149522, 149537, 149587, 149588.

BuNos of A-4Bs known converted to TA4S-1/TA-4SUs
142814, 142839, 142881, 142936, 144916, 144966, 144977, 145021, 145033, 145041, 148493.

BuNos of A-4Cs known converted to TA4S-1/TA-4SUs
147742, 148311, 148483, 148525, 148529.

A-4PTM/ TA-4PTM for Malaysia

In 1979 the Malaysian government obtained twenty-five A-4Cs and sixty-three A-4Ls from US surplus stocks with the intent of upgrading the majority for service with the

Tentara Udara Diraja Malaysia (TUDM) or Malaysian Air Force. Budgetary problems scaled the programme back to where only forty aircraft were upgraded by Grumman at St. Augustine, Florida, emerging as thirty-four A-4PTM single-seaters and six TA-4PTM two-seaters. PTM is usually said to stand for 'Peculiar To Malaysia' but more correctly stands for Persekutan Tanah Melayu, or Federation of Malay States. The PTMs had a limited avionics upgrade, mainly adding a new Saab RGS-2A lead computing gunsight and the provision to carry AGM-65A Mavericks and AIM-9J Sidewinders on all pylons, which were increased to five. All the A-4PTMs retained the avionics hump of the A-4L, although the TA-4PTMs did not. The TA-4PTM was somewhat unique in that it was created from single-seat airframes by inserting a 28-in (71-cm) plug in the forward fuselage and fitting the standard two-seat canopy and windscreen (with wiper). The A-4PTM canopy was slightly bulged for better rearwards and downwards view. Although both versions retained the J65 engine, the TA-4PTMs had separated intakes with splitter plates as on the J52-engined models. The Malaysian A-4s all had a drag chute, the straight refuelling probe and an undernose ECM fairing.

Deliveries of the PTMs took place in 1984 and 1985 and they equipped two squadrons (No.6 and No.9) by 1986. Malaysian A-4 service was relatively brief. In 1989 it was announced that they would be replaced by British Aerospace Hawk Mk 208s, and most were withdrawn by 1994. Six A-4PTMs were retained for use as tankers with the D-704 refuelling pod for a few more years. As an aside, the Hawk 208 carries less useable load over a shorter distance than the A-4, at a slightly lower speed.

A-4PTM BuNos

149594, 145101, 148479, 149531, 148306, 148588, 149506, 145141, 149551, 149633, 149518, 149607, 148611, 145092, 147798, 147780, 148555, 148436, 145119, 149536, 145121, 147706, 147827, 149573, 145078, 147796, 147736, 149497, 149583, 145114, 147782, 147703, 147807, 149608

TA-4PTM BuNos

149630, 150593, 145065, 149626, 147802, 145103

OA-4M for the Marines

Twenty-three TA-4Fs were converted to OA-4Ms for fast forward air control (fast

Built as an A-4C and updated to an A-4L, M32-01 finally became a TA-4PTM for Malaysia in 1984. This version retained the J65 engine but had intake splitters. Grumman via TRH Pictures

The OA-4M was a dedicated forward air control variant for the Marines. Essentially it was a TA-4F with an avionics hump. This OA-4M served with H&MS-32 from 1984 to 1989 and was retired to storage in 1991. Harry S Gann, McDonnell Douglas

FAC) missions as a follow up to the TA-4Fs used by the USMC in the Vietnam War. The first of the reworked aircraft flew in 1978, and the first unit to operate this version was Headquarters and Maintenance Squadron H&MS-32 at Cherry Point.

The OA-4M was a TA-4F equipped with the electronics of the A-4M, including the dorsal avionics hump, which was faired into the rear of the canopy, plus additional radios for communicating with soldiers on the ground. ARBS and LST equipment was not included and armour plate was added to the cockpit sides, but the OA-4Ms retained the J52-P8 engine of the TA-4F so had lesser performance than the A-4M. The four OA-4Ms put into service by Argentina were redesignated as TA-4ARs.

OA-4M BuNos (Converted from TA-4F)

152856, 152874, 153507, 153510, 153527, 153529, 153531, 154294,154306, 154307, 154328, 154333, 154335, 154338, 154340, 154623, 154624, 154628, 154630, 154633, 154638, 154645, 154651

A-4AR and TA-4R for Argentina

Refused approval to buy surplus A-4s from Israel in the late 1980s by the US (under pressure from the UK), Argentina was finally permitted to buy ex USMC A-4Ms and OA-4Ms in 1994.

In the hands of Lockheed Martin Aircraft Services at Ontario, California, the first seven of the 'new' Argentine A-4s (including one two-seater) underwent an upgrade programme similar to that performed on the RNZAF Kahu aircraft. A modified APG-66 multi-mode radar, designated ARG-1 replaced the APG-53 or the ARBS set, depending on which was fitted to a particular A-4M. The ARBS sets were kept for installation in the USMC's AV-8B Harriers.

The upgrade involved the installation of GPS/INS, a Mil-Std 1553 databus, a Sextant HUD, HoTaS controls, LCD screens, onboard oxygen generating system (OBOGS), a Horizon computerized mission planning system and a refurbished J52-P408 engine.

The remaining twenty-six A-4Ms and one OA-4M were refurbished in Argentina by Lockheed Martin Aircraft Argentina SA (LMAASA) at Cordoba under a $US 208 million contract and entered service in 1998.

A-4AR (A-4M) BuNos

158161, 158165, 158167, 158171, 158178, 158193, 158413, 158414, 158417,

C-905 lands at Palmdale, apparently before conversion to A-4AR standard, judging by the ECM blisters on the nose. A-4M BuNo 158161 served with VMA-331, VMA-223, MAG-49 Det Willow Grove and VMA-311.
Denny Lombard, Lockheed Martin

158419, 158423, 158426, 158428, 158429, 159470, 159471, 159472, 158473, 159475, 159478, 159483, 159486, 159487, 159493, 159778, 159780, 159783, 160025, 160029, 160032, 160035, 160039, 160040, 160042, 160043, 160045

TA-4AR (OA-4M) BuNos
153531, 154294, 154328, 154651

Skyhawks that were never built

Although just under 3,000 Skyhawks were built by Douglas and McDonnell Douglas, a number of other proposed versions were not ordered by the US military, and efforts to sell A-4s to several foreign air arms failed. The stories of those Skyhawks that were not to be, add some interesting sidelines to the long history of the 'Scooter'.

A4D-3

During production of the A4D-2, Douglas proposed an improved version with better avionics and the much more powerful and economic Pratt & Whitney J52-P-2 engine. This A4D-3 would have had a cambered leading edge in place of the slats, the AJB-3 low-altitude bombing system (LABS), APG-53 terrain-following and fire-control radar, improved instrumentation and a PB-20 autopilot. A contract for four aircraft was actually signed in 1957, but after six months work and three million dollars spent, the Navy ran into funding difficulties and the project was cancelled. Budget cuts had also slowed development of the J52. The Navy was still interested in many of the improvements promised by the A4D-3 and accepted a Douglas proposal to produce a 'poor-man's'

A TA-4AR (former OA-4M) leads. a line-up of A-4ARs preparing for the delivery flight to Argentina.
Denny Lombard, Lockheed Martin

A-4AR Fightinghawk C-908, depicted in full Grupo 5 markings is the one-time A-4M 158419.

version without the new engine or cambered wing as the A4D-2N.

A4D-4

Another very different Skyhawk proposal appeared in 1958. The A4D-4 was designed for low-level nuclear attack and featured swept wings with afterbodies in place of the delta wing. The new wings would have been 10ft (3.3m) longer with three hardpoints and would have required folding for carrier use. The A4D-4 would have resembled the Grumman F11F Tiger in some respects, including its enlarged canopy. The project was not funded.

A4D-6 (A-4F)

In 1963 Douglas made an unsolicited proposal for a further version known internally as the A4D-6 and as the A-4F to the Department of Defense. This differed from the A-4F which eventually emerged by having an 11,500-lb (51.2-kN) thrust Pratt & Whitney TF-30 turbofan engine as later used on the F-14 among other aircraft, and was the first proposal offered by Douglas when the Navy opened its VAL light attack aircraft

A model of the proposed A4D-4 low-level attack version. Author's collection

competition in May 1963. VAL was won by the Vought A-7 and there appears to have been no further development of a TF-30 Skyhawk.

Extended span A-4

Not a great deal is known about this proposal, although the accompanying drawing, dated 28 August 1973 has survived and shows that the 'extended span A-4' (its only known designation) would have been based on the fuselage of the A-4F with the big P408 engine.

This proposed variant would have had a wingspan twice that of a standard A-4. Another Douglas Company document has provided a partial idea of dimensions, weights and performance as shown in the table below. The fuel weight figure shows that the new wings would not contain any extra fuel, but their greater efficiency at high altitude would have given a time on station of around 3.2 hours and a combat radius of 740 nautical miles (1370km).

Submarine-launched Skyhawk

In the early 1950s, the US was very concerned about the vulnerability of its land bases and surface ships to a Soviet missile attack. One way to ensure survival of a retaliatory capability was to mount missiles on submarines. The Regulus and Regulus II were radio guided weapons. The prototypes of the Regulus II were powered by the J65 engine as used on the early Skyhawks and was intended to be carried operationally by the nuclear powered USS *Halibut*, which had an enormous hangar, 80ft (24.m) long and able to carry two of the missiles, which were 57ft (17.4m) long with a 20ft (6.1m) span and fired with the assistance of JATO rocket boosters. At some time in the 1950s, Ed Heinemann made studies into adapting the A4D for carriage in the *Halibut*'s huge hangar. Sketches were done that showed the Skyhawk could fit into the submarine's hangar with 'minimum modification'. An all-new aircraft, the Douglas Model 640 with a flying-boat hull was also outlined by Heinemann, but the cancellation of the Regulus II in favour of the Polaris ballistic missile in 1958 ended any plans for the sub-launched A-4.

CA-4E/F for Canada

In 1964-5 Skyhawk sales efforts centred around Canada. On 22 April 1964, the

An R.G. Smith depiction of the CA-4F loaded with bombs and Bullpups. This version would have been similar to the OA-4M but with fuel in the hump. McDonnell Douglas via TRH Pictures

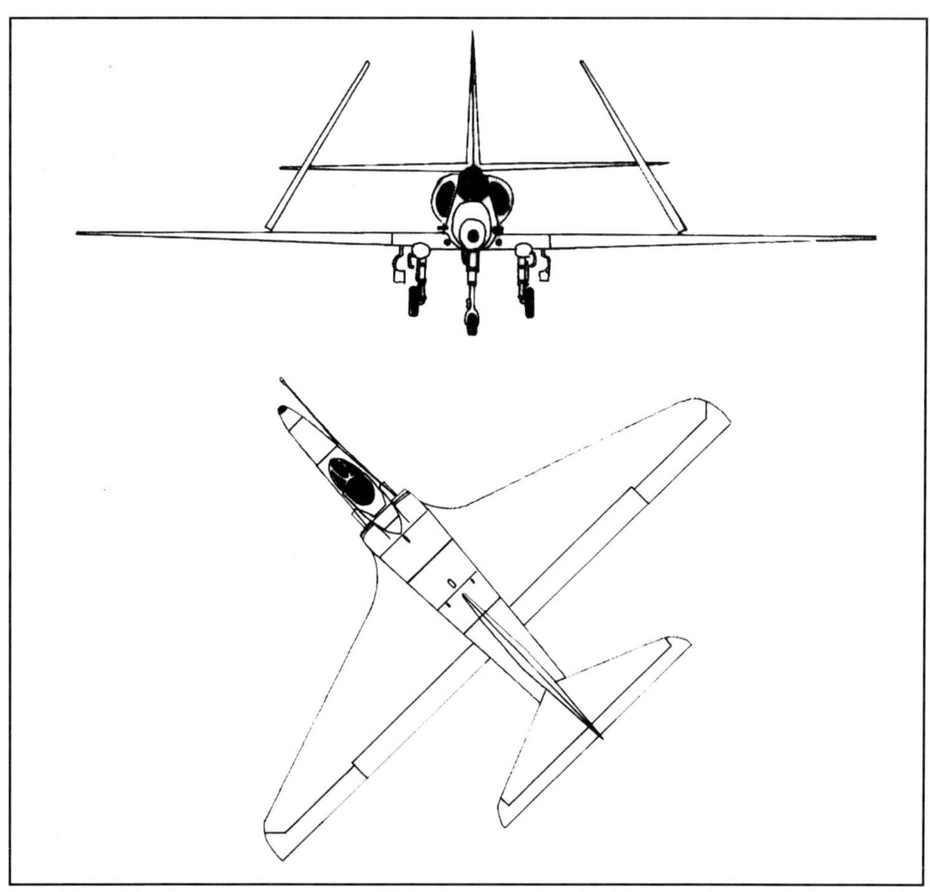

Comparison of standard A-4F and Extended Span A-4

	A-4F	Extended span
Engine	J52-P8	J52-P408
Thrust	9,300lb (41.4kN)	11,200lb (49.8kN)
Combat weight	13,801lb (6266kg)	16,000lb (7264kg)
Fuel weight	5,440lb (2470kg)	5,440lb (2470kg)
Wing span	27ft 6in (8.38m)	55ft (16.76m)
Wing area	260sqft (24.2m^2)	463sqft (43.0m^2)
Aspect ratio	2.91	6.53
Combat ceiling	45,000ft (13,716m)	c. 60,000ft (18,288m)
Approach stall speed	91kts (168km/h	75 kts (139km/h)
Normal approach speed	107kts (198km/h)	89kts (165km/h)

Canadian carrier HMCS *Bonaventure* (CVL-22) docked at Norfolk, Virginia following a cruise to the Mediterranean and loaded two A-4Es aboard for a series of flight trials. The borrowed USN Skyhawks had no difficulties in operating from the *Bonaventure*, which at 720ft (219.5m) long by 112.5ft (34.26m) wide, was considerably shorter than the US 'Essex'-class ships, but slightly longer (if marginally narrower) than HMAS

Melbourne, which later successfully operated A-4s.

The Royal Canadian Navy (RCN) evaluated the A-4 as a replacement for the McDonnell F2H-2 Banshee, which had been retired in 1962. A fleet of twenty-five Skyhawks was considered adequate for operations, training and attrition replacement. Their role would apparently have been anti-submarine attack, rather than as fleet defence fighters like the Banshee. The A-7 Corsair II was also considered (without onboard evaluation), but was too long for 'Bonnie's' elevators without a modification to allow the nose radar unit to fold. In the end, the Canadian government chose not to have a jet component on its carrier, retaining Grumman Trackers and helicopters for anti-submarine warfare.

The Royal Canadian Air Force (RCAF) also showed an interest in the Skyhawk, and to this end a new version was proposed under the designations CA-4E (single-seaters) and CA-4F (two-seaters). At least one drawing shows the CA-4F with a hump similar to that on the later OA-4M, although it was not for avionics but for extra fuel. This replaced some of the capacity of the fuselage fuel tank that had been displaced by the second seat.

A McDonnell Douglas cutaway of the CA-4E proposed for Canada shows few differences from the standard A-4E, at least in this incarnation, although there appears to be no IFR probe.
McDonnell Douglas via TRH Pictures

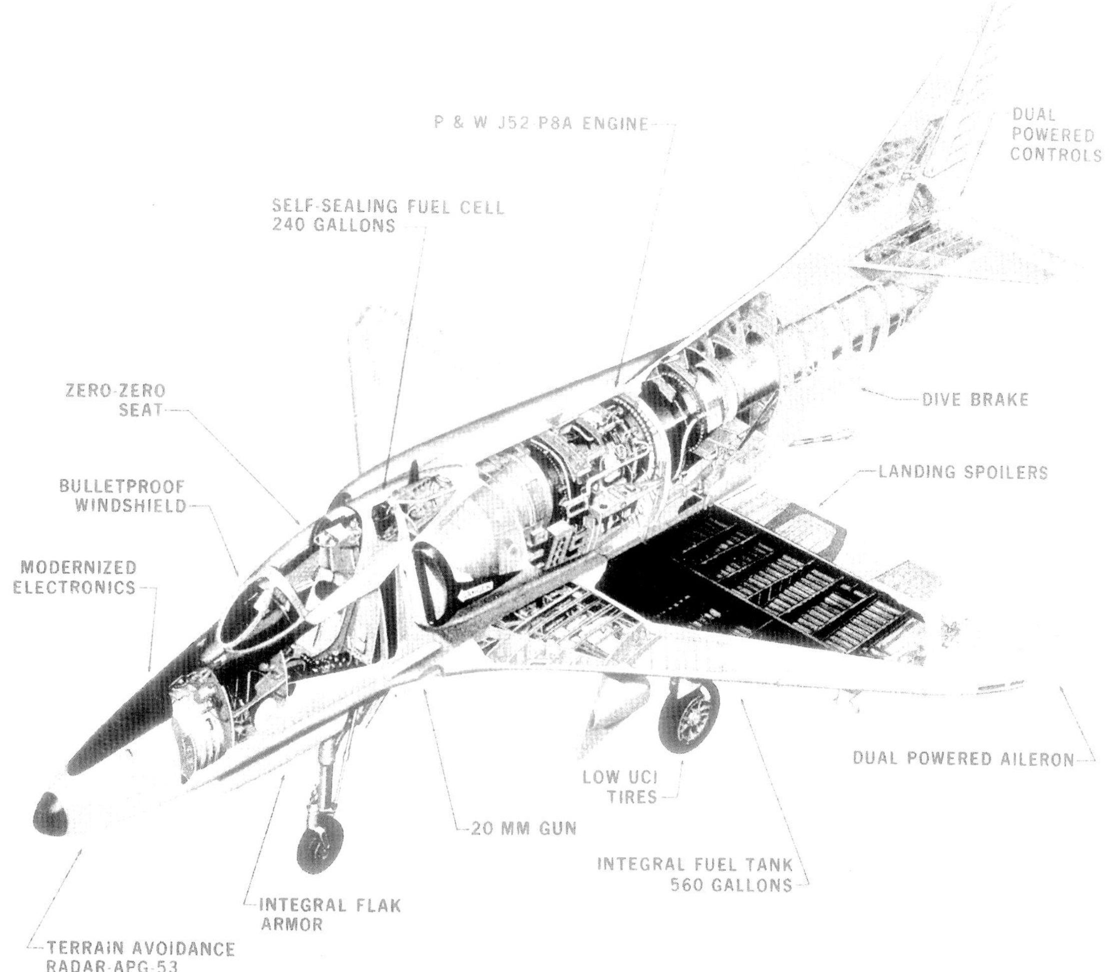

Documents from late1964 suggest that the two-seater, sometimes referred to as the TA-4E, was Canada's preferred choice.

Douglas proposed modifying the TA-4E/CA-4F to give it the capability to fire the Sparrow III medium-range air-to-air missile for 'small area point defence' and escort missions where supersonic speed was not required. The Navy agreed that a 'podded' installation based on previously proven components as used in fighters was practical. What fire-control radar was to be installed for search, track and missile guidance is unknown. Other documents of the time (circa 1964) refer to the 'Skyhawk International' as a marketing name for an export version of the A-4E with Sparrow III provisions.

The USN was prepared to support a Canadian A-4 purchase with logistical and training support. Canada considered the A-7 as well, presumably under the same terms, but eventually selected the F-5A Freedom Fighter as the CF-116 to meet its requirements.

As proposed by Douglas, the CA-4E and F would have shared many improved features of the TA-4F two-seater (known in 1965 as the TA-4E), such as nosewheel steering, wing spoilers and the zero-zero ejection seat. It would have weighed 53lb (24kg) less empty than a standard A-4E, mainly due to lighter electronics and armament related equipment.

Spey-engined Skyhawk

After failing to sell the Skyhawk to Canada, Douglas looked at developing a version of the CA-4 proposal with a Rolls-Royce Spey turbofan engine. The R.B.168-20 version proposed for the Skyhawk was a non-afterburning version of that specified for the Royal Navy's F-4K Phantoms. As such it was rated at 12,000lb (53.4kN) thrust, offering forty one per cent more thrust than the J52-P6A and between seventeen and twenty-four per cent better specific fuel consumption in the cruise. The Spey Skyhawk would have weighed nearly 900lb (408kg) more empty than the standard A-4E, with the new engine contributing most of the extra weight. Strengthened hardpoints would have permitted an increased take-off weight of 27,420lb (12,440kg). Low-pressure tyres would have been fitted for operation from unprepared landing strips.

The Spey was not only heavier than the J52, but of greater diameter. To accommodate it the fuselage would have been deepened by 5in (12.7cm) behind the cockpit, and

The only Skyhawks ever to feature folding wings were a number of surplus A-4As so equipped to serve as recruiting aids at airshows, parades and so on. The identity of this example seen at NAS Lemoore is unknown.
Harry Gann via TRH Pictures

lengthened by 10in (25cm) in the same area. The intake diameter would have been increased from 3.3 square feet (0.31m^2) to 5 square feet (0.46m^2) and the fin would have become slightly higher and broader.

Co-production and cost-sharing deals for the Spey A-4 were proposed to Belgium, the Netherlands and Italy, and possibly also to Switzerland and one other undeclared European nation. These would have replaced F-84s, F-86s and other obsolescent jets and could have been delivered in quantity less than two years from a go-ahead.

Preliminary design and initial flight tests would have been carried out in the USA, but the remainder of testing, research and development would have been shared between participating nations. The unit cost was stated as $764,000 in 1966 money. Although the Spey A-4 came to nothing, a version of the Spey was eventually used in its successor in the US Navy, the Corsair II.

Switzerland

Searching for a replacement for the de Havilland Venom, the Swiss Government evaluated the Vought A-7 Corsair II, Saab 105, Fiat G.91Y, F-5A and the A-4M. In 1970 the A-7 was declared the winner after a further evaluation against the Dassault Milan, a version of the Mirage 5, but Switzerland actually purchased refurbished Hawker Hunters instead. The Venoms themselves lasted until 1990.

Belgium

Apart from the proposal for licence production of a Spey A-4, not much is known of Belgium's interest in the Skyhawk, at some time in 1968 a USMC A-4E was flown by Belgian Air Force (BAF) Major Gustave Declercq at Yuma, Arizona. The aircraft (probably BuNo 151071) wore Belgian fin flashes and roundels alongside VMA-121 markings and US insignia. The BAF were looking for a replacement for the Republic F-84F Thunderstreak, but eventually chose the Dassault Mirage V.

Brazil

The Brazilian Air Force wanted to buy up to fifty new A-4Ms as early as 1968. Congressional and State Department objections to the sale on the basis that it would create a regional imbalance of power caused Brazil to choose French Mirages instead. Thirty years later the Brazilian Navy would purchase Skyhawks – ex-Kuwaiti A-4KU aircraft based on the A-4M airframe.

Colombia

In a very similar case to Brazil, Colombia negotiated for the sale of eighteen A-4Ms, but was also frustrated by US political considerations.

Uruguay

In 2000, Uruguay began to consider acquisition of a more potent combat aircraft to replace its tiny existing fleet of FMA Púcara and Cessna A-37 light attack aircraft. Second-hand Skyhawks or Northrop F-5s are said to be under consideration for purchase by 2005.

Other countries

In addition to those potential customers already mentioned here the late Harry Gann of Douglas listed the following countries as interested in the A-4 at one time or another: Greece, Lebanon, India, Peru, the Philippines, Spain, Tunisia and Zaïre.

Folding-wing Skyhawks

Like an earlier Douglas product, the SBD Dauntless, the Skyhawk was compact enough to allow carriage on aircraft elevators without the need for wing folding. Folding-wing A-4s did exist, and caused no end of head scratching over the years.

As a recruiting and promotional aid, NAS Lemoore painted an A-4A from their 'boneyard' in 'Blue Angels' colours and put it on the Navy float in local parades. The 27ft 6in (8.38m) wingspan was just too wide for California highway regulations, so the outer 6ft (1.8m) of each was torched off and fitted with a hinge, as was the tailfin. The aircraft was taken to the parade on a flatbed trailer along with an aircraft tow tractor. Once there, the aircraft was towed in the parade by the tractor. NAS Jacksonville and Atlanta also had folding-wing A-4s, and there was an all white A-4A at Lemoore at one time but it is not certain who had the idea first or the exact time period these aircraft were in 'service'.

Army A-4

The Skyhawk could have become the post-war US Army's first tactical jet aircraft following studies under Phase III of the 'Man/Machine Project' conducted by the Army Aviation Board at Fort Rucker.

The Man/Machine Project was referred to in official documents as an evaluation of the survivability probability of a deep-penetration manned surveillance aircraft and to refine requirements for such a low-altitude, high-speed (LAHS), adverse weather aircraft. Mention of such concepts as 'attack', 'close air support' or 'bomber' were studiously avoided to avoid upsetting the Air Force. Phase I studies began in 1959 and Phase II, which established some basic requirements involved testing of the T-28B Trojan and T2V-1 SeaStar trainers. Phase III, which took place in 1961 saw extensive test flying, adding the A4D-2N, Fiat G.91R and Northrop N-156 (F-5A prototype) and Grumman YAO-1 turboprop. A lack of compatible sensors precluded the conduct of simulated surveillance missions, but a large number of flights were conducted to evaluate gust response in low-level flight. The Skyhawk, despite encountering the most turbulent conditions, was the most stable at low level of all the types. The tests showed that speeds over flat terrain at up to Mach 0.96 at very low level were within the capabilities of pilot and aircraft and the recommendation was to develop a version of one of the three high performance jets (A4D, G.91 and N-156) for the Army.

As a follow-on, the Army conducted a nine week trial of the three contenders. All had revised undercarriage and drag chutes and proved able to operate from sod runways and other unprepared landing strips. The Navy helped support the project and allowed the use of an auxiliary field belonging to NAS Saufley, near Pensacola. Two A4D-2Ns (148483 and 148490) were bailed to the Army and were modified with dual-wheel main undercarriage legs, which retracted into revised fairings. The main gear doors were removed. A large ribbon-type drag chute from an A3D Skywarrior was fitted, which was the first to be used on a Skyhawk, and various cameras were installed on the centreline or wing pylons. Douglas test-pilot Drury Wood flew the modified Skyhawks for the trials.

A contemporary 'Aviation Week' account of the trials described an 'interim fighter programme to equip the Army until a projected V/STOL [vertical/short take-off and landing] tactical fighter with transatlantic ferry range is developed'. The tests raised 'the question of whether the interim fighter is to be operated by USAF Tactical Air Command (TAC) or the Army'.

It was probably at about this point that TAC started asking the same question. Jet fighters and air power projection were their business. The Army used helicopters and a few tactical transport and communications aircraft. At this time there were no gunships or attack helicopters and the Army relied on TAC, the Navy or Marines for close air support in the field.

Douglas promotional material for an Army close-support Skyhawk stressed the portability and durability of ground equipment and test equipment and the general low maintenance requirements of the A-4. Couching it in terms the Army understood, Douglas claimed that the latest model (A4D-5) Skyhawk required only nine enlisted men per aircraft, versus ten for the F-8A Crusader, sixteen for the F-4A Phantom and seventeen for the A-6A Intruder. It will be noted that none of these aircraft were really comparable to the Skyhawk or likely to be considered by the Army.

After considerable debate, the Army agreed to stick to rotorcraft and began development of what was to become the AH-56 Cheyenne attack helicopter, although the USAF saw even this high-performance machine as impinging on their territory and it too was to be cancelled. The AH-1 HueyCobra and AH-64 Apache eventually provided the Army with organic air support capability.

The two dual-wheel Skyhawks were de-modified and returned to Navy service. Both served in Vietnam, making at least three combat cruises between them. After the war, 148490 was converted to A-4L configuration and flew with the Navy Reserve. After retirement it was mounted on a high pole at the Santa Rosa rest stop on Interstate highway 10 near Pensacola where it remains today, painted in 'Blue Angels' markings. Its sister ship, 148483, served with at least three Atlantic Fleet squadrons, was supplied to Singapore, converted to A-4SU standard (as '903') and is today one of the aircraft based in France to train pilots for the RSAF, and still going strong after nearly forty-five years of eventful service.

The US Army trialled two A-4Cs modified to operate from rough strips near the front line as close suppport aircraft. The dual wheel main landing gear and their associated fairings were the main changes. The large fairing for the drag chute can just be seen under the tail.
Via Gary Verver

DOUGLAS A-4 SKYHAWK
BLUE HAWKS
ATKRON 72
HAWAIIAN ADVERSARY
VC-5 CHECKERTAILS
VF-43 CHALLENGERS
VC-8
4 and 20
VF-45
THE PROFESSIONALS PREFERENCE
DOUGLAS A-4 SKYHAWK
SKYHAWKS
FOREVER

A small selection of the many insignia worn by Skyhawk pilots over the years.

Opposite page top left to bottom centre: ***generic Douglas patch; VA-34: VA-72; VC-1; VC-5; VA-43; VC-8; generic Training Command patch; VF-45; Skyhawk sunset patch.***
This page: ***Argentine A-4AR; Israel 109 Sqn; 115 Sqn; 110 Sqn; 140 Sqn, 147 Sqn; Flight School; generic Malaysian; RNZAF 75 Sqn; RSAF Super Skyhawk; RSAF 150 Sqn.***

Author's Collection and via José M. Ramos.

Skyhawks from Oriskany *attack the Phuong Dinh railway bypass bridge on 10 September 1967. Although the attack wa successful with no losses, a VA-163 A-4E on a tanker mission ditched when it suffered power loss on launch.*

US Navy via TRH P

CHAPTER THREE

US Operations

The Skyhawk will always be associated with the Vietnam War, seeing action from the beginning to the end of 'official' US involvement in the conflict, and this chapter deals mainly with the Vietnam period. The US Navy and Marine Corps' Skyhawk squadrons were, however, involved in a number of international crises and made several operational deployments long before the USA became embroiled in the long and costly South-East Asia conflict.

In the period October 1957 to December 1958, several Carrier Air Groups (then called CVGs, later Carrier Air Wings or CVWs) incorporating Skyhawk squadrons operated in the Formosa Straits between Formosa (Taiwan) and mainland China. These included VA-93 'Ravens' on USS *Ticonderoga* (CVA-14) and VA-113 'Stingers' on *Shangri-La* (CVA-38), both with A4D-1s, and VA-83 'Rampagers' on *Essex* (CVA-9) with A4D-2s. For much of this time these early Skyhawks were standing nuclear alert in case of a full-scale invasion by China.

The Skyhawk was 'blooded' for the first time during the 1958 Lebanon Crisis, when an internal Muslim rebellion led to a Syrian incursion into Lebanese territory and a call for US assistance by the Christian president. On 18 July the A4D-1s of VA-34 'Blue Blasters' of CVG-3 aboard USS *Saratoga* (CVA-60) and the A4D-2s of VA-83 of Air Task Group (ATG) 201on *Essex* supported landings by US Marines. After the Marines were ashore the Skyhawks flew armed reconnaissance patrols over the Israel/Lebanon border. Two VA-83 aircraft were slightly damaged by small-arms fire, and became the first of the breed to taste combat. At one time, thirteen of the squadron's fourteen A4D-2s were in the air, the other being under repair for two bullet holes, inflicted by a rebel gunner while it was being flown by Lieutenant (Junior Grade) N.A. 'Butch' Swenson. The aircraft was symbolically awarded a giant cardboard 'Purple Heart' to mark its 'wounding' in combat. The Lebanese political crisis was solved without serious fighting, and the carriers withdrew on 23 August.

On several occasions in the early 1960s the Cold War nearly reached boiling point and Skyhawks were readied for launch on the first missions of World War 3. Lieutenant (Junior Grade) Pat Patrick was a pilot with VA-172 'Blue Bolts' aboard the Franklin D Roosevelt (CVA-42) in 1960 when tensions over the divided city of Berlin escalated. He gives a flavour of what many pilots must have felt strapped into their Skyhawk awaiting the signal to unleash atomic destruction on the enemy.

'We were operating in the Eastern Med when we [the US] went to a higher Defcon [national alert status] and stood down from normal operations. The captain moved the carrier into the entrance to the harbour at Souda Bay, Crete to provide protection from radar detection and attack by bombers and subs. There was a lot of natural wind (twenty-five or more knots) blowing directly into the harbour, so he let the carrier swing at anchor and planned on launching us when called upon from anchor. I thought at the time that that was a hell of a clever plan and still do. I only had one watch in the cockpit on the starboard bow catapult in an A4D-2 at the time with a Mk 7 weapon (20 kiloton) loaded on the centreline station (our only nuclear capable weapon station). I spent about four hours in the cockpit prepared to go on call and had some interesting thoughts during the time. I felt fully prepared to complete the mission, because my target was one of the easier ones. It was an airfield in Bulgaria only about forty-five miles north of the Greek border. I would have had a very short run in from the Greek border at low level with plenty of rolling hills to interfere with radar detection and tracking. I felt that there was almost no chance of a fighter intercept and didn't really believe they could hit me with flak at less than 100 feet and 500 knots. Furthermore, I had scored very high on the competitive exercises that I had flown simulating nuclear weapons delivery against targets in the Pinecastle target complex and a target near Key West. Consequently, I knew that I had the skills to do it right and the determination to deliver the weapon when ordered to do so. What really bothered me about that time were the thoughts about what would happen to Western Europe and the USA once that nuclear cat was let out of the bag. I would have done my part believing that if we got the first set of strikes in quickly the damage to the USA and Europe would have been minimized.

'Our participation in the crisis did not last more than a day and a half and I stood only one watch in the cockpit. Interestingly, when we stood down the CO and CAG took advantage of the training opportunity and we ran our full sequence of strikes after the war reserve weapons were downloaded. I got to fly my full mission minus the penetration and weapons delivery and I was catapulted off while at anchor for the only time in my career. When I popped up from the low level run through northern Greece 12 nautical

VA-93 was one of four A-4C squadrons on Enterprise *on its 1965-66 Vietnam War cruise. The aircraft in the foreground became an A-4PTM for the Royal Malaysian Air Force in the 1980s. It appears to be carrying Mk 83 1,000-lb bombs as well as two 150-gallon fuel tanks.* US Navy via TRH Pictures

Wearing a rarely seen sharksmouth marking, this A4D-2 of VA-43 was pictured on Independence *in February 1960.* Author's collection.

miles south of the Bulgarian border I could see my target and the full route in to the IP because the weather was so clear.

'It was a hell of an interesting experience and the memories are burned into my brain forever. I can still picture myself sitting in the cockpit going over my maps and check lists and getting very uncomfortable from sitting on the torso harness straps for that long. I can also still see the full colour image of the coast of Bulgaria between the Greek border and my airfield target with just a few fair weather cumulus clouds along my route. I never had any doubt that I would have delivered the weapon successfully and probably even got back to the ship. A lot of my targets were effectively one way trips but this one was pretty much a piece of cake'.

At around the same time, events in the Caribbean were beginning to occupy US carrier forces. In the latter part of November 1960, the governments of Guatemala and Nicaragua requested that the US supply a coastal patrol to prevent infiltration by communist insurgents from Cuba. VA-106 'Gladiators' contributed their A4D-2s to this mission from *Shangri-La* (CVA-38), and six months later also flew missions off the Dominican Republic following the assassination of dictator General Trujillo.

During the 'Bay of Pigs' invasion by US-backed Cuban exiles in April 1961 VA-34, now with A4D-2Ns, operated from *Essex* (now redesignated CVS-9). Otherwise the carrier had only ASW aircraft and helicopters and this was the first jet deployment on an anti-submarine carrier. During this period, Marine attack squadron VMA-331 'Bumblebees' deployed ten Skyhawks to the US base at Guantánamo Bay in the extreme east of Cuba. The original plan for the USN to provide air cover to the invasion was changed at the last minute by the CIA, and the exile-flown B-26 Invader bombers went in unescorted and suffered heavy losses to the Cuban Air Force (FAR), as did their ships, landing craft and ground forces. Not permitted to take a more active role, two VA-34 Skyhawks interposed themselves between a FAR Sea Fury and a counter-revolutionary B-26 on the afternoon of 17 April, but were unable to prevent the bomber being shot down.

With the failure to oust Castro, Cuba was soon to cause the USA trouble again, and involve many Skyhawk squadrons in operations that came just short of war. In October

August 1964 and A-4Cs from VA-146 on Constellation *(CV-64) fly past* Kearsage *(CVS-33). These Skyhawks would have taken part in the first naval strikes of the Vietnam War. The near aircraft survived at least two war cruises to be converted to an A-4L and then an A-4PTM. Its companion collided with an RF-8A Crusader in November 1964.* US Navy via Gary Verver

and November 1962, the Cuban Missile Crisis, in which the Soviet Union attempted to build ballistic missile bases on the island to threaten the United States 'from its own backyard' was the closest the Skyhawk came to being used in its original nuclear strike role.

Once the existence of the missile launch sites had been established by reconnaissance overflights, US Navy Task Forces 135 and 136 were sent to establish a blockade around Cuba. These included the carriers *Independence* (CVA-62) with Skyhawk squadrons VA-72 'Blue Hawks' and VA-86 'Sidewinders', *Enterprise* (CVN-65) with VA-94 'Shrikes' and VMA-225 'Vagabonds', *Shangri-La* with VA-46 'Clansmen' and VA-106 'Gladiators', *Wasp* (CVS-18) with VA-64 'Black Lancers', and *Essex* (CVS-9) with VA-81 'Sunliners'. All operated the A-4C version, until recently known as the A4D-2N. As well as these shipboard deployments, VMA-331 was deployed to NS Roosevelt Roads, Puerto Rico to stand alert duties for possible strikes against Cuba.

Although events in the Caribbean occupied many of the Atlantic Fleet's carriers in the early 1960s, developments on the far side of the world were soon to see the Skyhawk heavily involved in lands that few Americans could locate on the map. In May 1962, the *Hancock* (CVA-19) with VA-212 'Rampant Raiders' supported Marines landing in Thailand to support the Thai government forces protecting their border against Pathet Lao rebels. The same squadron had flown reconnaissance missions over Laos with their previous equipment, the FJ-4B Fury the previous March. In September 1963, 'Hanna' and the Rampant Raiders were again involved in Asian waters when they operated off Taiwan during further tensions with China. Two months later they were in the Tonkin

Gulf again, operating off the coast of South Vietnam following the coup that overthrew President Diem.

Cold War operations

Even after regular naval combat operations began in Vietnam in 1964, Cold War hot spots occupied USN Skyhawk squadrons in other parts of the world.

During the revolt in the Dominican Republic in April-June 1965, VA-76's A-4Cs flew armed reconnaissance missions out of Roosevelt Roads. Carrier-based combat aircraft were not involved in what was primarily a Marine Corps and USAF operation to restore order. In August 1965 VA-46 operated off Cypriot waters during Greek-Turkish unrest over the Mediterranean island. Following the attack on the USS *Liberty* (AGTR-5) by Israeli jets and torpedo boats on 8 June 1967, four A-4Cs of VA-66 'Waldos', armed with AGM-12 Bullpup missiles, were part of a strike group launched from *America* (CVA-66) in response. Their target was apparently the Haifa torpedo-boat base, but all aircraft were recalled by orders from Washington when the Liberty attack was declared a mistake. In September 1969, VA-81 'Sunliners' was one of the Air Wing One (CVW-1) squadrons that operated off the Libyan coast after the coup that overthrow the monarchy and saw Captain (later Colonel) Gaddafi take power.

Other notable peacetime events for A-4 squadrons included several 'cross-deckings' where the USN demonstrated its interoperability by flying aircraft aboard Royal Navy carriers and vice versa. Such cross-decks occurred numerous times in the 1950s and 60s. Two of the first such operations were in March 1958, when VA-34 from *Saratoga* (CVA-60) conducted operations on HMS *Ark Royal* (R09) with the squadron's new A4D-1 Skyhawks, and in July 1959 during Nato exercise Riptide when VA-106 'Gladiators' from *Essex* (CVA-9) flew their A4D-2s from HMS *Victorious* (R38). In October 1961 VA-56 'Champions' also flew from *Victorious*, as did VA-55 in October 1962 during

VA-34 'Blue Blasters' were the first A-4 squadron to deploy with the AGM-12 Bullpup missile, making the first operational (as opposed to test) firings in June 1959. In combat the Bullpup proved somewhat disappointing, partly due to its small warhead. US Navy via Mike Hooks

Operation Crosstie. In August 1962 VA-76 'Spirits' on *Enterprise* took A4D-2s over to *Centaur* (R06) in the Mediterranean. The same month VA-66 went aboard *Illustrious* (R12), followed by VA-95 'Green Lizards' in January 1963. In September 1966 during a break in Vietnam combat operations, *Oriskany* with VA-163 'Saints' and VA-164 'Ghostriders' aboard cross-decked with *Victorious* near Subic Bay.

As well as proving the compatibility of flightdeck procedures, these cross-deck operations also provided the opportunity for buddy refuelling to be practised. Skyhawks frequently topped up Fleet Air Arm Scimitar and Sea Vixen fighters and vice versa, using the Heinemann-designed D-704 buddy pod and their British equivalents built by Flight Refuelling Limited.

Anti-submarine fighters

Although the Skyhawk had been designed solely as a bomber, it was not long before its potential as a fighter was recognized. In the early 1960s the US carrier force was divided into attack carriers (CVAs), which operated the full range of fighter and attack aircraft, and those 'Essex'-class ships retaining hydraulic catapults and which were used for the anti-submarine warfare (ASW) mission. These were designated CVS and operated S2F/S-2 Trackers and helicopters. For effective air defence they needed to remain within the fighter umbrella of the CVAs. Soviet patrol and bomber aircraft often made probing flights and flew simulated missile launch profiles against the ASW carriers and their escorts. These 'snoopers' needed to be deterred, or at least watched.

In 1963 the commanders of the various US fleets were directed to provide an 'anti-snooper' capability for their ASW carriers by assigning four A-4Bs or Cs to each. The Chief of Naval Operations expressed his concern that the A-4 as it was had limited potential in the air-to-air role. Deficiencies cited included: the lack of radar or air-to-air ranging equipment for firing AIM-9 Sidewinder AAMs within the range envelope; the limited speed and altitude capabilities; no lead-computing gunsight or gun ranging capability and limited gun ammunition. The Bureau of Naval Weapons (BuWeps) was asked to examine both quick-fix and long-term modifications to the A-4B and/or A-4C to provide the best feasible anti-snooper capability, but it seems that little or nothing was actually done.

The main action taken was to form four-aircraft detachments (dets) of several attack squadrons for deployment to the CVS carriers. One of the first of these was VA-93 Det

An A-4E of VA-144 'Roadrunners', part of CVW-5 on USS Bon Homme Richard, *1969.*

A VA-56 A-4E lands aboard Ticonderoga during work-ups for their first Vietnam War cruise in February 1964. Two of the squadron's Skyhawks were lost in accidents during this cruise. The following year they were to lose an A-4E over the side of 'Tico' near Japan complete with pilot and a B61 nuclear bomb. Via Gary Verver

Q, formed at Lemoore in September 1963 and assigned to the USS *Bennington* (CVS-20). Complement was four A-4Bs, six pilots and sixty-five maintenance crew. Prior to deployment, the pilots learned about air combat manoeuvring (ACM) tactics at NAS Miramar and flew practice dogfights with F-4 Phantoms, followed by a gunnery deployment to MCAS Yuma. The cannons were fired against 40ft banner targets towed by a T-33, but as pilot Bob 'Creeps' Krall recalled 'We couldn't hit shit. As you know the Skyhawks guns were only for strafing and not air to air. But we tried.' Each pilot fired a live Sidewinder against a 5-in rocket fired from his own aircraft. 'Our Sidewinder firing evolution consisted of launching a 5-in rocket, getting a lock on with the Sidewinder weapons system and launching the Sidewinder. We had one hundred per cent success. We fired the rocket, got a growl, counted two seconds then fired the Sidewinder. That sweet Sidewinder hit the ass end of the rocket and detonated. Yes, the rocket motor was still burning when the Sidewinder was fired. Remember, the Sidewinder accelerated to around Mach 2 so it caught up with the rocket with no problem. Also, I think the effective range of the Sidewinder was from 1800 feet minimum to two miles maximum, so you couldn't fire too soon or too late'.

'Det Quebec' deployed in January 1964 on a WestPac (western Pacific) cruise, and entered the Sea of Japan in June. 'We spent some time in long-range recon assignments' recalled Bob Krall. 'That is, we would be vectored out a few hundred miles to investigate surface contacts and do some ship rigging [low passes]. Some of us caught submarines on the surface and split-s'd down and surprised them and took some great photos'.

A Sidewinder-armed A-4B of VA-93 Det Q meets a Soviet Navy Tu-16 'Badger' over the Sea of Japan.
Robert 'Kreeps' Krall

Submarines were not all that the A-4s encountered, as Soviet Tu-16 'Badgers' were following the *Bennington*'s progress. 'We were kind of expecting intercepts out of the Soviet Naval Base on Vladivostok. Sure enough, they came. We set up Condition One [armed] Skyhawks on the cats and we pilots sat in the cockpit with huffers [external power generators] hooked up. When radars detected inbound aircraft, we were launched and immediately picked up by controllers on the ship. We were vectored to intercepts and joined up on Badgers practising their air-to-sea missile launching missions. Those of us who were lucky to be launched to intercept Badgers took some photos from a safe distance so as not to pose a threat over international waters. However, when our "hot film" was developed and viewed by Flag intelligence, we were told that the Flag wanted some "close" pictures, not post card type shots.' Krall and his fellow pilots followed orders and came back with pictures in which the nervous expressions of Soviet tail gunners are clearly visible.

The *Bennington* returned to the US shortly before the Tonkin Gulf Incident and Det Q was not deployed in Vietnam. Other ASW fighter detachments of the period included VA-64 Det 48 (USS *Wasp*), VA-81 Det 45 (*Essex*) VA-22 Det R and VA-153 Det R, which made different cruises on USS *Kearsage.*

One of the more unusual aircraft ever intercepted by the ASW fighter Skyhawks was the Beriev Be-6 'Madge' flying-boat. Predecessor of the better known Be-12 'Mail', this one got a very close escort by VA-93 Det Q over the Sea of Japan on 16 July 1964.
Robert 'Kreeps' Krall

The early versions of the 'Madge' had two 23-mm cannon in the tail turret. The gunner (and friend) of this Be-6 keep a close eye on Bob Krall as he takes a one-handed photo from very close range.
Robert 'Kreeps' Krall

Vietnam

From the first day of what was regarded as the Vietnam War proper, as opposed the long involvement of 'advisors' in combat operations, the Skyhawk was in the thick of the action. From what was to become the first combat cruise of a carrier to Vietnam, which sailed on 14 April 1964, to the last, which returned on 8 January 1974, A-4s were to fly more bombing missions than any other naval aircraft. A total of thirty different USN squadrons flew attack missions with Skyhawk models from the A-4B through the TA-4F, although the great bulk were flown by A-4Cs, Es and Fs. Flying from land bases, the Marine Corps were to develop further new roles and new techniques for the 'Scooter', and nearly nine years after the first US combat missions dropped the final US bombs of the Vietnam War.

America's full involvement in the war is usually dated to the so-called Gulf of Tonkin Incident on 2 August 1964 when US destroyers came under fire from North Vietnamese patrol boats, and were believed to have faced a second attack two days later. As a response, President Lyndon Johnson directed a 'limited' response in the form of strikes on coastal targets by aircraft from USS *Ticonderoga* and *Constellation* (CVA-64). In the

VA-113 was one of the CVW-11 squadrons to conduct combat trials of green camouflage schemes aboard Constellation *in 1965-66. The camouflage was effective when seen from above over the jungle but silhouetted the aircraft against the sky. On this cruise CVW-11 lost at least thirteen aircraft including two A-4s to ground defences. This A-4C survived to be converted to A-4SU standard.*

US Navy via TRH Pictures

first 'Alpha Strike' of the war, named Operation Pierce Arrow, Phantoms, Crusaders, Skyhawks and Skyraiders were involved. Meeting fierce resistance from anti-aircraft artillery (AAA), one of the Skyraiders was shot down and its pilot was killed. An A-4C (149578) of VA-144 'Roadrunners' was also destroyed by AAA near the torpedo boat base at Hon Gay, and Lieutenant (Junior Grade) Everett Alvarez ejected to be made the first US aviator prisoner of the Vietnam War. He was not to be released until February 1973, eight and a half years later.

Naval air operations remained limited until Operations Flaming Dart I and II, retaliatory strikes against North Vietnam in February 1965. The sustained bombing campaign against the North, known as Rolling Thunder began in March, and by the end of 1965, ten different carriers had launched strikes against targets in Vietnam, North and South.

With an aviator lending a hand, redshirts assemble and load a Walleye missile on Station 4 of a VA-212 A-4E, mid 1967.

Via Gary Verver

VA-144 'Roadrunners' made a Vietnam cruise with the A-4C aboard Kitty Hawk *in 1966-67, losing one aircraft to AAA with its pilot made prisoner.* Author's collection

For the A-4 squadrons, the war became mainly a matter of Alpha strikes and armed reconnaissance by day and night, missions repeated again and again, often against the same targets, for day after day and year after year. The mood of the pilots on the carriers on 'Yankee Station' in the Tonkin Gulf and 'Dixie Station' off the coast of South Vietnam swung from a degree of gung-ho optimism to one sustained mainly by a sense of duty.

There were few great triumphs or victories for the attack squadrons in Vietnam, although there were many tragedies, big and small. Nearly 100 Skyhawk pilots were killed while flying, and another fifty suffered the depredations of the 'Hanoi Hilton' and other North Vietnamese prisons.

Skyhawk roles and missions

The types of missions flown by the Skyhawk were many and varied, and evolved as the conflict progressed. Closest to the pre-war doctrine of carrier-based (nuclear) attack of the enemy's main industrial and infrastructure targets was the 'Alpha strike', so named because the targets were on the Pentagon's 'A' or 'Alpha' list. because ofthe heavily defended nature of these targets, a full package of fighter escort, defence suppression, jamming and photoreconnaissance aircraft was needed to support the strikers, and tankers were needed to support all of them. The term Alpha strike came to mean a full air wing strike, with 'mini Alpha' sometimes used for a smaller version.

Armed reconnaissance missions were flown by day and night along the 'Ho Chi Minh Trail' (actually a collection of roads, tracks and trails weaving in and out of South Vietnam, Laos and Cambodia), and against waterways where materiel would be barged across or carried up and down by sampan. Pontoon bridges would also be laid at night and removed by dawn. A-4s acting in pairs would drop flares to illuminate such activities and the movement of vehicles, and strike them in the limited time before the flares burned out.

Interdiction encompassed planned attacks on targets along the Ho Chi Minh Trail such as truck parks, but were mainly aimed at fixed lines of communication such as bridges and railway lines, as well as transshipment points and POL (petrol, oil and lubricant) storage facilities.

When permitted by the policy makers in Washington, the A-4 could lay mines in North Vietnamese harbours using the DST-36 Destructor mine, essentially a Mk 82 bomb with a magnetic sensor and a tail fuse. These were also used against river traffic.

The first S-75 Dvina (SA-2 'Guideline') surface-to-air missiles (SAMs) were used by the North Vietnamese in July 1965, bringing down a USAF F-4C on the twenty-fourth. This was the first of 195 US fixed-wing aircraft to be lost to SAMs, thirty of which were A-4s. From early 1966, the A-4 added the 'Iron Hand' mission to its repertoire, using the AGM-45 Shrike anti-radiation missile (ARM), cluster bombs and other weapons to destroy the Fan Song radars that guided the SA-2.

The threat from SAMs and MiG fighters saw constant upgrading of the A-4's ECM

A heavily loaded A-4C of VA-36 roars down one of Enterprise*'s catapults, some time in 1966. On 14 June 1967, when assigned to Air Wing 21 on the* Bon Homme Richard *it was struck by a SAM and the CO of VA-76, Commander Robert Fuller was made POW.*

US Navy via 'Aeroplane'

An A-4E (151106) of VA-93 'Blue Blazers' waves off from the Hancock *in May 1967. It is configured for the 'Iron Hand' mission with AGM-45 Shrike anti-radar missiles.* US Navy

equipment from a baseline of nothing to a fairly sophisticated suite given the space constraints of the airframe. The so-called 'shoehorn' ECM installation on A-4Bs and Cs during 1966 necessitated the removal of one of the cannons altogether as the electronics occupied the ammunition bay. ALQ-51 deception repeaters were taken from A-3 Skywarriors for installation in A-4s. The Navy, Sanders Electronics and Douglas worked urgently to design and test the 'hump' installation for the ALQ-51 and the APR-25 SAM warning system. This first appeared on the A-4F, but was retrofitted to many A-4Es. ALQ-76 noise deception jamming pods were taken to Vietnam waters by at least one air wing but were not actually used, as there was suspicion that they acted as a beacon for the enemy if not used by aircraft that were flying in strict formation.

Not everything arrived in a timely fashion, and sometimes it arrived just in time. All the antennas, wiring, and black boxes for the APR-25 radar-warning receiver were in place on the A-4Fs of VA-23 and VA-195 when they deployed aboard *Ticonderoga* in 1968, but the scopes that supplied the visual direction warning information were not fitted. The basic missile warning unit provided a flashing 'SAM' warning caption and an 'oodle, oodle' sound when a missile was launched, but no indication of bearing or distance from the aircraft to the SAM, which might be targeting any or none of the aircraft in a formation. The APR-25 scope gave missile bearing and distance on a small circular grid. Two scope units arrived for VA-23 the day before Lieutenant Commander Pat Patrick and his CO, Commander Charlie Bush took part in a minelaying mission on a canal in North Vietnam. Only one unit functioned, and by chance it was fitted to Patrick's A-4F. As the A-4s of two squadrons approached the target area, a pair of SA-2s was fired at the VA-192 aircraft, led by Sam Chessman, which evaded successfully by hard manoeuvering.

Pat takes up the story: 'at this point Skipper Bush and I were in a left turn and belly-up toward the west. All of a sudden I was aware of the rattlesnake sound [from] another Fan Song. It was louder than the first. I glanced at the APR-25 scope and saw a three-ringer strobe pointing at 2 o'clock. I immediately lost interest in Sam's fight and got to work on ours. I dropped the right wing back down to level and looked down the strobe toward the ridges to our west. There it was. A single Guideline had dropped the booster and was levelling off at our altitude. There was a bright red ring around the dark circle

At the Marine bases in Vietnam Viet Cong rocket and sapper attack were constant threats. These A-4Cs of VMA-214 at Chu Lai in February 1966 are snug in blast pens, which in reality offered only a limited degree of protection. China Lake via Gary Verver

of the body of the SA-2, and it was dancing around the same spot on the canopy. It was close and there was no angle-off – it was clearly on a collision course. I screamed out to Commander Bush, "Skipper, break hard down and right NOW!" He didn't waste a second. As soon as the words came out, he rolled to his right, pulled hard into about a five-*g* descending barrel roll to his right. I followed.

'The SAM warhead detonated a few hundred feet above the underside of my upside-down aircraft and the shock wave drove me down into the stiff padding of the ejection seat. The explosion had actually pushed the aircraft down into my butt, which was pointed toward the sky. Both the Skipper and I heard the loud "WOMP" of the warhead explosion as the pressure wave hit us. We were very fortunate that Skipper Bush had responded so fast. We cleared the business end of the missile just enough that the shock wave hit us but the warhead fragments carried beyond both of our aircraft.

'Without the strobe and aural warning from my APR-25 we would have added at least one, and probably two, more names to the black wall of the Vietnam War Memorial. Talk about "just in time delivery" of the APR-25 scope, that was it. This was the first coordinated shot we had seen from the NVA missile crews and they did it almost too well. They fired the first two missiles, got us into a maneuver with our attention focused on the first two, then fired another one from our blind side.'

Sam Chessman was credited with more combat missions than any other naval aviator in Vietnam, flying an eventual total of 306. The runner-up was Commander Charles Hathaway, Chessman's predecessor as CO of VA-195, who flew over 280 missions.

VMA-311 arrived at Chu Lai in May 1965 with eight A-4Es and was active from this and other Vietnam bases until 1973. This 'Tomcats' Skyhawk carries Mk 82 bombs on multiple ejector racks.It was destroyed in an aborted take-off at Chu Lai on 17 October 1969. US Marine Corps

Fire on the *Forrestal*

The worst days for the Skyhawk community during the Vietnam War came not as the result of enemy action but from tragic accidents in the dangerous environment of the carrier deck. On the morning of 29 July 1967, only five days after arriving on Yankee Station, USS *Forrestal* (CVA-59) was preparing to launch aircraft for the second time that day. The A-4Es of VA-46 'Clansmen' were to lead the air wing on a strike against North Vietnam. The launch was just about to begin when a stray voltage sparked in a Zuni rocket launcher on an F-4B Phantom of VF-11 'Red Rippers', causing it to fire one rocket. The 5in projectile shot across the deck and struck an underwing fuel tank on the Skyhawk of Lieutenant Commander Fred White of VA-46 and sent debris flying into other aircraft. Among the nearest group of Skyhawks was the A-4E of Lieutenant Commander John McCain. Many sources say that it was his aircraft that was hit by the rocket, but whichever aircraft it was, the initial explosion punctured many fuel tanks. Rivers of JP-5 jet fuel ran across the deck and ignited. A 1,000lb bomb knocked from an aircraft lay in the flaming pools of fuel. Pilots in nearby aircraft including McCain shut down their engines and abandoned their cockpits. Others were unable to egress before the bomb exploded, destroying their aircraft. Fire crews running with hoses were knocked down by further blasts

The fantail of the carrier was engulfed in flaming jet fuel, which spread to six lower decks and into the ammunition storage areas through holes blown in the 3in (76mm) armoured decks by further detonations. Many pilots were killed when they were trapped in their ready rooms by the fires. Enlisted crew from VA-46 were instrumental in efforts to control the fire, which was eventually defeated after thirteen hours of struggle.

On the *Forrestal*, 134 sailors and aviators were killed and sixty-two were injured. Twenty-one aircraft were destroyed and forty-three others damaged. The aircraft lost comprised seven F-4B Phantoms, eleven A-4Es (from both VA-46 and VA-106) and three

Wisely wearing running shoes, a Marine 'shooter' gives the signal for the launch of a VMA-211 A-4E from the SATS catapult at Chu Lai, South Vietnam. The system allowed heavy ordnance loads to be carried from a strip only 4,000ft (1232m) long. US Marine Corps

This is one of the few good action shots of a Skyhawk in Vietnam.Despite the lack of unit markings, this A-4E is known to have belonged to VA-23 aboard Midway *in October 1965.* US Navy via TRH Pictures

USS Bon Homme Richard *(CVA-31) steams in the Gulf of Tonkin in 1969. Aboard were VA-22 with A-4Fs and VA-94 and -144 with A-4Es. Air Wing 5 lost one A-4E in combat and three in accidents during this cruise between March and October 1969.* US Navy via TRH Pictures

Despite the intensity of the October 1966 Oriskany *fire, only one A-4 was lost and three damaged. The scorched aircraft went to Alameda for rework alongside many other battle damaged Skyhawks.* Via Robert 'Creeps' Krall

RA-5C Vigilantes. Repairs to the ship took seven months and cost $72 million. This was the only Vietnam combat cruise for the *Forrestal*.The disabled supercarrier limped to Subic Bay in the Philippines for immediate repairs, from there sailing to Norfolk, Virginia where it arrived on 14 September. The responsibility for Vietnam operations was left to the World War 2-vintage *Intrepid* and *Oriskany*.

Oriskany herself had suffered a serious fire in October 1966 which killed forty-four men including many aircrew, four of them pilots of VA-163. The fire, which started in a flare locker, caused a huge fireball to fly across the hangar bay. Two UH-2 Seasprite helicopters and one VA-163 A-4E were destroyed. Several other aircraft including three more A-4Es were badly damaged. The heat scorched the aircraft, melted canopies and

The heat caused the ejection seat of the VA-163 A-4E shown below to partially fire as seen here. Despite the damage, this Skyhawk was later returned to service. Via Robert 'Creeps'Krall

Illustrated elsewhere in this book in VC-1 colours, A-4E BuNo 151194 is seen at Lemoore when with VA-164 in May 1969 in a short respite between war cruises on Hanna. *The figure in the bomb symbol quietly proclaims 101 combat missions.*

TRH Pictures

fired ejection seats. Despite this, the Naval Air Rework Facility (NARF) at Alameda worked miracles and was able to return the damaged aircraft to service.

In general, NARF Alameda was kept extremely busy throughout the Vietnam War with Skyhawk work, although not all of it was directly related to the conflict. The NARF conducted complete overhauls, progressive airframe reworks, in-service repairs, emergency repairs and battle damage repairs. About 100-125 Skyhawks were overhauled or repaired each quarter. Two full-time test pilots were employed just for the Skyhawk and each flew forty to sixty test flights per month. Bob Krall became one of these pilots after his stint with VA-93 Det Q. He recalled that; 'The workload was so great that we had to solicit the services of a Marine Major from another tenant command to help, as well as a Navy Commander who was also a flight surgeon but qualified in the Skyhawk. We even had to transition a P-2 Neptune pilot to the Skyhawk. The reasoning here was that the P-2 had two auxiliary jets'. Krall himself flew 637 different A-4s, most of them during his time at NARF. This represents nearly one in five of all the Skyhawks built.

Anti-submarine fighters

As the Vietnam conflict intensified, the Navy revised the ASW fighter concept as developed by VA-93 Det Q and its sister units and created one large squadron dedicated to the role. This was Anti-Submarine Fighter Squadron One (VSF-1) 'War Eagles', which formed in late 1965 at Alameda and made two cruises to the Mediterranean (1966-7 and 1968-9). Shortly before the 1966 cruise on *Shangri-La* (CVS-38), the squadron was split in two, leaving VSF-1 Det Alameda ashore. This detachment was soon given full squadron status as VSF-3 'Chessmen'.

The Chessmen deployed aboard *Intrepid* (CVS-11) in May 1967 with A-4Bs and began its first combat line period on 21 June, ending its fourth and last on 23 November. It was soon realized that there was little or no submarine threat in the Gulf of Tonkin and VSF-1 took part in regular attack missions. It was during these that the only two A-4B combat losses occurred. On 2 July 1967 Lieutenant (Junior Grade) Fredrick Kasch was hit by AAA fire during an attack on the Hai Duong rail yard. Although he nursed his Skyhawk (145002) a further 35 miles towards safety, he was killed when it crashed among a group of houses. On 3 October Lieutenant (Junior Grade) A.D. Perkins was wounded by AAA when making Zuni rocket pass on a bridge near Haiphong. He was

After TR Swartz's MiG-killing exploits, all the A-4Cs of VA-76 were marked with a MiG-17 silhouette. This 'Charlie' is now displayed in VA-76 colours at the National Air and Space Museum in Washington DC and has been seen by millions.
TRH Pictures

able to eject from his A-4B (142114) and was rescued from Haiphong harbour by a UH-2A Seasprite.

While there was no real submarine threat, there was at least a theoretical air threat to ships on Yankee Station. At least two American warships were damaged by MiG-17s, and a North Vietnamese fighter was shot down by a ship-launched SAM, but the effectiveness of the A-4B as an interceptor was questionable. They had no radar and could only carry 75 rounds of 20mm ammunition per gun. There was only a fixed gun/bomb sight that was set depending on whether the A-4 was firing rockets, dropping bombs or strafing. The pilots were trained to do 'slashing' runs on an aerial target if needed or attempt a direct astern shot. With limited airspeed and altitude performance compared to a possible incoming bomber, the method of attacking a higher target was to do a 'pop up' attack, that is, pull the nose up, get a Sidewinder 'growl' then fire away.

Although the VSF-3 pilots did not intercept any attacks on their carriers, they were involved in at least one air battle with MiGs alongside other *Intrepid* squadrons as outlined below. Following *Intrepid*'s return to the US in December, the Chessmen disbanded in February 1968. VSF-1 followed in July 1970, thus effectively ending the ASW fighter experiment, although two Naval Reserve squadrons (VSF-76 and –86) continued into 1971.

Dogfighting the MiGs

Even though the A-4 was used primarily in Vietnam as a bomber, with a limited use as a fighter on anti-submarine carriers, there were a number of air combats between Skyhawks and Vietnam People's Air Force (VPAF) MiG fighters. VPAF records claim several A-4s destroyed by MiGs, but as the following table shows, only one loss tallies directly with a claim.

On 25 April 1967 a raid on fuel and ammunition storage sites at Haiphong by Skyhawks from the *Bon Homme Richard* was engaged by several MiG-17s from the nearby forward airfield at Kien An. The Skyhawks had just completed their bombing

An A-4B of VA-22 Det R 'Fighting Redcocks' embarked on the Kearsage *in 1963.*

Air combat claims by VPAF against A-4s in Vietnam

Date	Regiment	Claimed by	Against	A-4s lost on date
20 Sep 65	921st	MiG-17	A-4E	One to AAA
13 Jun 66	921st	MiG-17	A-4E	None
15 Jun 66	921st	MiG-17	A-4E	One to AAA
17 Jul 66	923rd	MiG-17s	2 A-4s	None
25 Apr 67	923rd	MiG-17	A-4E	Two to SAMs
25 Apr 67	923rd	MiG-17	A-4C	A-4C 147799 NP-603
11 Jul 67	921st	MIG-21	A-4	No US losses

runs when the enemy struck. A MiG soon got behind one Skyhawk and in turn Lieutenant Charles Stackhouse of VA-76 'Spirits' manoeuvred his A-4C behind the MiG. Just as he was about to fire his guns, a burst of cannon fire from another MiG hit his aircraft. The engine spooled down and the Skyhawk caught fire. Rapidly losing control, Stackhouse ejected and was captured on landing. On the same mission, Lieutenant (Junior Grade) Dick Crebo's VA-212 A-4E was hit by a SAM but made it out to sea before he ejected. A well-known photograph shows Crebo's Skyhawk with its rudder

Bombs from A-4s of CVW-16, which included VA-163 and VA-164 fall on the infamous Than Hoa bridges, November 1967. Despite many accurate strikes like this, the main bridge was not destroyed until 1972 when hit by LGBs dropped by USAF F-4s. US Navy via TRH Pictures

missing and only its nose gear extended as it struggles away from the Vietnamese coast. The VPAF claimed this as another MiG kill and credited it, along with Stackhouse's aircraft, to a group of four pilots including their top ace Nguyen Van Bay. Charles Stackhouse himself remained a prisoner until March 1973.

The 'Spirits' were not slow to exact their revenge on the MiGs of the 923rd Regiment. Less than a week later, on 1 May, Lieutenant Commander Theodore 'TR' Swartz, an ex-Crusader driver and a fighter pilot at heart brought down a MiG by a very unusual method. Swartz was flying a flak suppression mission for a strike on Kep airfield near Hanoi. His aircraft was armed with pods of Zuni rockets, each containing four shots of the large 5in (70mm) diameter projectiles with their 53lb (24kg) warheads. The rockets could be fired singly or in salvo, and Swartz had saved three from one pod, as he 'kind of felt naked' near a MiG base with nothing more than the cannon for self-defence. It would appear that Swartz's A-4C (148609/NP-685) was one of those that was fitted with only one cannon and seventy-five rounds of ammunition. One of the A-4s suppressing flak sites at the other end of the airfield called in a MiG sighting near Swartz's flight. 'TR' saw the two MiGs over his left shoulder in close formation firing both their 37mm and 23mm cannon at him. Pulling his Skyhawk into a high-*g* barrel roll at 425 knots, Swartz found the MiGs ahead and off his right shoulder as he came over the top. He shot one Zuni at the wingman, missed, shot another, missed again and shot his third and last, which hit the MiG and blew it to pieces. The leader was still ahead of Swartz, so he went after it with the cannon, which jammed repeatedly. Despite the flight manual's injunctions against recharging a jammed gun, lest a round explode in the barrel, Swartz recharged it about four times, getting only a few shots off each time, before realising what a bad situation he was now in and 'getting the hell out of there'.

Although many considered Swartz a hero for bringing down a MiG, others were less charitable. Some thought that his decision not to fire all his rockets at the flak sites compromised his primary mission and jeopardised his colleagues. Others said that the event caused half the attack pilots on Yankee Station to go running around after MiGs instead of concentrating on their attack missions. The Navy in fact awarded Swartz's initiative with the Silver Star, their third-highest decoration for bravery.

After this incident, all VA-76's A-4Cs were marked with a diving MiG-17 silhouette on the fuselage side. The actual MiG-killing aircraft made at least one subsequent Vietnam cruise before being issued to Fleet Composite Squadron Two (VC-2). It was lost in an accident at Oceana on 23 June 1972.

TR Swartz nearly got a second MiG on 21 July 1967 when a group of 'Iron Hand' Skyhawks from *Saratoga* was bounced by eight MiG-17s. In a hectic seven-minute engagement, four MiGs were destroyed by the escorting Crusaders. Two of the F-8s used Sidewinders, one destroyed his target with cannon and the fourth F-8 pilot, Lieutenant Commander Ray Hubbard of VF-211, took a leaf from Swartz's book and blasted his MiG with Zuni rockets as well as cannon fire. Swartz himself was armed with one Shrike and a Zuni pod, and fired two rockets almost head on at a pair of MiG-17s to deter them from pressing an attack on an F-8. The rockets missed, but the MiGs left in a hurry. No US losses were recorded in this battle, although several Crusaders were damaged, one of them by a US Sidewinder.

On 5 October 1967, a large but inconclusive dogfight took place between MiG-17s and A-4Bs and Cs of VSF-3, VA-15 and VA-34 from Air Wing 10 on USS *Intrepid*. The

This is one of a series of photos taken at the time of the first combat use of the AGM-62 Walleye in March 1967. On the left is Tom Taylor, on temporary loan from China Lake. At right is Homer Smith, VA-212 CO, who made the first Walleye combat drop and was awarded the Navy Cross for heroism during another Walleye mission at Bac Giang on 20 May 1967. On this mission he was shot down and made POW, but was killed within days by his captors.
China Lake via Gary Verver

strike group of twenty-three A-4s was attacking the slipway for a river ferry near Loi Dong when jumped by at least ten MiG-17s from Kien An. The battle split into three engagements, one of them centred around a VA-15 A-4C which had been damaged by ground fire. After several firing passes by both sides, Commander Dick Wigent of VA-34 scored hits with his remaining cannon rounds on a MiG-17, but the 'Fresco' apparently escaped, despite Wigent giving fleeting consideration to ramming him. The A-4s were generally able to out-turn the MiGs, but several pilots were frustrated by jamming cannons or by running out of ammunition. One pilot, Lieutenant Ed Gilreath, fired eight Zuni and thirty-eight 2.75in rockets at one MiG in two attacks, but failed to score any hits. Despite the aggressiveness of the pilots on both sides, no aircraft were lost. The only claim on the US side being one MiG-17 damaged. With just a little more (or a little less) luck, this encounter could have been as well known as those of April and May 1967. As it is, it has taken the efforts of writer Mike O'Connor, author of 'MiG

Each armed with a Walleye and a bomb for balance, A-4Es of VA-212 are loaded and ready for a strike mission. The aircraft on the left was piloted by Homer Smith when he was shot down.
Via Gary Verver

Air combat claims by A-4s in Vietnam

Date	Unit	Model	Identity	Against	Pilot	Weapon
01 May 67	VA-76	A-4C	148609	MiG-17	LCDR T R Swartz	Zuni rockets
05 Oct 67	VA-34	A-4C	AK-307	MiG-17 damaged	CDR Dick Wigent	20mm

Killers of Yankee Station' (New Past Press 2003) to uncover the details of this wild encounter, probably the last battle involving US aircraft to be fought without use of guided missiles on either side.

Marine Skyhawks in Vietnam

In 1964 the A-4 equipped twelve US Marine Corps attack (VMA) squadrons, and seven of these were to be rotated through land bases in Vietnam during the war. One of the first things the Marines did when they landed in Vietnam in May 1965 was to construct a new airfield at Chu Lai, 55miles (89km) south of their main base at Da Nang, which was incapable of handling all the jet aircraft pouring into the country.

Although the first combat missions were flown by VMA-311 'Tomcats' from Chu Lai on 1 June, using Jet-assisted take-off (JATO) assist, the base was not fully operational until July with the completion of the SATS (short airfield for tactical support) system. This allowed take-offs with a full ordnance load without the need for immediate refuelling by KC-130s from Da Nang.

The SATS system consisted of a 4,000ft (2480m) aluminium plank runway, or 'tinfoil strip' laid by the Navy Construction Battalions (Seabees). The arresting gear was installed quickly but installation of the catapult was delayed until May 1966. Until the catapult was ready, the A-4s relied on JATO. As well as a catapult and arresting gear, the

Covers still on to protect the TV seekers of the Walleyes, a VA-212 Skyhawk awaits a tow to the catapult. This A-4E was shot down by AAA 20 miles NE of Kep Airfield on 31 May. LCDR Arvin Chauncey became a prisoner.
Via Gary Verver

Through seemingly peaceful skies, a VA-212 A-4F approaches the broken span of the Phuong Thuong bridge, brought down by the Skyhawks of Air Wing 21 in April 1972. US Navy via TRH Pictures

SATS system had a Fresnel lens optical landing system (FLOLS), similar to the 'meatball' used on aircraft carriers. . In 1968 a 10,000ft (3048m) runway was built, which took some of the excitement out of operations at Chu Lai.

Some of the first missions flown out of Chu Lai were in defence of the base itself, as the Vietcong launched major attacks in mid August. A-4s and F-4s successfully supported Marines on the ground in the effort to drive off the attackers, and no fixed-wing aircraft were lost.

After this event, the A-4s settled down to the 'routine' business of close-air-support for Army and Marine troops on the ground, using bombs, rockets and napalm. The most active of the squadrons rotated through Chu Lai was VMA-311, which flew over 50,000 missions by 1973 and expended 105,000 tons of ordnance. During one three-day period in May 1968, the 'Tomcats' flew 240 sorties. Chu Lai-based pilots were regularly flying 600-700 combat hours a month. By way of comparison, a more common peacetime average today would be 24-30 hours. Most USMC units used the A-4E, but VMA-223 also used A-4Cs for a time, alongside their Es. Alert aircraft were often armed with weaponry (usually Snakeye bombs and napalm canisters) on every pylon – the close proximity of the aircraft obviated the need for external fuel tanks.

In the 1967 period, forward air controllers (FACs) preferred to work with the A-4 over any Air Force aircraft. The A-4 could always put the bombs on target, which was essential for close air support work in close proximity to friendly troops. The only attack aircraft they preferred was the South Vietnamese (VNAF) A-1 Skyraider. Other jet aircraft were often called off the target by FACs who weren't happy with their ability to put their bombs in exactly the right spot.

An unidentified Marine A-4 shows the sort of damage the Skyhawk could take and still come home, thanks to the strength of its three-spar wing structure.
US Marine Corps

Although the Marines were primarily land based, two USMC squadrons detached Skyhawks on combat cruises aboard carriers during the war. They were VMA-223 Det T on *Yorktown* (CVS-10) in 1964-65 and H&MS-15 on *Hornet* (CVS-12) in 1965-66, acting as fighter support for these ASW carriers. No combat or operational losses were suffered by either unit.

The last combat mission by Marine Skyhawks was flown on 27 January 1973 when four VMA-311 A-4Es flying from Bien Hoa attacked Vietcong positions around a former rubber plantation. One of the bombs on the Skyhawk flown by squadron commander Colonel John Caldas was painted red, yellow and blue and inscribed with the message 'The Last Bomb' and the date. Dropped at 1145 local time, a quarter-hour before the armistice, this was not only the last bomb dropped by the unit, but probably the last bomb dropped during American involvement in the Vietnam War.

'Lady Jessie'

US Navy combat aircraft have not been noted for names and nose-art in the way that their Air Force and Army Air Force counterparts traditionally have been. One exception was 'Lady Jessie' of VA-164 'Ghost Riders'. In fact, Lady Jessie was a name worn by at least five Skyhawks in turn, and how it came about is an interesting, if somewhat sad, story.

Born in the little Nevada town of Carlin, Richard Perry worked his way through the

Back from a tanker mission, one of the two A-4Fs named 'Lady Jessie' traps aboard Hancock. *This May 1972 image was captured by Photographer's Mate Jessie Cralley.*
US Navy via TRH Pictures

Although this photo depicts a China Lake A-4C during pre-war testing, it represents the many thousands of AGM-45 Shrikes fired on Iron Hand missions over Vietnam.

NWC China Lake via Gary Verver

University of Nevada as an employee of Mrs Jessie Beck, who ran the Keno concession at the famous Harold's Club casino. Perry was like a son to Mrs Beck and he never forgot the encouragement she provided when he most needed it. After graduation, Perry went through naval flight training and eventually became an A-4 pilot, based at Lemoore in Northern California.

Mrs Beck adopted Perry's squadron, VA-164 and hosted its members during their periodic deployments to NAS Fallon, near Reno. When the squadron was at sea, she would send regular care packages of playing cards from the casino, as well as cakes and pastries which Dick Perry shared with his shipmates. Dick Perry marked the name Lady Jessie on the fuselage below the canopy of his assigned A-4E (151180/NP-407) in tribute to Mrs Beck

When the Ghost Riders deployed to Vietnamese waters aboard the USS *Oriskany* (CVA-34) in June 1967, A-4E 152048 AH-406 was aboard, wearing the name of Lieutenant Commander Perry under the canopy, and prominently marked as Lady Jessie on the intake trunking.

This, the third war cruise of the *Oriskany* was one of the costliest for any air wing in the entire Vietnam conflict. The squadrons of Air Wing 16 lost twenty-nine aircraft to enemy action and a further ten in operational accidents during its seven-month cruise, which included 122 days 'on the line'. A total of twenty-seven aircrew were killed, declared missing or taken prisoner. Among the latter was Lieutenant Commander John McCain of VA-163, who had transferred from VA-46 rather than wait for the squadron to be rebuilt after the *Forrestal* fire. He was to achieve fame for his resistance as a POW, and later as a senator for Arizona and a candidate for the Republican Party presidential nomination in 2000.

One of those lost was Lieutenant Commander Dick Perry. He was shot down by an SA-2 SAM over North Vietnam on August 31, 1967 while flying another A-4E (151991/AH-402). Three *Oriskany* Skyhawks were brought down that day during an attack on a rail bridge at Vat Cach Thuong near Haiphong.

A-4E BuNo 155062 is seen at the May 1968 Edwards AFB Open House with a load of napalm and 'slick' bombs, shortly after VA-155 returned from a costly war cruise on Coral Sea. *Sold to Australia in 1971 as N13-155062 coded '875'; on 2 October 1980 it made the last Skyhawk launch from HMAS* Melbourne *and crashed in the Andaman Sea due to a catapult failure. The pilot ejected safely.*

TRH Pictures

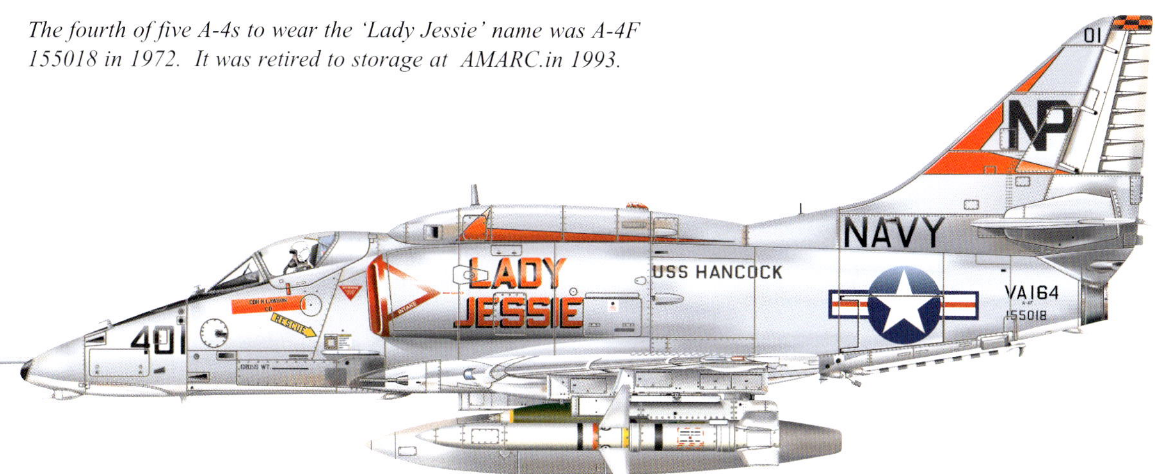

The fourth of five A-4s to wear the 'Lady Jessie' name was A-4F 155018 in 1972. It was retired to storage at AMARC.in 1993.

Two pilots from VA-164 were able to escape from their aircraft (one being blown from the cockpit by a SAM explosion) and were captured by the North Vietnamese, but Perry, leading the VA-164 element was seriously wounded by missile fragments before he was able to nurse his crippled jet over the water and eject. A rescue helicopter reached him, but the SAR swimmer determined he was dead as mortar shells from shore positions splashed all around. The helicopter could not recover Perry's body, which was tangled in the parachute lines, before it was forced to leave the area.

Perry's 'own' aircraft, the one named Lady Jessie was itself shot down by AAA near Haiphong on 18 October 1967 while attacking a SAM site. The pilot, Lieutenant Commander John F. Barr did not eject and was killed.

When the squadron returned stateside in January 1968 and was reassigned to Air Wing 21 on *Hancock* but retained the tradition of naming an A-4 Lady Jessie. Jessie Beck herself continued to support the pilots of VA-164. The next Skyhawk to bear the name was another A-4E, BuNo 151098/NP-415, followed by two A-4Fs in succession (155018 and 155022, each assigned to the squadron commander as NP-401). The latter two aircraft served until the squadron was disestablished in December 1975. Both subsequently served with a variety of USMC units and were retired from VFC-12 and VF-126, respectively, in the second half of 1993. Both the A-4Fs remained in desert storage at Davis-Monthan AFB in 2004. Given the popularity of Lady Jessie among artists and model builders, it would seem that these veteran Scooters deserve preservation and display in their Vietnam configuration.

Mrs Beck later became the first female owner of a major Nevada casino, an establishment in Reno known as Jessie Beck's Riverside Casino, and was known locally as 'The Gambling Grandmother'. To the men of VA-164, she was always known as 'Lady Jessie'. A performance by the 'Blue Angels' was dedicated to her at the opening of the Richard Perry Administration Building at Fallon in 1971. Jessie Beck died aged eighty-three in July 1987, a few months after the remains of Dick Perry were finally returned from Vietnam.

Two-seat Skyhawks in combat

The TA-4F replaced the elderly Grumman TF-9J Cougar in the fast forward air control (Fast FAC) role with the Marines in early 1968. Some areas of South Vietnam were deemed too dangerous for propeller driven FACs such as the O-1 Bird Dog and the O-2 Skymaster, and so jet aircraft were used to mark targets for close air support strikes. Armed mainly with pods of white phosphorous marking rockets, the TA-4s of

H&MS-11 'Playboys' flew the TA-4F in the fast FAC role from Da Nang in the years 1967-73. Additional tasks included helicopter escort and spotting for naval gunfire.
US Marine Corps

H&MS-11 'Playboys' at Da Nang were widely respected for their quick response and accuracy in target marking. Other missions for the TA-4s were as airborne tactical co-ordinators between helicopters and their bases, fighter escort for helicopters, and gunfire spotting for Navy ships, notably the battleship *New Jersey* (BB-62) in 1968-69.

Less well known is that Navy TA-4Fs also made two combat cruises aboard one carrier at the tail end of the war. For its 1972 WestPac cruise, Air Wing 21 aboard the *Hancock* had three squadrons equipped with A-4Fs, each of them specializing in a different guided weapon, although each also used unguided ordnance when required. VA-55 'Warhorses' had the 'Iron Hand' mission with the AGM-45 Shrike, VA-212 'Rampant Raiders' employed the AGM-62 Walleye glide bomb, and VA-164 'Ghost Riders' mainly used laser-guided bombs (LGBs), but also flew Iron Hand missions. This last squadron flew the TA-4 alongside its single-seat Skyhawks as detailed below after a quick summary of the main precision weapons used by Vietnam A-4s.

Guided weapons in Vietnam

The AGM-62 Walleye unpowered glide bomb entered full service in 1968 on USAF Phantoms and on the A-4E. The A-4E's cockpit radar screen was replaced by a tiny black and white Sony TV monitor. The pilot guided the Walleye using the TV camera in the weapon's nose. The first live test was made from a YA-4B at China Lake in January 1963, production was authorized in 1966 and combat trials were undertaken in Vietnam in March 1967. Commander Homer Smith of VA-212 put the first one through a window of the barracks at Sam Son on 11 March.

The best Walleye results were achieved against targets that gave high contrast on a TV

A veteran of 225 combat missions by the time this image was made, probably in early 1974 after the squadron's last war cruise, this VA-212 A-4F was retired to desert storage in 1993.
Author's collection

Seen in 1966 after a cruise with VA-216, A-4C 148514 was shot down on 4 May 1967 when with VA-113. Lt (jg). James Scott Graham ejected but is believed to have been killed after landing. Author's collection

screen, but were lightly defended. Bridges fell into the first category, but usually not the second. The Air Force in particular had less success with the original Walleye I, particularly as defences improved. The Navy persisted and achieved better results. In one seven-month period, sixty-five of sixty-eight Walleyes dropped were determined to have hit their target.

The Walleye had an 825lb (374kg) warhead based on that of the Mk 84 bomb, which had good hitting power but was still not enough to destroy the heaviest targets such as the bridges at Than Hoa. A heavier Walleye II, sometimes called 'Fat Albert' was developed for use on the A-7 Corsair and A-6 Intruder. A rocket-powered variant called Condor (AGM-53) was tested but did not enter service.

Shrikes and LGBs

The AGM-45 Shrike anti-radiation missile (ARM) was developed at China Lake from 1961 and entered service in 1965 and as such was the first successful weapon designed to home in on and destroy enemy radar emitters. Using the same basic aerodynamics as the AIM-7 Sparrow AAM, the Shrike had a 170lb (77kg) high explosive warhead. The Shrike carrying aircraft had a special antenna to work the side and back lobes of the SAM radar pulse, particularly the search radars. This allowed the A-4 to set up for the Shrike shot without having to approach head on, risking the SAM radar locking up the aircraft and firing first. 'If you ever had a shoot out with a SAM site trying to get your shot off before he gets his intercept [missile launch solution] it got real interesting' according to VA-164 pilot Dennis Carroll.

Effective use of the relatively new laser-guided bombs was a demanding task for a single pilot, and this is where the TA-4 came in. VA-164 acquired two Marine Corps TA-4Fs (152877 and 154622) from MCAS Iwakuni so as to fly a backseater who could designate the target for the single-seat A-4s. The backseater used a hand-held device developed at China Lake known as an Airborne Laser Designator (ALD), sometimes known as a 'zot box'.

The backseaters were recruited from other squadrons in the *Hancock*'s air wing, either E-1 Tracer NFOs (Naval Flight Officers) or F-8J Crusader pilots. The A-4 pilots themselves were flying up to three missions a day and were 'maxed out' for flying hours.

The graffiti on the centreline tank of this VA-94 A-4E appears to read 'Bad Blivet', a blivet being another name for a fuel tank. This aircraft was stricken from the inventory in August 1971 and supplied to a foreign country (most likely Israel) under the Military Assistance Program (MAP). TRH Pictures

The Ghost Riders' A-4Fs were modified with a laser spot tracker (LST) in the nose. This was evidenced by a narrow black ring just behind the tip of the nose and a new access panel atop the nose cone. The APG-53 terrain avoidance radar was generally removed on A-4s in the Vietnam theatre, leaving room for new equipment. The gunsight was a modified unit with a 'HUD-type' floating reticle that would lock onto the laser spot on the target as acquired by the LST. Prior to the installation of the LST, the pilot would only know if the target was accurately designated by way of radio communication with the laser operator, who was either on the ground or in another aircraft.

The first combat use of the TA-4F from carriers in Vietnam came in August 1972. Targets for LGBs were generally preplanned and fixed, such as bridges. The A-4s normally carried either 500lb GBU-12 or 1,000lb GBU-16 Paveway I bombs on stations 2 and 3 with a 400-gallon tank on the centreline. As the A-4s did not use the bigger 2,000lb GBU-10 bombs, the largest bridges were not usually attacked. Using two aircraft, one to bomb and one to designate required some co-ordination, and there were plenty of things that could go wrong, from the designator through the cabling and bomb rack to the LGB's single electrical tail fuse. The tracker in the bomber nose was not essential, but gave VA-164 much better results than those squadrons employing LGBs without being able to lock onto the laser spot. In general, as one VA-164 pilot estimated, each LGB was ten to one hundred times more effective than a 'dumb' bomb, depending on target size. The TA-4s were also used for conventional bombing missions. Although they had slightly less power than the A-4Fs they performed just as well in combat.

On the 1972 cruise, between January and October 1972, the *Hancock* spent 165 days on the line in Vietnamese waters. Her squadrons suffered eight combat losses, six of which were A-4s. VA-55 lost two A-4Fs and one pilot to AAA and another to a SAM, with the pilot made prisoner. Another VA-55 jet became an operational loss. VA-212 suffered two losses to AAA, with one pilot killed and another made prisoner. In May 1973, the *Hancock*, again with CVW-21 and the same squadrons returned to the war. This was the last combat cruise for the A-4.

Marine Losses

Between 1964 and 1972, the Marines lost eighty-one single-seat A-4s and had twenty-nine pilots killed, with one taken prisoner. The great majority of these losses (seventy) were in South Vietnam. A further ten TA-4Fs were destroyed, all but three of them in the south. The majority of TA-4 losses were to AAA, although one was brought down by an SA-7 SAM in unusual circumstances on 26 May 1972. This was an aircraft of H&MS-15 (153508), which was on a reconnaissance mission near Hué when the crew of Captain W. E. Ramsbottom and Warrant Officer Bruce Boltze spotted a North Vietnamese armoured vehicle, most likely a PT-76 amphibious tank. Not wanting to turn up such a rare opportunity but having no heavy weapons, they attacked the tank with 20mm cannon. Pulling up from the target, the TA-4 was struck by a shoulder-fired SA-7 'Grail' missile. The Skyhawk was badly damaged and struggled back to Da Nang to attempt an emergency landing. USAF forward air controller Darrel Whitcomb saw the TA-4 approach the airfield with one main landing gear down and the canopy missing; 'What a mess. I do believe that they tried to land but could not get the gear down, so they went out over the water and ejected' Whitcomb recalled. The two Marines were rescued on this occasion, but Boltze was killed in October while flying in the back of a USAF OV-10 FAC which exploded over the sea while directing naval gunfire, likely the accidental victim of a warship's main guns.

Medal of Honor - Mike Estocin

Numerous A-4 pilots distinguished themselves by their courage in Vietnam, reflected in the many combat decorations awarded to their number, including two of the Medal of Honor and seven of the Navy Cross, the second highest award.

James Stockdale, the commander of Air Wing 16 on *Oriskany* who was shot down in an A-4E of VA-163 received the Medal of Honor for his leadership and resistance as a prisoner from 1965 to 1973, but the only US Navy jet pilot to be awarded the Medal of Honor by Congress for heroism in combat was an A-4 pilot of VA-192 on USS *Ticonderoga*.

Michael Estocin was born in Turtle Creek, Pennsylvania in April 1931. In April 1967, he was a second-tour aviator and VA-192's operations officer, although he had only arrived on the 'Golden Dragons' shortly before the 'Tico' sailed for Vietnam. He was one of only a handful in the squadron to have Shrike missile training and as such he was often

This A-4E was the 'CAG bird' of VA-155 'Silver Foxes' in May 1966. Returning to Vietnam with VA-192 in October, it was the aircraft in which Mike Estocin was flying on his last mission on 26 April 1967.

TRH Pictures

assigned leader of the dangerous 'Iron Hand' SAM suppression missions.

On 20 April 1967, Mike Estocin was leading a flight of three Skyhawks on an 'Iron Hand' mission against thermal power plants in Haiphong defended by SA-2 'Guideline' SAMs and multiple anti-aircraft guns. The 'Iron Hand' A-4s were typically armed with two or four AGM-45 Shrikes and a centreline fuel tank, or two Shrikes and two rocket pods. Flying ahead of the strike package, Estocin kept up a continuous commentary on the location of SAM threats while making Shrike attacks against their radar transmitters. One SA-2 however was launched accurately and exploded close to his Skyhawk, riddling it with shrapnel. Despite the damage, Estocin carried on into the AAA barrage to prosecute his Shrike attack, which was successful in destroying a radar site, one of three he was credited with that day. Estocin's A-4 was badly damaged, however and was losing fuel at a rapid rate through holes in the wings. Only five minutes' gas remained as he left the target. A KA-3 Skywarrior tanker was close at hand and was able to make a rendezvous just in time to prevent the A-4's engine flaming out. The two aircraft remained plugged together for over 100 miles and flew a completely non-standard long, straight approach to the carrier. Reportedly, Estocin was calling glideslope corrections to the 'Whale' pilot until the tanker disengaged three miles aft of the ship. By this point the Skyhawk was not just leaking fuel but was on fire, nevertheless, it was brought in to a successful landing into the crash barricade. The Skyhawk was said to have looked like a sieve with an uncountable number of holes in the airframe.

Six days later, Estocin led two wingmen once again to the Haiphong power plants. Washington's micro-management of the war meant that target selection and even approach paths were dictated from afar with little regard to the safety of aviators or even tactical effectiveness. The defences were well prepared when the Iron Hand A-4s arrived in the target area. Not willing to expose themselves to Shrike attack, the SAM operators kept their radars shut down until the bombers were outbound and over the coast. Suddenly, Estocin's radar warning equipment came alive and he turned back towards the source of the emissions. About eight miles from the target, an SA-2 was launched at a head-on aspect to Mike Estocin's A-4 (151073/NM-208). Although the range of the AGM-45A was about 10 miles, Estocin held off to ensure a higher probability of a lethal hit. Unfortunately, he waited just a little too long and the SAM exploded to the left of the Skyhawk's nose and rolled his aircraft almost inverted. Streaming fuel, and with the left intake smashed in, the A-4 dived towards the ground. Estocin managed to pull the A-4 out of its steep dive and turn it towards the coast, but the aircraft, and probably its pilot, were mortally wounded. Three miles from the coast, the Skyhawk rolled to 90 degrees, the centreline tank blew off and both Shrikes fired, then it rolled inverted and dived into the ground from 500 feet. Other pilots circled the wreckage, but could see no sign that Estocin had ejected.

VA-192's commander and its admin officer wrote up a citation for Estocin to receive the Navy Cross for the 20 April mission. The *Ticonderoga* left Yankee Station two days later and berthed in Hong Kong. While there, Seventh Fleet asked for the mission to be resubmitted for a posthumous Medal of Honor award, and this is what happened. The medal itself was not presented until 1978 because the Estocin family disputed Mike's KIA (killed in action) status, holding out hope that he was still a prisoner in Hanoi.

As well as the Medal of Honor, Mike Estocin is remembered by the Estocin award for the top attack (now top F/A-18) squadron in the US Navy, and by the frigate USS *Estocin* (FFG-15), which was commissioned in 1989.

Vietnam losses

The A-4 carried the burden of the naval air war over South-East Asia, and suffered the brunt of the losses. US Navy Skyhawk squadrons made 107 cruises, compared with eighty-four for F-4 squadrons, fifty-seven for F-8s and fifty-six (or slightly over half as many) for the A-7, the second most numerous pure attack type. The Navy flew just over half the fixed-wing combat sorties by all services over North Vietnam, the most heavily defended area. Of the 538 USN fixed-wing combat aircraft losses caused by enemy action, 195 were Skyhawks, all single-seaters. This compares to seventy-five F-4 Phantoms, which suffered the next highest loss rate. Operational accidents accounted for a further seventy-six Navy A-4s.

Comparative figures for the USMC were 173 fixed wing combat losses, of which sixty-two were A-4s or TA-4s, the vast majority (fifty-one) of which were over South Vietnam. Nineteen single-seat Marine Skyhawks were destroyed in non-combat accidents or by Viet Cong attacks on Chu Lai. Many other damaged Navy and Marine A-4s were stricken (written off) after suffering battle or accident damage and are not included in the loss figures.

because of the low-level nature of the light attack mission, the majority of Skyhawk losses were caused by anti-aircraft gunfire, including small arms fire. Only thirty-two were lost to SAMs, and one to a MiG. The remainder involved crashes not directly attributable to flak or missiles, collisions, and the premature explosion of the A-4's own ordnance or ingestion of bomb or rocket debris, which happened on a distressing number of occasions.

At the time of 'Pierce Arrow' in August 1964, VA-55 'Warhorses' led the retaliatory strikes for the so-called Gulf of Tonkin incident from the 'Essex'-class carrier *Ticonderoga* (CVA-14). This squadron was one of three Skyhawk units aboard the 'Tico's sister-ship *Hancock* (CVA-19) for the last Vietnam War cruise nearly a decade later, from May 1973 to January 1974. In total, this one squadron out of many made eight war cruises, lost thirteen Skyhawks (A-4Cs, Es and Fs) in action and six in operational accidents. Only one pilot was listed as killed in action and another as missing, but one of the squadron's six prisoners died in captivity.

A-4Es of VA-55 are seen aboard Ticonderoga *shortly before its during its first war cruise in 1964.* Via Gary Verver

The Kahu upgrade programme gave New Zealand's A-4Ks the capability to launch precision weapons including AIM-9L Sidewinders, AGM-65 Mavericks and GBU-16 LGBs.

RNZAF Official

CHAPTER FOUR

A-4s for Everyone

The Skyhawk had reasonable degree of export success over the years, both as a shore-based and a carrier-based attack aircraft and fighter. The Skyhawk was popular because of its low cost, high load-carrying capability and relatively low maintenance requirements. It was chosen or considered by several navies not least because of its ability to operate from the small ex-British aircraft carriers of World War 2 vintage that were in use in some parts of the world. New-built A-4s were sold to four nations, namely Australia, Israel, Kuwait and New Zealand. Another five countries (Argentina, Brazil, Indonesia, Malaysia and Singapore) bought fleets of refurbished aircraft. Australia, Israel and New Zealand later topped up their purchases of new Skyhawks with second-hand or refurbished aircraft.

The use of the A-4 by non-US air arms is described here, along with tables of Bureau Number and user serial number tie-ups. This is the most comprehensive attempt to catalogue all exported A-4s published to date. Four foreign nations have used their A-4s in combat, details of which are in the following chapter.

Fuerza Aérea Argentina

To replace the elderly Avro Lincolns and the slightly more modern Gloster Meteors and F-86F Sabres in the Fuerza Aérea Argentina (FAA), the Argentine government ordered the Skyhawk, signing an initial $7.1 million contract for fifty surplus A-4Bs in late October 1965. The first twenty-five aircraft were transferred from storage at NAF Litchfield Park, Arizona to the Douglas factory at Tulsa, Oklahoma in February 1966. Here they were refurbished and modified with some features then appearing on the new A-4F, such as wing spoilers and nosewheel steering. Engines were zero-timed and ejection seats were modified to give a zero-altitude, 90-knots capability. Douglas and the US government gave these models the designation A-4P, but they seem to have been universally known as the A-4B in FAA service.

Initial training for pilots and ground crews was carried out at the Naval Reserve base at Olathe, Kansas. One aircraft was lost at Olathe before delivery and never replaced, but the remaining twenty-four were delivered to Villa Reynolds by flights from Olathe via Cecil Field Florida, Guantanamo Bay Cuba, Howard AFB Panama, Chiclayo and Pisco, Peru and San Miguel de Tucumán in Argentina. The first group arrived on 31 October 1966 and the second on 18 March 1967. They entered service with IV and V Escuadrones de Caza-Bombaredo of Grupo 5 de Caza (G5C) 'Halcones' (Hawks) at the V Brigada Aérea, based at General Pringles Air Base, (also known as Base Aérea Militar – (BAM) Villa Reynolds) in San Luis Province.

Delivery of the second batch of twenty-five Skyhawks was delayed until 1970 because

Argentina's A-4Ps were refurbished by Douglas' factory at Tulsa, Oklahoma, which had produced B-17s and B-47s under licence to Boeing among other things. Some of these Skyhawks, seen before delivery in 1969, had seen combat in Vietnam and would do so again over the Falklands.

Douglas via Mike Hooks

Fuerza Aérea Argentina A-4B/P

Bu No	c/n	FAA	Del.	Fate
142799	11861	C-201	Oct 66	Crashed 27 Jul 77 San Luis. Pilot ok
142127	11381	C-202	Oct 66	Damaged 55% 27 Jul 70
142421	11606	C-203	N/A	Crashed Olathe Kansas 1 Aug 66. Pilot ok
142126	11380	C-204	Oct 66	Shot down by AIM-9L from Sea Harrier XZ499 8 Jun82. Pilot killed
142694	11756	C-205	Oct 66	Damaged 30% 10 Nov 67 wings to C-212 1986
142762	11824	C-206	Oct 66	Shot down by Seawolf 12 May 82. Pilot killed
142688	11750	C-207	Oct 66	Halcón. Preserved National Aviation Museum, Morón.
142139	11443	C-208	Mar 67	Shot down by Seawolf HMS *Brilliant* 12 May 82. Pilot killed
142684	11746	C-209	Oct 66	Halcón. Forced landing 23 Jun 94 Salar Tolilar. Pilot ok
142128	11382	C-210	Mar 67	Crashed 25 Oct 74 Santa Fe. Pilot killed
142701	11763	C-211	Oct 66	Crashed 13 Nov 71 San Luis. Pilot killed
142773	11835	C-212	Oct 66	Halcón. Damaged 10 Dec 85 received wings C-205.
142129	11383	C-213	Oct 66	Crashed 1Jul 80. Pilot ok
142109	11363	C-214	Oct 66	Halcón. Preserved Villa Reynolds.
142102	11356	C-215	Oct 66	Shot down 40-mm HMS *Fearless* 27 May 82. Pilot ok
142098	11352	C-216	Mar 67	Crashed 31 May 68. Pilot ok
142747	11809	C-217	Mar 67	Damaged 85% 26 Nov 77. Pilot ok
142099	11353	C-218	Mar 67	Crashed 19 Oct 81 San Luis. Pilot ok
142416	11601	C-219	Mar 67	Crashed San Luis 8 Sep 77

Bu No	c/n	FAA	Del.	Fate
142796	11858	C-220	Mar 67	Damaged 40% 6 Mar 79. Wreck at Córdoba
142108	11362	C-221	Mar 67	Stored Villa Reynolds
142752	11814	C-222	Mar 67	Halcón. Preserved museum Rio Cuarto.
142110	11364	C-223	Mar 67	Crashed 23 Oct 74. Pilot ok
142132	11386	C-224	Mar 67	Preserved Ezezia
142803	11865	C-225	Mar 67	Halcón. Ground Instructional, Córdoba.
142090	11344	C-226	Jun 69	Shot down AIM-9L (ZA177) 8 Jun 82 Pilot killed
142104	11358	C-227	Jun 69	Crashed 3 Aug 87. Parts stored at Rio Cuarto
142728	11790	C-228	Jun 69	Shot down AIM-9L (ZA177) 8 Jun 82 Pilot killed
142734	11796	C-229	Jun 69	Crashed 18 Jul 78
142736	11798	C-230	Jun 69	Crashed 21 Sep 82. Pilot killed
142748	11810	C-231	Jun 69	Retired 10/86. Preserved Villa Reynolds
142749	12011	C-232	Jun 69	Preserved Grupo V HQ, Villa Reynolds
142757	11819	C-233	Jun 69	Damaged – to technical school Mendoza as 'C-301'
142760	11822	C-234	Jun 69	Crashed 31 Oct 84. Pilot ok
142765	11827	C-235	Jun 69	Crashed 12 Jul 83. Pilot ok
142784	11846	C-236	Jun 69	Crashed 4 Oct 88. Pilot ok
142788	11850	C-237	Apr 70	Crashed 19 Nov 84. Pilot ok
142830	11892	C-238	Apr 70	Crashed 14 Aug 74. Pilot killed
142838	11900	C-239	Apr 70	Retired May 1991. Under restoration IMPSA plant, Maipu, Mendoza
142855	11917	C-240	Apr 70	Retired August 1991.Displayed at FAA HQ, Buenos Aires
142859	11921	C-241	Apr 70	Crashed 31 Oct 78. Pilot killed?
142862	11924	C-242	Apr 70	23 May 82 Shot down by multiple weapons. Pilot killed
142866	11928	C-243	Apr 70	Crashed 27 Dec 78. Pilot ok
142883	11945	C-244	Apr 70	Shot down Sea Dart 25 Aug 82. Pilot killed
142893	11955	C-245	Apr 70	Crashed 5 Sep72. Pilot Killed
142901	11963	C-246	Apr 70	12 May 82 Shot down by Sea Wolf from HMS *Brilliant*. Pilot killed
142902	11964	C-247	Apr 70	Crashed 15 Dec 81. Pilot ok
142910	11972	C-248	Apr 70	Shot down by Argentine AAA 12 May 82. Pilot killed
142911	11973	C-249	Apr 70	Crashed 25 Jun 73. Pilot killed
142914	11976	C-250	Apr 70	Crashed 12 Nov 82. Pilot killed
144932	12178	-n/a-		To Argentina for spares recovery
145017	12263	-n/a		To Argentina for spares recovery
unknown		-n/a		To Argentina for spares recovery
unknown		-n/a		To Argentina for spares recovery

some US congressmen argued that the Argentine purchase was forcing the US Naval Reserve squadrons to use obsolescent A-4As. The second batch was delivered by way of Jacksonville, Key West, Kingston Jamaica, Panama, and Talara and Pisco, Peru. The last arrived in April 1970.

The second batch of Skyhawks was issued to two new squadrons. These were I and II Escuadrones of IV Brigada Aérea at El Plumerillo Air Base, Mendoza. A further four A-4Bs were later obtained for use as spares sources. At least some of the FAA's A-4Bs had their refuelling probes removed during their early years as the FAA then had no tanker aircraft or buddy refuelling pods. Two KC-130Hs entered service in 1969.

A-4Ps C-231 was one of several Grupo 5 de Caza Skyhawks to wear ship-kill silhouettes following the Falklands/Malvinas conflict. It is displayed today beside an Avro Lincoln at Villa Reynolds air base. TRH Pictures

Pleased with their A-4Bs, in 1975 the FAA ordered a batch of twenty-five A-4Cs from storage at Davis-Monthan Air Force Base. They were delivered to Lockheed Aerial Services at Ontario Airport, California, who refurbished them for further use by Argentina. All the A-4Cs were well-used surplus USN and USMC aircraft. As an example, 147806 (C-316) is known to have served with VA-83 aboard the USS *Forrestal* and with Marine squadrons VMA-224, -211, -121, and -223 before going into storage in 1974.

Unfortunately, the A-4Cs were bought 'as is' and were not upgraded greatly beyond fitting two additional pylons, wing spoilers and nosewheel steering. Many items of equipment were in a poor state. The APG-53 radars were functional on only six of the A-4Cs by the time they reached Argentina. The radar was deleted from all the A-4s by 1980, as was the radio altimeter and TACAN. Unlike the A-4Bs, which were ferried by air, the A-4Cs were shipped in containers to Buenos Aires port and on to the Rio Cuarto

Fuerza Aérea Argentina A-4C

Bu No	c/n	FAA	Del.	Fate
147714	12478	C-301	Apr 76	30 May 82 Shot down by Sea Dart fired by HMS *Exeter* off East Falkland. Pilot killed
148438	12631	C-302	Apr 76	Preserved Rio Cuarto. Halcón
149526	12851	C-303	Apr 76	9 May 82 Probably crashed into sea NW of West Falkland. Pilot missing
149618	12943	C-304	Apr 76	25 May 82 Shot down by Sea Dart from HMS *Coventry* over San Carlos Water. Pilot ejected but not recovered.
148562	12755	C-305	1976	24 May 82 Damaged by gunfire and shrapnel over San Carlos Water. Crashed in King George Water. Pilot killed.
148435	12628	C-306	1976	13 Jul 78 crashed Mendoza province

Bu No	c/n	FAA	Del.	Fate
148452	12645	C-307	1976	18 Feb 82 crashed 30km west of IV BA. Pilot killed
148612	12805	C-308	1976	29 Sep 76 crashed at San Juan. Pilot killed
147747	12511	C-309	1976	21 May 82 shot down by AIM-9L from XZ492 or XZ496 over Christmas Harbour. Pilot ejected but killed
148450	12643	C-310	1976	30 May 82 Shot down by Sea Dart fired by HMS *Exeter* off East Falkland. Pilot killed
148517	12710	C-311	1976	19 Aug 81 crashed Mendoza, pilot ejected.
147765	12529	C-312	1976	25 May 82 damaged by Sea Harrier cannon fire. Halcón. 01 Oct 91 Crashed 2.5 miles from Villa Reynolds. Pilot ejected.
150595	13006	C-313	1977	09 May 82 crashed into high ground at NW of South Jason Island. Pilot killed.
149564	12889	C-314	1977	Stored, Mendoza. Halcón
148531	12724	C-315	1977	09 Jul 80 crashed at Morón. Pilot ejected
147806	12570	C-316	1977	(Date unknown) Collided with C-317 near Luis Palacios y Aldao. Pilot ejected
147830	12594	C-317	1977	(Date unknown) Collided with C-316 near Luis Palacios y Aldao. Pilot ejected
148556	12749	C-318	1977	02 Dec 87 crashed at Villa Reynolds. Pilot ejected
148533	12726	C-319	1977	25 May 82 hit by multiple weapons over San Carlos. Pilot ejected
149642	12967	C-320	1977	18 Dec 80 crashed Mendoza. Pilot killed
147741	12505	C-321	1978	Halcón. 10 Mar 95 Crashed 0.5 mile short of Villa Reynolds. Pilot ejected but killed due to seat failure
149514	12839	C-322	1978	Halcón. Preserved National Aviation Museum, Morón.
148467	12660	C-323	1978	09 ? 81 crashed at Mendoza.
148559	12752	C-324	1978	Halcón. 10 Dec 97 crashed at Villa Reynolds. Pilot ejected
149585	12910	C-325	1978	21 May 82 shot down by AIM-9L from XZ492 or XZ496 over Christmas Harbour. Pilot killed

*Delivered from Rio Cuartos to unit

maintenance base at Córdoba. Remedial maintenance was needed to make them airworthy and bring the avionics and engines up to standard. The same Bendix navigation and communications package as used on Argentina's A-4Bs was fitted to the Cs. In April 1976 the first four A-4Cs were ready for delivery to IV Brigada Aérea. Rio Cuarto delivered eight more in 1976, another eight in 1977 and the remaining five during the first half of 1978. The A-4Cs replaced F-86F Sabres with 1 Escuadron of Grupo 4. At the end of that year, tensions with Chile saw several A-4Cs fitted with Rafael Shafrir I AAMs, although this was may have been a propaganda tactic.

Spare parts shortages, particularly of such items as ejection seat cartridges affected serviceability and by the time of the Falklands War, only fourteen A-4Cs and thirty A-4Bs were available. A US arms embargo against Argentina's military government prevented deliveries of twenty-nine more A-4Bs and thirty-two spare J65 engines that had been earmarked for Argentina and which the FAA desperately needed. Ironically, the embargo was lifted just before the Argentine landings on the Falklands, but not in time to improve the situation before the US announced its moral, (and to a lesser degree material) support for Britain in April. Release of AIM-9L Sidewinders to the UK was to

A-4Ps C-231 was one of several Grupo 5 de Caza Skyhawks to wear ship-kill silhouettes following the Falklands/Malvinas conflict. It is displayed today beside an Avro Lincoln at Villa Reynolds air base.
TRH Pictures

spell the end for four of the nineteen FAA and one of the three CANA Skyhawks lost in the war, as well as many other Argentine aircraft.

Shortly before the war, the A-4Bs and Cs were concentrated in a composite unit, often known as 'Escuadron Skyhawk', but usually regarded as being under Grupo 5 command. In April 1982 they were deployed to the civil airport at San Julian in the extreme south of Argentina, also known as BAM Rio Gallegos. Twenty-six A-4Bs and twelve A-4Cs could be mustered to meet the British task force and were deployed to Rio Gallegos. Nineteen (nine Cs and ten Bs) were lost during the conflict.

Post war operations

Eighteen months after the war, the remaining fourteen or so serviceable A-4Bs were combined with the six remaining A-4Cs at Colonel Pringles airbase under the Grupo 5 banner. By then four more A-4s had been lost in accidents and some of the surviving but non-airworthy Bs gave up their wings to keep the Cs flying. Following the crash of A-4C C-321 in March 1995, severe restrictions were placed on the fleet. This aircraft suffered an engine failure and the ejection system also failed to work, killing the pilot. Time-expired seat cartridges had resulted in a low ejection success rate during the Falklands conflict.

Various weapons were integrated or tested on the A-4 fleet post-war, including Magic 2 AAMs, Durandal anti-runway bombs and Belouga cluster bombs. The French firm Matra produced all of these and appears to have been eager to step in to the gap in the market left by the British and Americans. The navigation system was upgraded and the ejection seats were modified to give true zero-zero capability. Some of the Bs were given the higher-rated engine of the C and were marked with a white tip to the nose to denote this.

Project Halcón (hawk) in 1988 saw 30-mm DEFA-534 cannon replace the 20mm Colt guns on the remaining Skyhawks. A-4C C-318 was the prototype, but crashed soon after conversion. At least some of the twelve production conversions were equipped with an Omera 110 reconnaissance camera. The modified aircraft were sometimes known as Halcónes and are identified in the accompanying tables. In 1997 a GPS receiver was added to the small number of remaining aircraft.

A few A-4Bs and Cs remained in service as trainers for the upcoming A-4Ms. On 15 March 1999 an Old Skyhawks Farewell ceremony saw flypasts by four aircraft (C-207, –214, –314 and –322) to mark the end of thirty-two years of A-4B/C operations. These were the last J65-engined Skyhawks to see service.

Argentina's A-4Ms

After the war, the US maintained an arms embargo on Argentina, preventing replacement of lost aircraft or replenishment of spare parts. From 1986 Argentina tried to have the embargo lifted and negotiate the purchase of more Skyhawks from US stocks. Israel offered to supply between twenty and thirty of its surplus A-4E and H models. Around 1989, suitable aircraft were taken out of desert storage and concentrated at Tel Aviv's Ben Gurion Airport for export, having been covered with a tan coloured protective material. This sale never went through. It is likely that the US exerted pressure on Israel and would not approve the transfer of aircraft supplied under the Military Assistance Program (MAP). The British government's objections to rearming the FAA while Argentina still held a claim on the Falklands no doubt also influenced the US over the sale of A-4s.

Finally in 1993, with the achievement of a decade of democratic government in Argentina, the arms embargo was lifted. Kuwait offered it's A-4KUs to Argentina (which of course eventually went to Brazil) and McDonnell Douglas proposed a deal whereby surplus A-4Ms would be overhauled by a facility in Spain. Lockheed Martin offered the winning proposal, which would bring surplus A-4Ms and OA-4Ms brought up to modern standard with a rebuild and upgrade programme along the lines of New Zealand's Project Kahu. This would see the A-4Ms and OA-4Ms emerge as A-4AR and TA-4AR Fightinghawks respectively.

In 1994 an agreement was signed to supply the FAA with thirty-two surplus A-4M and four OA-4M aircraft from aircraft stored at Davis-Monthan AFB. Under a US $208 million contract the first eighteen aircraft were to be refurbished by Lockheed Martin at Ontario, California, and the remainder in Argentina. This was later modified so that only eight were completed in the US. The first A-4M (C-906, dubbed 'Gaucho 01') was flown out of AMARC on 1 August 1995. This aircraft was later found to have severe corrosion and was later relegated to instructional duties. The rework encompassed fitting of a version of the APG-66 radar designated ARG-1, a new HUD, a computerized mission

Fuerza Aérea Argentina (O)A-4M

BuNo	C/n	FAA	Model	Delivered
154328	13716	C-901	TA-4AR	21 Feb 00
154294	13682	C-902	TA-4AR	04 Jun 98
154651	13769	C-903	TA-4AR	23 Dec 97
153531	13597	C-904	TA-4AR	04 Jun 98
158161	14198	C-905	A-4AR	07 Jan 00
158167	14204	C-906	A-4M*	23 Dec 97
158178	14215	C-907	A-4AR	04 Jun 98
158419	14241	C-908	A-4AR	23 Dec 97
158193	14230	C-909	A-4AR	30 Sep 99
158429	14251	C-910	A-4AR	05 Nov9 9
159471	14412	C-911	A-4AR	26 Nov 99
159493	14434	C-912	A-4AR	20 Dec 99
159778	14477	C-913	A-4AR	01 Dec 99
159780	14479	C-914	A-4AR	30 Sep 99
159472	14413	C-915	A-4AR	20 Dec 99
160029	14531	C-916	A-4AR	07 Jan 00
158165	14202	C-917	A-4AR	23 Dec 97
158423	14245	C-918	A-4AR	23 Dec 97
158171	14208	C-919	A-4AR	05 Oct 98
158426	14248	C-920	A-4AR	07 Sep 98
159475	14416	C-921	A-4AR	03 Nov 98
160045	14547	C-922	A-4AR	11 Aug 98.
159470	14411	C-923	A-4AR	11 Dec 98
160025	14527	C-924	A-4AR	31 Mar 99
158413	14235	C-925	A-4AR	27 Dec 98
160032	14534	C-926	A-4AR	07 May 99
160035	14537	C-927	A-4AR	11 Jun 99
160039	14541	C-928	A-4AR	11 Jun 99
160040	14542	C-929	A-4AR	05 Jul 99
160042	14544	C-930	A-4AR	21 Jul 99
160043	14545	C-931	A-4AR	23 Jul 99
159478	14419	C-932	A-4AR	11 Feb 99
159483	14424	C-933	A-4AR	26 Aug 99
159486	14427	C-934	A-4AR	09 Aug 99
159487	14428	C-935	A-4AR	20 Feb 99
159783	14482	C-936	A-4AR	03 Sep 99
-	-	'C-937'	Hybrid A-4P/F/M	

Displayed at Rio Cuartos museum

** Not converted because of corrosion. Stored at V BA

planning system, onboard oxygen generation and a HoTaS control system. The aircraft were completely rewired and the engines zero-timed. The OA-4Ms received A-4M tail sections complete with braking parachutes. Pilot and mechanic training and spares support was included in the package. Four more aircraft (two A-4Ms and two OA-4Ms) were retained at AMARC for spare parts reclamation By November 1997 all of the first batch were undergoing a test programme at Lockheed's Plant 2 at Palmdale, California. The first five Skyhawks, including one TA-4R, were flown to Villa Reynolds supported by a KC-130, and arrived on 23 December 1997.

The remaining twenty-seven Skyhawks were reworked in a new facility at Córdoba. This was the former Material Area privatized as Lockheed Martin Argentina Aircraft Services S.A. (LMAASA). The first of these arrived in Argentina by sea in September1995 and the first refurbished example (C-922) rolled out on 3 August 1998.

The new FAA Skyhawks achieved initial operating capability (IOC) with Escuadrones I and II of Grupo 5 in mid-2000. The A-4ARs brought radar warning, ECM, IFF and a stand-off weapons capability to the FAA. The J52-P408 engine, modern multi-mode radar and all-aspect Sidewinder missiles offered a quantum leap in capability compared to the A-4Bs and Cs of 1982. The A-4ARs can launch the AIM-9M/N versions of the Sidewinder and drop the Argentine CITEFA FAS 250kg, 280kg and 800kg standard bombs, as well as the FAS 300A runway-destroying

The first overseas appearance by an A-4AR in service was to the 1998 FIDAE airshow at Santiago, Chile. Robert Hewson

A-4AR C-918 served as an A-4M with VMA-214, VMA-223 and VMA-311 before it was sold to Argentina in 1995. Note the modified radome, which accommodates the ARG-1 radar.
Denny Lombard, Lockheed Martin

bomb, similar to the Matra Belouga. For dogfight training the A-4ARs can carry the Israeli 'Ehud' ACMI (Air Combat Manoeuvring Instrumentation) pod.

Since entering FAA service, the new Skyhawks have taken part in a number of exercises, including Glaciar I and II at Rio Gallegos in 1999, which saw navigation exercises over the South Atlantic and the Beagle Channel. In 1999, during Exercise Vigla III in the northern Chaco province, operational patrols were flown to detect drug smuggling aircraft and secret airstrips in the border region with Paraguay and Bolivia. During Exercise Aguilla II in 2001 A-4ARs operated alongside FAA Mirages and US Air National Guard F-16Cs. A long planned participation in a 'Red Flag' exercise in Nevada has been cancelled several times because of budgetary difficulties. To preserve airframe life and reduce costs during Argentina's financial crisis half the Skyhawk fleet was put into storage at Rio Cuarto.

Following the acquisition of the Fightinghawks, the

A-4s supplied to Argentina for spares recovery

BuNo	c/n	Model
152874	13420	OA-4M
154306	13694	OA-4M
154307	13695	OA-4M
154645	13763	OA-4M
158166	14203	A-4M
158170	14207	A-4M
158174	14211	A-4M
158176	14213	A-4M
158184	14221	A-4M
158414	14236	A-4M
160244	14587	A-4M
160248	14591	A-4M
160258	14601	A-4M
160261	14604	A-4M
158126	14163	TA-4J
158477	14282	TA-4J
154173	13630	A-4F
154970	13786	A-4F
154976	13792	A-4F
154997	13813	A-4F
155034	13850	A-4F
155064	13880	A-4F

FAA planned to acquire twenty-three surplus TA-4Js and make eighteen of these operational to replace the MS.750 Paris jet trainer, which had been in Argentine service even longer than the A-4B. Just as the deal was almost completed Argentina withdrew, citing the poor condition of the chosen aircraft.

Two TA-4Js and six A-4Fs have been transferred to Argentina in January 1997 as spares sources and have been seen at Rio Cuarto. Eleven A-4Ms and three OA-4Ms have also been identified in Argentina, probably acquired for the same purpose.

Argentine Navy (Comando Aviación Naval Argentina)

The Argentine Navy (Armada Republica Argentina) was offered refurbished A-4A Skyhawks as early as 1964, but at that time apparently would have preferred A-1 Skyraiders, perhaps because they would have represented a less difficult transition from the F4U Corsairs then in shipboard service. Skyraiders were not available and the Armada Argentina retained its Corsairs until 1966 for use aboard ARA *Independencia* (V1). The Comando Aviación Naval Argentina (CANA) acquired twenty-four F9F-2 Panthers in 1958, but these were never operated from the carrier.

In 1968 Argentina bought the carrier Hr.Ms *Karel Doorman* (also a 'Colossus'-class ship, formerly HMS *Venerable*) from the Netherlands and renamed her ARA *Veintcinco de Mayo* (25 May, the Argentine national day). The *25 de Mayo* (V2) was 697ft 7in (212.6m) long with a maximum width of 133ft 5in (40.66m).

CANA followed the FAA by ordering refurbished J65-engined A-4s from surplus US stocks. At least one of the aircraft had seen combat in Vietnam and been damaged in action there. After refurbishment by Douglas at Tulsa, the sixteen A-4Bs were redesignated A-4Qs. The rework programme included the same modifications as applied to the FAA's Bs, including spoilers, nosewheel steering and a saddle-type ADF antenna.

The sixteen Skyhawks were originally issued to 2a Escuadrilla within 3a Escuadra. The A-4 operating unit was redesignated 3 Escuadrilla de Caza y Ataque (3a Esc) by March 1971 and known as the Tábanos (horseflies). The much greater performance of the A-4 allowed expansion of roles to include close air support for marine amphibious operations, anti-shipping strikes and air-to-air interception. For the latter role AIM-9B Sidewinders could be carried, a capability not initially shared by the FAA's A-4s. Modifications during service allowed six of the A-4Qs to mount the D-704 buddy pod and refuel the Navy's A-4s and Super Etendards.

Six of the Armada's A-4s had been lost in accidents by March 1982 and two of the remaining ten were not serviceable at the start of the war, although they were subsequently repaired. Like the FAA, CANA made strenuous efforts to obtain further A-4s in the late 1970s, but were thwarted by the US arms embargo against the military government.

Three A-4Qs were lost in the 1982 conflict, all destroyed by Sea Harriers within a twenty-minute period on 21 May. With a further aircraft lost later in 1982, only six remained by the end of that year and 3a Esc lost its operational commitment, being relegated to training. The unit disbanded in late 1987 but at least a few of the final five A-4Qs continued flying into the first months of 1988. The 25 de Mayo was finally retired in 1997, but had seen no operations since 1988. This left the remaining CANA fixed-wing fleet of Super Etendards and Turbo Trackers land based apart from occasional operations from Brazil's carriers.

A pre-war formation of CANA A-4Qs, only ten of which were available for the 1982 conflict. Three were lost in action, including two of those seen here. The nearest aircraft is under restoration to fly in Texas.

TRH Pictures

Argentine Navy (Comando Aviación Naval Argentina) A-4Qs

BuNo	C/n	CANA	Code	Fate	Details
144872	12118	0654	3-A-301	Groundnstructional	Technical School, La Matanza, Buenos Aires
144882	12128	0655	3-A-302	Ground instructional	BAN Bahía Blanca .Made last A-4Q flight Apr 88
144895	12141	0656	3-A-303	w/o 09 Aug 81	
144915	12161	0657	3-A-304	preserved	CANA HQ Edificio Libertad, Buenos Aires
144929	12175	0658	3-A-305	w/o 22 May 86	
144963	12209	0659	3-A-306	w/o 11 Nov 82	
144983	12229	0660	3-A-307	w/o 21 May 82	Shot down by AIM-9L from Sea Harrier XZ457
144988	12234	0661	3-A-308	preserved	Flying Club, Batán (Displayed as 3-A-314)
144989	12235	0662	3-A-309	Sold to USA.	Registered N82079 to James Ritchie Sep 98
145001	12247	0663	3-A-210	w/o 29 Sep 75	
145004	12250	0664	3-A-311	w/o 16 Aug 77	
145010	12256	0665	3-A-312	w/o 21 May 82	Damaged by cannon of XZ457, shot down by Argentine AAA
145025	12271	0666	3-A-313	w/o 13 Mar 75	
145050	12296	0667	3-A-314	w/o 21 May 82	Shot down by cannon of XZ500 pilot killed
145053	12299	0668	3-A-215	w/o 25 Jun 73	
145061	12307	0669	3-A-216	w/o 16 Jan 73	
-	-	'0667'	'3-A-312'	preserved Tigre	Hybrid aircraft

The nose of an A-4B is preserved at Bahía Blanca in USN markings

*23 May 82 ran off runway, pilot ejected but killed.

Seen about to launch from HMAS Melbourne *2A-4F 155052 flew with VA-212 in Vietnam, then as 871 with VF805 of the Royal Australian Navy and NZ6215 of the RNZAF.* Laurie Hillier

Australia (Royal Australian Navy)

Australia became the first nation to purchase new Skyhawks from Douglas when it ordered eight A-4Gs and two TA-4Gs to replace the de Havilland Sea Venom for use on the carrier HMAS *Melbourne* in October 1965. Cost of the ten aircraft was £9.2 million.

The *Melbourne* (CVS-21) was laid down in 1943 as HMS *Majestic* (R21), the name ship of its class and commissioned into the Royal Australian Navy (RAN) in October 1955. Although the largest ship ever operated by the RAN, the *Melbourne*, at 701ft 6in (213.8m) long with a 125ft 9in (38.3m) deck width was, by a narrow margin, the smallest carrier to regularly operate Skyhawks.

The first A-4G was handed over to the RAN in a ceremony at Long Beach on 28 July 1967. In October the *Melbourne* collected the Skyhawks from NAS North Island and took them as deck cargo to Australia before undergoing an extensive refit.

The A-4s were issued to the operational 805 Squadron and training unit 724 Squadron and based at Nowra (HMAS *Albatross*) south of Sydney. The RAN adopted US-style designations in 1969 and *Melbourne* became CVS-21, 805 Squadron became VF805 and 724 Squadron became VC724. The RAN Skyhawks' first carrier landings and take-offs were made aboard the visiting British carrier HMS *Hermes* in November 1968. The Skyhawks first embarked on their own carrier the following year but a Skyhawk had already been aboard *Melbourne*. In May 1965 'somewhere in South-East Asian waters', an A-4B of VA-113 (BuNo 144874, later destined for Singapore) came aboard from the USS *Bennington*. This evolution proved beyond the doubts of some that Skyhawks could be operated safely from the Australian carrier and its rather short (93ft/28m) catapult. A bit of extra steam pressure was applied for the launch to ensure adequate 'end speed' for the launch and prevent any suggestion of a marginal operation. The unknown US pilot's exclamation of 'Holy shit!' as he climbed away entered RAN folklore.

The A-4G was employed primarily as an air defence fighter and was equipped to carry AIM-9Bs on stations 1, 2, 4 and 5, although only ever carried them on the outboard pylons (1 and 5) in service. The air-to-ground weapons options were limited to dumb

Depicted here with with a D-704 buddy refuelling pod, VF805 A-4G 887 later became NZ6216 with the RNZAF.

bombs and rockets. Bombs were American-designed 250lb, 500lb and 750lb models carried either singly or on triple ejector racks (TERs). Four-shot 5in Zuni and seven-shot 2.75in folding-fin aircraft rocket (FFAR) pods and the cannon completed the A-4G's offensive capability. Fuel tanks were either 150- or 300-gallon capacity, the former usually being carried when embarked. The D-704 buddy pod gave the RAN an air-refuelling capacity many years before the RAAF had one.

In 1971 Australia acquired ten more Skyhawks, eight A-4Fs and two TA-4Fs modified to G standard. Four of the new single-seaters had seen combat in Vietnam. The new aircraft were picked up in July by HMAS *Sydney*, Australia's other carrier, which was used as a logistics ship and troop transport.

Despite now having twenty Skyhawks, *Melbourne* could only operate an air wing of eight A-4Gs alongside its Trackers and Sea Kings. because of their different centre of gravity and slower elevator response, the 'T-bird' could not be assured of a successful 'bolter' in the event of missing a wire on the short deck, and so the TA-4Gs remained shore based.

The Skyhawk did not have a very good safety record in RAN service. Ten of the twenty aircraft were destroyed in accidents between 1973 and 1980, including two of the

An 805 Squadron A-4G traps aboard Melbourne. *The only store is a rocket pods on the port outboard station.*
Laurie Hillier

Royal Australian Navy (RAN)

Bu No	c/n	RAN	Del.	Fate
A-4G				
154903	13734	882	Nov 67	To RNZAF NZ6211 Jul 84
154904	13735	883	Nov 67	To RNZAF NZ6212 Jul 84
154905	13736	884	Nov 67	To RNZAF NZ6213 Jul 84
154906	13737	885	Nov 67	Crashed in sea near Colombo 21 Oct 80. Pilot ejected
154907	13738	886	Nov 67	Fell off *Melbourne* 24 Sep 79. Crewman aboard rescued
154908	13739	887	Nov 67	To RNZAF NZ6214 Jul 84
154909	13740	888	Nov 67	Went overboard from *Melbourne*. 23 May 79 pilot ejected
154910	13741	889	Nov 67	Crashed in sea near Singapore 08 Nov 73. Pilot rescued
TA-4G				
154647	13926	878	Aug 71	Crashed 28 Apr 80 near Nowra. Pilot ejected
154648	13927	879	Aug 71	Crashed in sea off Nowra 16 May 74. Pilot killed
154911	13732	880	Nov 67	To RNZAF NZ6255 Jul 84
154912	13733	881	Nov 67	To RNZAF NZ6256 Jul 84
A-4F				
155051	13867	870	Aug 71	Crashed near Braidwood NSW 23 Jan 79. Pilot ejected
155052	13868	871	Aug 71	To RNZAF NZ6215 Jul 84
155055	13871	872	Aug 71	Collided with 870 near Beecroft Head 17 Jul 75. Pilot killed
155060	13876	873	Aug 71	Crashed in sea 05 Jun 73 near Williamtown. Pilot ejected
155061	13877	874	Aug 71	To RNZAF NZ6216 Jul 84
155062	13878	875	Aug 71	Crashed Andaman Sea 02 Oct 80. Pilot ejected
155063	13879	876	Aug 71	To RNZAF NZ6217 Jul 84
155069	13885	877	Aug 71	To RNZAF NZ6218 Jul 84
A-4B				
142871	11933	'885'	n/k	Nowra museum, marked as N13-154906

Note: the RAN issued serials using the prefix N13 to the Bureau Number ie 'N13-154903', as well as the coding system '882' etc

TA-4s. Six of these were lost between January 1979 and October 1980, leaving the RAN again with an available air wing of only eight fighters. Three of the A-4s were lost due to equipment failure aboard *Melbourne* and another fell overboard when the ship rolled in heavy seas. Five suffered engine failures, one crashed into the sea during a mock attack and one crashed after a collision. Two pilots were killed in these accidents.

The shrinking A-4 force hastened the end of carrier operations from *Melbourne*. In 1980 the Australian government made plans to replace the carrier and agreed to purchase HMS *Invincible* and a number of STOVL aircraft (presumably Sea Harriers, but never specified), which the UK had deemed surplus as part of a planned round of defence cuts. The 1982 Falklands War changed all that and the *Invincible* was no longer on the market. *Melbourne* had been paid off even as the Falklands were being retaken and the Skyhawks permanently stationed at Nowra. An offer of the much older HMS *Hermes* was

Unlike the 'Blue Angels' the RNZAF's 'Kiwi Red' display team used standard aircraft with the leading-edge slats active. The only modification was a smoke system. RNZAF Official

considered, but an election in Australia saw the incoming government decide to not replace *Melbourne* at all. In June 1983, six of the A-4Gs were withdrawn from service, but the remainder (two A-4Gs and two TA-4Gs) carried on with VC724 for a further year as target tugs and for other fleet support duties.

The last RAN Skyhawk mission was a target-towing flight to test the Phalanx close-in weapons system of the frigate HMAS *Sydney*. On 30 June 1984 a flyby by the last four Skyhawks marked the end of VC724 and fixed-wing aviation in the Royal Australian Navy. The ten remaining RAN A-4s were sold to New Zealand for A$28.2 million (at that time NZ$40 million).

New Zealand (Royal New Zealand Air Force)

Following consideration of several aircraft types, including the Northrop F-5 and the McDonnell F-4 to replace the English Electric Canberra in the strike role, the New Zealand government announced an order for fourteen Skyhawks in June 1968. The deal, valued at NZ $23 million (or NZ$933,000 for each basic aircraft plus spares, support and initial training), was for ten single-seat A-4Ks and four TA-4K trainers, which were based on the A-4F and TA-4F, respectively.

The initial group of ten RNZAF pilots and forty-eight maintenance personnel were among the last to train with VA-44 at Cecil Field, Florida before the squadron disbanded in May 1970.

The Skyhawks were able to 'hitch a lift' as deck cargo aboard the USS *Okinawa* (LPH-3) from North Island, San Diego to Auckland, arriving on 17 May 1970. The aircraft were unloaded by crane and made their first journey in New Zealand towed from the waterfront to Whenuapai Air Base by a collection of aircraft tugs, Land Rovers and other vehicles, several of which overheated en route through the city centre and along Auckland's Western Motorway.

By mid-June the Skyhawks were in service with No. 75 Squadron at Ohakea in the

With a few markings changes, the RNZAF's Skyhawks remained in this version of the USAF's South East Asia colour scheme from 1970 until the mid-1980s. TRH Pictures

central North Island. At the same base No.14 Squadron also operated three of the TA-4Ks and one A-4K for conversion training from mid 1971 until 1975. Initial armament choices were Mk 80 series bombs, 2.75-in rocket pods and AIM-9G Sidewinders.

A few changes were made to the RNZAF Skyhawks in their early service. The straight refuelling probe was replaced with the 'cranked' probe as seen on most A-4Fs and many A-4Es. The short-lived silver fern roundel marking was replaced by the kiwi roundel still in use today. In order to fit a removable Minipan reconnaissance camera on the starboard landing gear fairing the fuel dump mast was relocated to the port fairing.

From March 1971 many overseas deployments were made by the RNZAF A-4s, initially to Australia, but later throughout South-East Asia using P-3 Orions for navigation, communications relay and SAR support. An extra Skyhawk used the D-704 buddy pod to top up the deploying A-4s before they made the long crossing over the Tasman Sea. Up to three C-130 Hercules would be needed to transport spares, support equipment and ground crew for a deployment.

New Zealand operations

As part of the Five Power Defence Arrangement (FPDA), RNZAF A-4s frequently participated in exercises held in Malaysia and Singapore alongside the forces of those nations as well as those of Australia and the United Kingdom. Under the now moribund ANZUS (Australia-New Zealand-USA) Treaty, A-4s took part in exercises in Australia, the Philippines, Hawaii and New Zealand, the last of which was TRIAD '84, held 'at home' in June 1984.

The Kiwi Skyhawks never saw combat, but on 30 March 1976 a pair of A-4Ks was despatched to enforce New Zealand's 12 mile (19km) territorial waters. The Taiwanese squid boat *Kin Nan* had been discovered fishing within 10 miles (16-km) of the east coast of the North Island. It had ignored all orders to stop and even warning shots from a Navy patrol boat. Two A-4Ks were launched from Ohakea armed with cannon and rocket pods. Several low runs were made over the recalcitrant squid boat directing it to head for the nearest port. Even these failed to stop the vessel so one Skyhawk, piloted by Flight Lieutenant Jim Jennings made a live gunnery run, firing a two-second burst 300 metres in front of its bows. The *Kin Nan* immediately put its engines in full reverse and was quickly boarded by an armed party from the patrol boat.

An A-4K with Maverick and Sidewinder training missiles is seen at uncharacteristically high level over an RAN warship during exercises off Australia's east coast.

RNZAF Official

A rocket-armed pre-'Kahu' A-4K (note the lack of ILS and RWR aerials) passes over the crater of Mt Ruapehu in New Zealand's central North Island.

RNZAF Official

The RNZAF had an opportunity to sink a ship for real on 16 December 1994. The *Dong Wong 513*, a Korean fishing boat that had caught fire and burnt out was drifting abandoned off the South Island of New Zealand and was regarded as a hazard to shipping that needed to be dealt with. Former RNZAF airman Calum Gibson recalled that the ship was supposed to be attacked the previous day but there was a disagreement between the ship's owner and the RNZAF about who was going to pay for the ordnance. While this question was resolved the aircraft remained 'bombed up' at Ohakea overnight and the sortie was flown on the last day of work for the year. Six A-4Ks of No. 75 Squadron made two attacks each. The weapons employed were MK 82s, most likely low-drag (not

With the RNZAF's strike force slated for disbandment in December 2001, expenditure of weapons by the Skyhawk squadrons was phased out by mid year. Here an A-4K fires off CVR-7 rockets during one of the last sessions on the Raumai range near Ohakea.

RNZAF Official

For some months after the RNZAF acquired the RAN's A-4s, they could be seen in hybrid colour schemes, such as NZ6255, seen here with kiwi roundels and the RAN late two-tone colour scheme with green, brow and grey coloured drop tanks. RNZAF Official

Snakeyes), recalls Gibson, as they were 'tossed' at the ship. The A-4s also tried rocket tossing (similar to bomb tossing but using CRV-7 rockets) to increase the range of the rocket. The *Dong Wong 513* was soon sent to the bottom, but during the attack one of the A-4Ks suffered a partial structural failure of its port aileron and had to divert to the civil airport at Dunedin.

A similar, but slightly less glorious event occurred in the 1990s. The RNZAF were informed of a shipping container adrift in the shipping lanes north of New Zealand. It was decided that eliminating the hazard with A-4s would prove their usefulness and get some good publicity for the Air Combat Force. A group of A-4s were sent to the area and started by tossing radar-aimed rockets at the container. When these hit but did not sink the bobbing metal box, the A-4s used their cannon, but this proved equally ineffective. One of the pilots flew low and slow over the container to see why it was proving so hard to despatch. The container was seen to be full of holes, but surrounded by many bright green objects floating in the water. These turned out to be a shipment of 'boogie boards' (polystyrene mini surfboards) and there was probably no way that this container could have been sunk short of being hit with a 500lb bomb. The expected press release was not issued.

In RNZAF service, the TA-4Ks were known, naturally enough as 'T-birds' and the A-4Ks were 'Models'. The Skyhawk pilots themselves were 'Knucks' – short for knuckleheads. Despite their primary attack role, the Kiwi A-4 drivers saw themselves as fighter pilots, and woe betide anyone who turned up at a social event with a 'bomber pocket' or knife pocket in the leg of their flying suit.

Kahu

The question of a replacement for the A-4 was considered on a number of occasions. In the early 1980s, the Northrop F-20 Tigershark was one aircraft seriously considered for New Zealand's needs. Other potential replacements included second-hand F-16s or F/A-18s, but when Australia finally retired its last A-4Gs, New Zealand purchased all the remaining aircraft and instituted an upgrade programme under the name Project 'Kahu', the Maori word for hawk. At a total cost of NZ$92 million, it was said that the same capability as the purchase of an equal number of F-16s could be achieved for one-

A view from the back seat as a TA-4K of No.2 Squadron makes a typically low-level attack on the French Navy helicopter carrier Jeanne d'Arc *off the New South Wales coast in February 2001.* Robert Hewson

sixteenth the cost.

The ten single-seat and two two-seat Australian Skyhawks were delivered across the Tasman Sea in July 1984 and operated alongside the A-4Ks in a mix of colour schemes until they went through the Kahu modification programme. This got under way in 1986 and lasted until 1991 when the last aircraft was delivered. Details of the modifications are given in chapter two, but in summary the programme, conducted by engineering firm Safe Air at Woodbourne saw the complete replacement of all wiring, the three wing spars and the lower wing skins. All the A-4Ks lost their (empty) avionics humps, bringing them into line with the A-4Gs. A new radar was installed, this being a version of the APG-66 used in the F-16A with extra maritime attack modes and designated APG-66(NZ). Also fitted were a HUD, a new navigation and attack system, an RWR, and a modern cockpit with HoTaS controls and two MFDs. An additional air scoop was later added to the nose to cure cooling problems caused by the tightly packed radar and computer equipment.

The Kahu A-4s were able to use a wider range of weapons which were purchased at the same time as the upgrade was conducted. These included Canadian-designed CRV-7 rockets, GBU-12 and -16 LGBs, AGM-65B TV-guided and AIM-65G Scene Mag infrared-guided Mavericks (purchased second-hand from Jordan) and AIM-9L Sidewinders. The remaining stocks of elderly AIM-9Gs were fired off at ground-fired flares and reportedly had a very low success rate.

In December 1984, the RNZAF reformed No. 2 Squadron to fulfil the training, operational conversion and research and systems evaluation and procedures development roles for the RNZAF Air Combat Force.

Royal New Zealand Air Force (RNZAF)

RNZAF	BuNo	c/n	Model	Fate
NZ6201	157904	14084	A-4K	Stored Woodbourne by Feb 2002
NZ6202	157905	14085	A-4K	Stored Woodbourne by Feb 2002
NZ6203	157906	14086	A-4K	Crashed near Ohakea 20 Jun 96. Pilot ejected
NZ6204	157907	14087	A-4K	Stored Woodbourne by Dec 01
NZ6205	157908	14088	A-4K	Stored Ohakea Dec 01
NZ6206	157909	14089	A-4K	Stored Ohakea Dec 01
NZ6207	157910	14090	A-4K	Crashed Ohakea 18 Oct 74. Pilot ejected
NZ6208	157911	14091	A-4K	Crashed 23 Jul 92 SE North Island. Pilot ejected
NZ6209	157912	14092	A-4K	Stored Woodbourne by Feb 2002
NZ6210	157913	14093	A-4K	Collided Ohakea with NZ6211 and crashed 24 Oct 89. Pilot killed
NZ6251	157914	14094	TA-4K	Stored Woodbourne by Dec 01
NZ6252	157915	14095	TA-4K	Retained at Ohakea as a demonstrator 2002
NZ6253	157916	14096	TA-4K	Crashed Ruhaine ranges 23 Mar 81. Pilot killed
NZ6254	157917	14097	TA-4K	Stored Woodbourne by Dec 01
NZ6211	154903	13776	A-4G	Crashed 16 Feb 01 Nowra. Pilot killed
NZ6212	154904	13777	A-4G	Stored Woodbourne by Dec 01
NZ6213	154905	13778	A-4G	Stored Woodbourne by Feb 2002
NZ6214	154906	13779	A-4G	Stored Woodbourne by Dec 01
NZ6215	155052	13868	A-4F	Stored Woodbourne by Feb 2002
NZ6216	155061	13877	A-4F	Stored Woodbourne by Feb 2002
NZ6217	155063	13879	A-4F	Retained at Ohakea as a demonstrator 2002
NZ6218	155069	13885	A-4F	Stored Woodbourne 2001
NZ6255	154911	13784	TA-4G	Retained at Ohakea as a demonstrator 2002
NZ6256	154912	13785	TA-4G	Crashed 20 Mar 2001 off Western Australia. Pilot ejected
Display aircraft				
'NZ6207'	149516	12841	A-4L	RNZAF Museum in K configuration
'NZ6257'	-	-	TA-4K	Ohakea Museum, composite airframe including parts of NZ6208

A 'Kahu'-standard A-4K armed with AIM-9L and AGM-65 missiles. In their latter years the aircraft usually wore No.2 Squadron markings (as seen here) on one side and 75 Squadron insignia on the other.

In early 1991 the New Zealand and Australian governments signed the Nowra Agreement, which saw some of the former RAN Skyhawks return to their former base. The agreement called for the Australian and New Zealand Defence Forces to share costs of the operation with 400 hours per year dedicated to providing the RAN, particularly their shipboard radar and missile operators, with realistic training. The same missions gave the Kiwi pilots excellent practice in the maritime attack role. Many of the missions were the same type flown by US Navy VC squadrons over the years, albeit with the addition of radar and precision weapons. Another difference was the height flown. While the US Navy rarely went below 250ft (75m), the RNZAF A-4s had a 'hard deck' of 50ft (15m), or 100ft (30m) for newly-qualified pilots. One problem with such low-altitude flying was that the seeker heads of the training (TGM) versions of the Maverick missiles became encrusted with salt spray, which obscured the picture on the cockpit display. When operating in concert with RAAF F/A-18s, the Hornet pilots were restricted to 250ft, or 'way up in the stratosphere' as the New Zealanders liked to say.

The Nowra Agreement was extended in 1996 with more hours allocated to training with Australian sea and air units. A New Zealand defence review the following year called for replacement of the A-4s from 2004 and the opportunity was taken to implement a deal to lease (and thereafter probably purchase) twenty-eight F-16A/B aircraft from the US Government. The particular aircraft involved had been bought by Pakistan but embargoed because of that country's nuclear weapons programme. Although the deal was signed in July 1999, a change of government in New Zealand saw a review of the deal and its cancellation in March 2000. Without public consultation or parliamentary debate, the new government announced the disbandment of the Air Combat Force altogether in May 2001. Despite protests from concerned groups, the three jet squadrons (Nos. 2 and 75 with Skyhawks and No. 14 with Aermacchi MB 339CB trainers) were disbanded on 13 December 2001.

Many of the RAF's combat pilots left to join other air forces that were eager to have their skills. At time of writing, former RNZAF pilots are flying RAAF F/A-18s. F-111s

A TA-4KU leads A-4KUs on a training flight over the US before delivery. The Kuwaiti Skyhawks were regarded as the nicest to fly by the company test pilots.

Harry S Gann, McDonnell Douglas via TRH Pictures

Kuwait Air Force (KAF)

BuNo	c/n	KAF	Fate
A-4KU			
160180	14548	801	Brazil Navy N-1001
160181	14549	802	Brazil Navy N-1002
160182	14550	803	lost prior to August 1990
160183	14551	804	Brazil Navy N-1003
160184	14552	805	damaged in Iraq/preserved Kuwait Airport
160185	14553	806	lost prior to August 1990
160186	14554	807	Brazil Navy N-1004
160187	14555	808	lost prior to August 1990
160188	14556	809	Brazil Navy N-1005
160189	14557	810	Brazil Navy N-1006
160190	14558	811	Brazil Navy N-1007
160191	14559	812	Destroyed in bombing raid in Iraq
160192	14560	813	Brazil Navy N-1008
160193	14561	814	Brazil Navy N-1009
160194	14562	815	lost prior to August 1990
160195	14563	816	Brazil Navy N-1010
160196	14564	817	Brazil Navy N-1011
160197	14565	818	Brazil Navy N-1012
160198	14566	819	Brazil Navy N-1013
160199	14567	820	Brazil Navy N-1014
160200	14568	821	Disassembled and trucked to Iraq – stored Kuwait Airport
160201	14569	822	Brazil Navy N-1015
160202	14570	823	Brazil Navy N-1016
160203	14571	824	Brazil Navy N-1017
160204	14572	825	Brazil Navy N-1018
160205	14573	826	Brazil Navy N-1019
160206	14574	827	Brazil Navy N-1020
160207	14575	828	Shot down by radar-guided SAM over Kuwait 17 Jan 91
160208	14576	829	Collided with high-tension lines post war. Wreck at Kuwait Airport
160209	14577	830	lost prior to August 1990
TA-4KU			
160210	14578	881	Preserved Kuwait Airport (also said to have been taken to Iraq and damaged beyond repair).
160211	14579	882	Disassembled and trucked to Iraq 1990. Nose used on the museum example
160212	14580	883	Brazil Navy N-1021
160213	14581	884	Brazil Navy N-1022
160214	14582	885	lost prior to August 1990. Wreck said to be at Kuwait airport
160215	14583	886	Brazil Navy N-1023

A hybrid TA-4KU was assembled for the KAF Museum using parts of several recovered/unflyable aircraft.

Kuwait's Skyhawks saw intense action in defence of their country in August 1990 and during the campaign to recapture it in early 1991. Most are now in service with Brazilian Navy. TRH Pictures

and PC-9s, and Harriers, C-130s, Jaguars and Tornado F.3s with the RAF. At the time of its retirement, A-4K NZ6218, which was the last single-seat Skyhawk built for the US Navy, and which had seen combat in Vietnam, two major accidents and service with three air forces, had a total of 5,594 airframe hours recorded.

The seventeen surviving RNZAF Skyhawks were put in storage, with one A-4K and one TA-4K kept airworthy for sales demonstration purposes. At one time five different Asia-Pacific nations were said to be interested in purchasing the aircraft, but the Philippines and Malaysia were the only ones to be publicly named. A New Zealand firm had its offer to purchase two Skyhawks for contract target support work for the Navy rejected. Eventually, in early 2003, Arizona-based Advanced Training Systems International (ATSI) announced they were to purchase the aircraft for an undisclosed sum, believed to be in the order of $60 million. It was suggested that some might be based once again at Nowra to support the RAN's training needs, this time on a commercial basis.

Kuwait (Kuwait Air Force and Free Kuwait Air Force)

In November 1974 the government of Kuwait announced that it intended to purchase thirty-six new-build Skyhawks along with AIM-9 Sidewinders, spare parts and support equipment for a total cost of $250 million. On 20 January 1975, McDonnell Douglas was given authority to proceed with the development of the A-4KU single-seat and TA-4KU two-seat models for the Kuwaiti Air Force (KAF).

The single-seaters were based on the 1974-model A-4N, although with the self-starter

The ex-Israeli Skyhawks of Indonesia's 11 Skuadron wore this unique camouflage scheme during their early years of service.

of the A-4M. The TA-4s had the same configuration as the OA-4M, but were structurally more akin to the 1972-model TA-4H, albeit with the P-408 engine and self-starter and a different avionics fit. For some reason, the ALR-45 'hot dog' tail fairing was only fitted to the two-seaters. Other equipment associated with the Shrike and Walleye missiles and with nuclear weapons delivery was deleted.

The first of 30 A-4KUs flew at Palmdale on 20 July 1976 in the hands of McDonnell Douglas pilot Fred Hamilton, followed on 14 December by the first of the six TA-4KUs. The manufacturer soon established a training programme at Yuma, Arizona for Kuwaiti air and ground crews mainly using borrowed Training Command TA-4Js, although at least three A-4KUs and one TA-4KU were operated there during 1977 with US insignia. American military and civilian contract personnel were also to help fly and maintain the Skyhawks in KAF service.

The Kuwaiti Skyhawks were delivered by air during 1977 and 1978, and although exact details of dates and numbers are sketchy, it is known that some passed through Prestwick, Scotland and Ramstein, Germany. Eight A-4KUs stopped over at RAF Bentwaters in eastern England in April and May 1977, followed by another batch in July and two more in September. These aircraft had come from Keflavik, Iceland and their next stop was Sigonella, Sicily en route to Kuwait.

Once integrated into full KAF service, the Skyhawks served with Nos. 9 and 25 Squadrons at Ahmad al-Jabr Air Base in Southern Kuwait. Five A-4KUs and one TA-4KU were written off prior to August 1990, leaving twenty-five A-4KUs and five TA-4KUs. In 1984 Kuwait put the A-4s up for sale but later withdrew the offer.

After the liberation of Kuwait in February 1991, the Free Kuwait Air Force remained in Saudi Arabia until the damaged Kuwaiti airfields could be restored, but they returned home to Al Jabr on 6 and 7 July 1991. They were flown for a short period after the war. One aircraft (KAF 829) was lost after the War when it collided with high-tension wires. The remainder were stored pending the delivery of F/A-18C and D Hornets that had been ordered prior to August 1990. In 1993 Nos. 9 and 25 Squadrons completed conversion to the Hornet.

Attempts by the US State Department to broker a deal to sell the A-4KUs to Bosnia in 1996, or to the Philippines came to nothing, but in 1998 Brazil agreed to purchase most of the surviving aircraft for its naval air arm. The twenty-three remaining aircraft, comprising twenty A-4KUs and three TA-4KUs, were sold and transported to Brazil.

Iraq

One source says that five of Kuwait's A-4s that were captured on the ground by Iraq in August 1990 were taken to Abu Ubaida Airbase near Kut. After the end of hostilities, all but one, which was destroyed in an Allied bombing raid, was returned to Kuwait by road. They are unlikely to have flown in Iraqi Air Force hands.

More recently, Indonesia's A-4Es have sported this toned down but still attractive three-tone scheme as seen on this A-4E at Hasanuddin in 1999. Alan Warnes, *Air Forces Monthly*

Tentara Nasional Indonesia-Angkatan Udara (TNI-AU)

BuNo	C/n	TNI-AU	Model	Delivered	Notes
		TL-0415	TA-4H	Nov 79	
		TL-0416	TA-4H	Nov 79	
154315	13703	TL-0418	TA-4J	1999	
158454	14259	TL-0419	TA-4J	1999	Damaged in take-off accident 10 Feb 03
		TT-0401	A-4E	Nov 79	
		TT-0402	A-4E	Nov 79	
		TT-0403	A-4E	Nov 79	
		TT-0404	A-4E	Nov 79	
		TT-0405	A-4E	Nov 79	Crashed 19 Jun 00 near Kendari, pilot killed
		TT-0406	A-4E	Nov 79	
		TT-0407	A-4E	Nov 79	
		TT-0408	A-4E	Nov 79	
		TT-0409	A-4E	Nov 79	
		TT-0410	A-4E	Nov 79	
		TT-0411	A-4E	Nov 79	
		TT-0412	A-4E	Nov 79	
		TT-0413	A-4E	Nov 79	
		TT-0414	A-4E	Nov 79	
		TT-0431	A-4E	1982	
		TT-0432	A-4E	1982	
		TT-0433	A-4E	1982	
		TT-0434	A-4E	1982	
		TT-0435	A-4E	1982	
		TT-0436	A-4E	1982	
		TT-0437	A-4E	1982	
		TT-0433	A-4E	1982	
		TT-0439	A-4E	1982	
		TT-0440	A-4E	1982	
		TT-0441	A-4E	1982	
		TT-0442	A-4E	1982	
		TT-0443	A-4E	1982	
		TT-0444	A-4E	1982	
		TT-0445	A-4E	1982	
		TT-0446	A-4E	1982	

Indonesia (Tentara Nasional Indonesia-Angkatan Udara)

By the late 1970s, Indonesia's fleet of Soviet-built Ilyushin Il-28 'Beagle' and Tupolev Tu-16 'Badger' bombers was largely grounded because of a lack of spare parts. US vice-president Walter Mondale offered Indonesia sixteen Skyhawks during a May 1978 visit to Jakarta. Fourteen single-seat and two two-seat Skyhawks were indeed delivered in November 1979, but these were A-4Es and TA-4Hs from Israeli stocks. It is possible that it was Israel who initiated the sale, but that it was brokered by the US to avoid local Muslim sensibilities. The A-4s were serialed TT-0401 to TT-0414 and the TA-4s were

TL-0415 and TL-0416. The former US or Israeli identities are not known for the Es, although one is believed to have been 819 in IDF/AF service, and one of the TA-4Hs was 66. Some of the Israeli-built avionics were removed, but the A-4s retained the DEFA 30mm cannon and extended tailpipes. Indonesia's pilots were trained by No. 141 Squadron at Etzion in Israel, and once this was completed, the squadron's aircraft were transferred to Indonesia.

These aircraft formed the complement of Skwadron Udara 11 (SkU11) at Madium-Iwahyudi Air Base on Java and later at Hasanuddin Air Base near Ujung Pandang on Sulawesi (the Celebes). In 1982 an additional sixteen surplus A-4Es were purchased directly from US stocks and were refurbished before delivery in a deal worth $27 million in total. This second batch was used to equip Skwadron Udara 12 (SkU12) at Pekanbaru Air Base, Riau Province, Sumatra. The TNI-AU serials were TT-0431 through TT-0446. Again, their previous identities remain unknown. With the arrival of BAe Hawk Mk 109s and 209s in 1996-7, SkU 12 gave up its remaining A-4s, and the approximately twenty-seven survivors were concentrated at Hasanuddin with SkU 11.

Down to only one TA-4 for conversion training by the late 1990s, Indonesia considered buying TA-4PTMs from Malaysia, but acquired a pair of ex-USN TA-4Js instead. The Malaysian aircraft were probably in too poor a condition, and also had different engines to the rest of the TNI-AU fleet. The TA-4Js were refurbished by Safe Air Engineering at Woodbourne, New Zealand in a contract that attracted some protest because of the political situation in East Timor and the New Zealand government's opposition to Indonesian policy there. Nonetheless, the work was completed, the aircraft were test flown by personnel from ATSI (q.v.), and the Skyhawks were disassembled and shipped to Indonesia in 1999. One of the two new aircraft was substantially damaged during an aborted take-off at Hasanuddin in February 2003 when its brake parachute failed. The two crew were not hurt.

One aircraft is known to have been written off in late 1991 and one or two in 2000.

As delivered, Israeli A-4Es were much the same as their USN counterparts. The squadron badge has been crudely censored, but 209 is believed to have belonged to 116 'Flying Wing' Squadron when photographed in 1970. This Skyhawk is stored as part of the Hatzerim Museum collection.
TRH Pictures

Known Israel Defence Force/Air Force A-4Hs

BuNo	C/n	Del.	IDF	Units	Fate/notes
155242	13937	1968	01	109	Written off.
155243	13938	12/67	03	109	Destroyed 2 MiG-17s 1970. Shot down 18 Oct 73 by Egyptian SAM or AAA
155244	13939	12/67	05	109,102	Damaged 1971. Stored Ovda. Last of first four to survive
155245	13940		07/107/207	109	
155260	13955	1968	08/108		
155246	13941	1968	09		
155254	13949	1968	22/122/222	102	Preserved Hatzerim
155269	13963	1968	29/129/229	109, FSAS.	Was at IAF Museum, Hatzerim
155271	13965	1968	30/130/230	102	IAF Museum, Hatzerim
155283	13976	1968	55/155/255		Stored Ovda
155284	13977	1968	56/156/256		
155287	13981	1968	61/161/261	FSAS	Was at IAF Museum, Hatzerim
155289	13983	1968	70/170/270		IAF Museum, Hatzerim
157918			88/188/288		

An A-4N of 116 'Flying Wing' Squadron shows all the pertinent features of this version, many of which were retroffitted to earlier versions, including various aerials, spoilers, 30-mm cannon and the tailpipe extension. IDF/AF

From thirty-two A-4s purchased, various sources give notional TNI-AU A-4 strength as twenty-eight in 1992, twenty-seven in 1996 and nineteen in 1999, including the two additional TA-4Js, and fourteen in 2002. Following the 2003 accident to TT-0419, First Air Marshal Edi Harjoko admitted that the Skyhawk was 'not in the best condition', saying that only four or five of the Air Force's Skyhawks were currently in airworthy condition because of a shortage of spares.

The arrival of the Sukhoi Su-27 in Indonesia in mid-2003 has probably spelt the end of the A-4 in TNI-AU service, particularly as the first delivery arrived wearing an SkU-11 badge. At the time of writing, it is believed the unit is operating with a mixed fleet of A-4s and the first four 'Flankers'

Israel (Israel Air Force/Defence Force)

Israel is and has been the largest A-4 operator outside the US. Up to 1976, the Israel Defence Force/Air Force (IDF/AF) is believed to have acquired 321 new and used Skyhawks. A further seventeen TA-4Js were delivered in the early 1990s for a total of

A-4Hs without known BuNos

IDF	units	IDF	units	IDF	units
07	109	55/155/255		94/194/294	110
11/111/211	Hatz Mus	56/156/256	110,147	255/755	102
15/115/215		58/158/258		267/767	102*
16/116/216	109, 102	59/159		271/771	102 **
17/117/217	109	61/161/261		266/766	FS
19/119/219	115	62/162/262	**		
21/121/221		63/163/263	147,110	262/762	
23/123/223		65/165/265		296/796	102
24/124		66/166/266		290/790	102
25/125/225	147, FSAS	68/168			
28/128/228		70/170/270			
29/129/229	109	71	115, FSAS, Hatz Mus		
30/130/230	Hatz Mus	72/172/272			
31/131/231		73/173/273	115**		
32/132/232	109, 102, 110	74/174/274	**		
33	109	77/177/277	109**		
34/234	109**	78/178/278	109, 147		
35/135/235	110, Hatz Mus	79/179/279			
36/136	109**	80/180/280			
38/138/238		182/282	**		
39/139/239		84/184/284	109 **		
40/140/240		88/188/288	116		
41/141/241	110	89	109		
42/142/242		91/191/291			
47/147/247	147	92/192/292	**		
52/152	109	93/193/293	110 Instructional, Haifa		

*Damaged Oct 73
**stored or dumped Ovda
Hatz Mus = IAF Museum, Hatzerim

A-4Es and Hs were progressively updated until they were very close to A-4N standard. Seen in 1970, this 116 Squadron example has the avionics hump but no drag chute and the original 20mm cannon. The tailpipe extension was added to A-4s from 1974.

TRH Pictures

Israel Defence Force/Air Force A-4E

A-4E deliveries consisted of sixty ex-USN/USMC aircraft supplied in 1971, twenty-five in 1969 and twenty-nine delivered in October/November 1973. The A-4Es were serialled in the 200 range, the survivors later being reissued with numbers from 800 upwards.

IDF	Units	Fate/notes
201/801		
202/802		
203/803		
204		Shot down 9 Oct 73
205/805		
207/807		W/o 2 Apr 81
208/808	147, 140, FSAS	
209/809	116	Stored Hatzerim
210/810		
211		Said w/o 7 Oct 73 but seen since
212/812		Damaged 1973.
213/813		Tail at Lod
215/815	116	Ground instructional Haifa
216/816		
217/817		
219/819		Damaged 1973. Sold to Indonesia
22019820	116	On electronics range SW of Dead Sea
221/821		Stored Ovda
222/822		Stored Hatzerim
223/823		
224/824	110	
225/825	FTS	Stored Ovda
228/828	116,102	Stored Ovda
229/829		
230/830	102	
231/831	102	
232/832	110, 147	
233/833	147	'Argentine store' Ben Gurion
235/835		
236/836	110	

338, although some sources give a figure as high as 355.

Israel first requested Skyhawks in 1964. In February 1966 the US agreed to supply Israel with A-4s if it agreed to certain demands and in August a contract was signed for the first twenty-four of a version of the A-4E to be designated A-4H. There was an option, soon taken up, for a further twenty-four. Israel had pledged to allow more and fuller inspections of the nuclear research facilities at Dimona and that their Skyhawks would not be equipped with nuclear weapons.

The first A-4H was flown at Palmdale by test pilot John Lane on 27 October 1967. Prior to delivery of the Skyhawks, Israeli pilots and groundcrew trained in Florida with VA-44 and VA-45, although this was interrupted somewhat by the Six-Day War in June 1967, which saw the first group of pilots urgently recalled to Israel to rejoin their units.

The initial delivery of four A-4Hs arrived at the port of Haifa on 29

IDF	Units	Fate/notes
238/838	110, 147	Stored Ovda
239/839	147, 102	Stored Ovda
240/840		Stored Ovda
241/841		Gate guardian Ramat David
242/842		
243/843	110	
245/845		
246/846		
247/847	116	Damaged 1973
248/848		
249/849	140	
250/850	140	'Argentine store' Ben Gurion
251/851		
252/852		
253/853	149,110	'Argentine store' Ben Gurion
254/854		
255/855		dumped Ovda
256/856		
257/857		
258/858		
259/859	110	
260/860	110	
261/861		
262/862		
264/864		
265/865		
266/866	149	Probably to Indonesia 1979
267/867		
268/868		
269/869		
271/871		
272/872		Wore ship kill mark
273/873		
274/874	140	
275/875		Collided with F-4E 13 Jan 74
276/876		
277/877		
278/878		
279/879		W/o 18 Dec 80
280/880		Hatzerim
282/882		
286/886	116, FS	Fire dump Ovda
287/887	115	Holz college (not 149990)
288/888		Stored Ovda
289/889	110	
294/894	102	Holz college
296/896		Stored Ben Gurion in 1989
298/898	140	
299/899	140	Stored Ovda

December1967, and the first was ready for flight by 1 January. These became the first American jets to enter service with the warring nations in the Middle East. Known as the 'Ayit' (Vulture) in IDF/AF service, they soon began to replace Dassault Ouragons and Mystères in the ground attack and close air support roles. The first unit to transition to the Skyhawk was 109 'Valley' Tayeset (Squadron) at Hatzor, with whom it replaced the Mystère IV. Compared to the older French jets. the A-4 offered greater lifting capability, better engine reliability (requiring a tear-down inspection each 200 hours versus every thirty hours for the Mystère IV), greater speed and longer range, and the option of aerial refuelling. Using J52-P8A engines supplied as spares with the A-4s Israel re-engined at least twenty-five of its Super Mystère B2s in 1969-72 to create the 'Sa'ar' (Tempest), which proved faster than the Skyhawk due to its slicker airframe and a very effective ground attack platform in the 1973 war.

The first Skyhawk combat missions came on 15 February 1968, when A-4s of 109 'Valley' Squadron attacked Jordanian artillery and Palestinian bases along the Israel-Jordan border following attacks on Israeli settlements. The proximity of the target to the A-4s' base at Hatzor meant that all five pylons could be used for carrying bombs, which at that time were 250lb and 500lb French-made weapons.

Known Israel Defence Force/Air Force A-4Es

BuNo	C/n	IDF	Units	Fate/notes
149647	12972	237/837	147	Stored Ovda. Delivered Oct 73
149964	13017	291/891		Hatzerim Museum
149984	13037	281/881	110,115	Holz college. Delivered Oct 73
149994	13047	280/880		Ground instructional, Haifa. Delivered Oct 73
150090	13143	293/893		
150091	13144	8??		Delivered Nov 73
150095	13148	283/883	116	Holz college. Delivered Oct 73
150099	13152	244/844	147,102	Hatzerim Museum in grey scheme
150127	13180	295/895	102, FSAS	Holz college
151056	13226	249/849	140	Stored Ovda delivered Sep 72
151139	13309	214/814		
151179	13347	285/885		Hatzerim Museum
151184	13354	292/892	110	Holz college
151994	13382	263/863		Stored Ovda
152009*	13397	244/844		Hatzerim Museum
152019	13407	206/806		Stored Ovda. Delivered 02/71
152030	13418	8??		Stored Ovda. Delivered 04/71
152050	12438	254/854		Hatzerim Museum
152097	13485	284/884		Hatzerim Museum. Delivered Oct 73

New squadrons formed as Skyhawk deliveries continued. No.102 'Flying Tiger' Squadron formed at Ramat-David in June 1968. Later it became the advanced jet training squadron. No.115 Flying Dragon' Squadron received A-4Hs in March 1969 at Nevatim. In March 1971, 116 'Flying Wing' Squadron converted to the A-4E from the Mystère IV, followed by 110 'Knights of the North' at Ramat-David with A-4Hs. Just before the Yom Kippur war in October 1973, No.140 'Golden Eagle' Squadron began forming with A-4Es as the advanced training unit, completing the process after the war. In April 1976 143 'Smashing Parrot' squadron began A-4E operations at Etzion in April

An A-4H of No. 102 'Flying Tigers' Squadron, upgraded with most of the features of the A-4N.

An A-4N and a TA-4H of No 140 'Golden Eagle' Squadron line up for take-off. This unit was based at Nevatim from 1982 to 1986 when it received F-16s. IDF/AF

1976. Finally, reserve unit No. 147 'Battering Ram' squadron was re-established in August 1978 with A-4Ns at Hatzerim. The Flight School at Hatzerim, also known as No 252 Squadron, used single- and two-seat A-4s from 1972, with the former mainly being aircraft borrowed from the 'Flying Tigers'.

The initial deliveries of forty-eight A-4Hs were followed by a further forty-two to make ninety of this model, derived from the A-4F. The last of these arrived in 1970. Somewhat surprisingly considering US losses in Vietnam and the political fallout from the Israeli attack on the USS *Liberty* in June 1969, the US government released twenty-five A-4Es for supply to Israel in 1969, followed by another thirty-five for a total of sixty. These came from Navy and Marine Corps squadrons, some of which were forced to revert to the A-4C because of shortages of A-4Es. The A-4Es were shipped in three

Israel Defence Force/Air Force A-4Fs

IDF	BuNo	c/n	units	fate/notes
601				
602			116	On electronics range SW of Dead Sea
603			147, 140	Displayed Ramon 2004
604			147	Stored Ovda
605			147, 102	Stored Ovda
606			102	Stored Ovda
607			147	
608				
609				
610			147	Stored Ovda
611	155010	13826	147	Hatzerim Museum. BuNo doubtful as lost in Vietnam
612				
613				
614			147	Stored Ovda
615				

Israel Defence Force/Air Force TA-4 two-seat Skyhawks

The serial pattern of the two-seaters remains unclear. It is likely that some aircraft were given new serials, and thus may appear here twice, but the pattern of re-serialling, if any, is not known. The following aircraft have been sighted

IDF	Model	Units	BuNo	c/n	Fate/notes
228	TA-4H	102			
40?	TA-4F				Shot down 1973
40?	TA-4F				Shot down 1973
404	TA-4F				Shot down 1973
406	TA-4F				Shot down 1973
481					W/o 01 Nov 92
542	TA-4H	102, FTS			Seen 1994-2001
543	TA-4H	FTS			Seen 2001
544	TA-4H	FTS			Seen 1995-1999
545	TA-4H	FTS			Seen 1997-2001
547	TA-4H	102, FSAS			
566	TA-4F	FSAS			Seen Oct 73
66	TA-4H				Sold to Indonesia
701	TA-4J	102, 115			
702	TA-4J	102			
703	TA-4J	116, FTS, 102			
704	TA-4J	102, FSAS			
705	TA-4J	FSAS			
706	TA-4J	FSAS			
708	TA-4J	FSAS			
712	TA-4J	FSAS			
715	TA-4J(H)	102, FSAS, 147, 116			
719	TA-4J(H)	140			
720	TA-4J(H)	110, 102			
721	TA-4J(H)	102			
723	TA-4J(H)	102			
725	TA-4J(H)	140, 102, FTS			
726	TA-4J(H)	102, 115			
728	TA-4J(H)	140			
730	TA-4J(H)	FSAS			
743		102			
44	TA-4H	115			
45/145/745	TA-4H	116, 102			
747	TA-4J	Museum	153500	13499	Delivered 1994. To ATSI N250WL
748	TA-4J		152853	13566	Delivered 1994. To ATSI N251WL
749	TA-4J		153672	13610	Delivered 1992. To ATSI N252WL

FSAS = Flight School Advanced Squadron
FTS = Flight Training School

batches during 1971 and were issued to 116, 110 and 102 Squadrons in turn.

Israel's A-4Es and A-4Hs were heavily involved in the 'War of Attrition' with Egypt of 1969-70. During this time the TA-4H joined the inventory. This was a version of the TA-4J with Israeli equipment, five pylons and a combat capability more akin to that of the TA-4F. In some US documents the last fifteen two-seaters built for Israel are referred to the TA-4J(H). Although mainly used for conversion training, the IDF/AF two-seaters were also employed in a combat role as and when necessary, including as forward air controllers. A total of twenty-five TA-4Hs were built for Israel. The following TA-4Fs are believed to have been transferred to Israel in the early 1970s: 153464, 153466, 153470, 153514, and these TA-4Js: 158492, 158493, 158497, 158502, 158503, 159101, 159102, 159103, 159104, 159546, 159547, 159548, 159549, 159550, 159551, 159552, 159553, 159554, 159555 and 159556. Following the First Gulf War, in 1992 fourteen TA-4Js were provided by the US as part of a package in payment for Israel's non participation in the war, including 153672. In 1994, these three were also delivered: 152853, 153500 and 153672, but it is not certain if they were ever used before being resold to ATSI in Arizona.

Despite their use in action on many occasions, there are only eight known A-4 losses before October 1973, three of which were caused by Egyptian ground fire or SAMs.

Israel was very impressed with the improvements made by McDonnell Douglas to create the A-4M for the US Marines, particularly its high powered and fuel efficient J52-P408 engine. In March 1971 the US government approved an Israeli request for supply of a new designated A-4N Skyhawk II version based on the A-4M. The first A-4N flew in June 1972 and the first was handed over to Israel in January 1973. The N was basically similar to the M but lacked the self-starting capability. Israeli avionics and 30-mm cannon were added once the aircraft were in Israel. Thirty A-4Ns had been delivered by October 1973 and they equipped 115 'Flying Dragon' Squadron at the outbreak of the Yom Kippur War.

Additionally, a programme was begun in 1972 to upgrade the A-4Hs in the inventory to a similar standard as the A-4N, with the P408 engine, slightly wider intakes, the new HUD and navigation system and an avionics hump as found on US A-4Fs. Also in 1972 the two squadrons operating A-4Es had their aircraft updated with 30mm cannon, nosewheel steering and a brake parachute.

Yom Kippur War

Following a fortnight of tension, on 6 October 1973, the Jewish holy day of Yom Kippur, Syrian and Egyptian forces crossed Israel's borders. The initial days of fighting were the most desperate for Israel and the IDF/AF. In the first three days alone, nearly sixty Israeli aircraft were lost, including twenty-four of the 162 A-4s of various models and configuration that were then in service.

The war situation quickly deteriorated and Prime Minister Meir made a direct appeal to President Nixon for immediate military aid to replace lost equipment and bolster the beleaguered IDF. It is possible that Meir hinted that the nuclear option might be used if there was a serious danger that Israel would lose the war.

Although impossible to confirm, some analysts believe that Israel assembled up to thirteen 20kt nuclear bombs for use in the event their forces were overrun and major population centres were threatened. Such a possibility was explored in the opening

Led by a TA-4H is a gaggle of TA-4s in the markings of the IDF/AF's Flight School Basic Squadron. When needed, the TA-4s were called on to perform attack, FAC and other combat missions. IDF/AF

chapter of the Tom Clancy novel 'The Sum of All Fears', which was filmed in 2001 using an A-4N owned by US private contractor ATSI.

On 15 October 1973 the Nixon administration began Operation Nickel Grass to supply Israel with much needed war materiel. C-141 StarLifter and C-5 Galaxy transports from Travis AFB delivered APCs, artillery guns, ammunition, CH-53 helicopters and parts for damaged and F-4s and A-4s. The latter included nineteen entire Skyhawk rear fuselages, which were rushed straight from the transport aircraft to the repair hangars and fitted to A-4s that had been damaged by SAMs and were lined up ready to receive them. They are said to have flown into battle before the new sections could be repainted in Israeli colours. At least one of the A-4s was flown in Israel, at least for a time in standard US colours with Star of David insignia. The A-4s that arrived in October 1973 were credited with eighty-five combat missions before the cease-fire on the twenty-fourth.

Aid to Israel included nearly fifty complete Skyhawks taken directly from US squadrons. One US airman recalled being on a Marine Reserve unit's flightline during October 1973 when the call came to urgently 'de-class' (remove classified equipment from) the unit's newly-received A-4Es and send them to Norfolk, Virginia for delivery to Israel.

A-4s were delivered via US Navy carriers in the Mediterranean. The assumption has often been that the aircraft belonged to a particular air wing and were just handed over as is where is. The actual process was more complicated. The USS *Franklin D. Roosevelt* (CVA-42) left port in the USA on 14 September 1973 with CVW-6 embarked, this being an air wing with no A-4 squadrons. On 30 October, the 'FDR' deployed off Crete (other sources say south of Sicily) and served as a jumping off or transhipment point for A-4s that had flown from the USA via the Azores. Personnel of former A-4 squadron VA-15, which by 1973 flew A-7s, serviced the incoming Skyhawks. One aerial refuelling was given to the A-4s between the FDR and Israel.

Thirty-six A-4s were delivered this way via the FDR. The *Kennedy* and *Independence* were also positioned in the Mediterranean and provided assistance during Nickel Grass.

Known Israel Defence Force/Air Force A-4Ns

A total of 117 A-4Ns were built and delivered to Israel 1973-76.

BuNo	C/n	Del date	ID	Units	Fate/notes
158726	14345	19 Jul 73	322	115	Shot down Oct 73
158728	14347	19 Jan 73			
158729	14348	1 Feb 73	324	102, FTS	
158730	14349	2 Apr 73	321	116, 115	To ATSI as N260WL
159051	14379	19 Oct 73			To ATSI as N267WL
159078	14384	13 Nov 73	335	116	To BAE Systems as N432FS
159523	14443	21 Nov 74	344	115	To ATSI as N263WL Crashed in Utah 10 May 2003
159530	14450				To ATSI as N268WL
159533	14453		413	140	To ATSI as N261WL
159534	14454				To ATSI as N266WL
159536	14456				To ATSI as N269WL
159542	14462		432	140	To BAE Systems as N437FS
159544	14464				To ATSI as N265WL
159545	14465		444	116	To ATSI as N262WL
159805	14504		305	102, 140	To BAE Systems as N431FS
159815	14514		373	116, 115	To BAE Systems as N434FS also quoted 373
159816	14515		379	116	IAF Museum, Hatzerim
159823	14522				To ATSI as N264WL

The figure of 'some fifty' A-4s delivered via carriers is also quoted by one source, and another breaks total war-related deliveries down into thirty A-4Es and Fs in October and another sixteen in November/December. These later deliveries are believed to have come via the *Independence*. Other sources quote up to eighty A-4 deliveries and speak of US Navy F-4J Phantoms joining F-4Es supplied from USAF stocks, although no evidence of Navy Phantoms in Israel has yet emerged.

A figure of forty-six deliveries tallies with the thirty A-4Es and sixteen A-4Fs struck off USN/USMC charge at Norfolk between 21 October and 2 November and allocated to the Military Assistance Program (MAP). The official 'strike' records of only twelve indicate that Israel was the recipient, the others only recording 'MAP'. A further six new A-4Ns were handed over at Long Beach during October 1973. Ex-US Skyhawks believed transferred to Israel include:A-4Es 149647, 149664, 149964, 149990, 149995, 149971, 150016, 150082, 150087, 150091, 150095, 150124, 150134, 151040, 151084, 149984, 149994, 150026, 150127, 150138, 151028, 151066, 151072, 151120,151163, 151177, 151184, 152006 and 152097. A-4Fs were: 154178, 154191*, 154990, 154997*, 154998, 154188, 154195, 145065, 155005*, 155007, 155008, 155010, 155040, 155043 and 155048. *Not confirmed

At roughly the same time as US Atlantic Fleet carriers were preparing to act as 'lily pads' for A-4 deliveries, the USS *Hancock* , then on her final cruise in Vietnamese waters, was ordered to the Indian Ocean and then to the Arabian Sea. Aboard were VA-56, -164 and –212 with A-4Fs. As they approached the war zone, CVW-21's pilots were warned that they would probably be asked to fly off their A-4s and F-8s and hand them

A-4Ns without known BuNos

IDF	units	IDF	units	IDF	units
301	140	351	116	386	102 w/o 15 Nov 98
306	140	353	116, 115**	388	w/o 15 Jan 80
302	115, 102	354	115	387	102
303	102	355	116 w/o 18 Feb 80	389	102
307	115, 116	356	116**	390	115
309	116	357	115	391	116
310	102	358		392	116**
312	109	361	115, 116	393	115 IAF. Museum
314	116	360	w/o 18 Feb 80	394	115**
315	w/o 29 Feb 76	362	**	395	**
318	115**	363	115, 116	396	FTS w/o 11 Feb 04
319	115 w/o 04 Jun 78	365	140	397	115, 140
20/320	102	366	115, 116	398	FTS
323	116 w/o 30 Aug 92	367	116	399	116, 115, FTS
25/325	102	368	116	401	116, 115
27/327	116, 102	369	115, 116	402	
28/328	116, 140, 110, 102*	371	115	404	
329	102	372	116, 115	405	115, 140**
330	116**	374	116, 115, 149	406	w/o 01 May 83
				407	102, 149 FTS IAF
331	115, 116, 102	375	115		Museum
332	115, 116, 102, FTS	376	116	408	
333	115, 116	377	116	409	140
334	116	380	116**	410	FTS**
336	116	381		411	102
338	116	382	w/o 11 Dec 77	413	140
339	w/o 14 Oct 79	383	**	415	140, 115**
341	102	384	**	417	115
342	149, 116, 102	385	116	419	102 FTS**
343	149	388	w/o 15 Jan 80	421	116**
346	116	381	w/o17 Dec 76	423	116**
348	348 w/o 29 Apr 81	383	115**	427	115, 116**
349	115	384	140**	438	102**
350	115**	385	116		

*preserved Ramat David
**Stored Ovda

over to the Israeli Air Force. It was never quite made clear what the rules of engagement might be if they met Arab air opposition on route or how the pilots were supposed to return, but in the end the situation stabilized before they were called upon, and the *Hancock* set sail for home.

Post war

It is generally accepted that fifty-three to fifty-five Israeli Skyhawks were lost in the

Possibly suffering from hot brakes, an A-4N of No. 140 Squadron is attended to by the base fire services. The rudder colours for the 'Golden Eagle' squadron were yellow with green ribs and leading edges. IDF/AF

Yom Kippur War. Many of the losses were caused by infrared-guided SA-7 SAMs. The Sa'ar survived many SA-7 hits in cases where the Ayit was lost. This was attributed to the Sa'ar's exhaust pipe extending aft of the tail surfaces, which were easily damaged by warhead fragments on the Skyhawk. To reduce their IR signature, Israel's A-4s were fitted with a tailpipe extension, called 'chavit' (barrel) in a post-war modification programme. This moved the heat source as seen by the missile seeker further aft and cooled it slightly. A missile that did explode in the heat plume was likely to be further behind the aircraft where its shrapnel could do less damage to the tail control surfaces. A variation of this idea had been tested at China Lake on the first production A4D-1 Skyhawk as early as 1963 using a long asbestos pipe that protruded from the exhaust. Although several variations of tailpipe extension and shield were tested as part of Project DIRTY, the concept was not applied to American A-4s.

Following the Yom Kippur War, nearly a decade of relative peace followed, and the A-4 was gradually supplanted by new supersonic attack types such as the Kfir and F-16s and by further F-4E deliveries. In June 1982 when Israel invaded Lebanon, five regular Ayit squadrons (102, 115, 116, 140 and 147) were in service, flying the A-4N or A-4Hs and Fs upgraded to N standards as well as the TA-4J/H. Although facts are sparse, three reserve squadrons of A-4s (137, 145 and 202), are believed to have existed in the 1980s and 1990s but since disbanded.

Various further upgrades were implemented to maintain the A-4's combat effectiveness. The Elisra self protection system integrated chaff, flares and radar warning receivers to defend against enemy missiles. In 1982-3 some A-4Ns of 116 Squadron, including Nos. 309, 331 and 337 were fitted with AN/ABS-19 angle-rate bombing system (ARBS), allowing them to designate LGBs including the Paveway I and II and IAI Griffin. Other weapons used by, or at least cleared for use by, IDF/AF A-4s include TAL-1 220 kg and TAL-2 250 kg cluster bombs, ATAP cluster bombs, Guillotine LGBs, Opher LGBs, Pyramid TV-guided bombs, PB-500 penetration bombs and Gabriel radar-guided air-to-surface missiles. AIM-9D Sidewinders and Shafrir II AAMs could be carried for self-defence.

At least thirty-five Israeli Skyhawks have been destroyed in non-combat accidents as of 2004, in addition to the sixty-five lost to enemy action. An independent 2002 estimate

Singapore's 'Black Knights' flew the A-4SU (and later also the F-16A) during the 1990s. They did not appear at the 2004 Asian Aerospace show and may be in abeyance. Air Forces Monthly

in the 'Military Balance' yearbook gave active IDF/AF A-4 strength as one squadron of twenty-four A-4Ns and a training squadron with a strength of twenty-six two-seaters, nineteen TA-4Js and seven TA-4Hs. A small number of additional TA-4Js were supplied to the IDF/AF in the 1990s, but are not known to have actually entered service.

In January 2003 a contract was awarded to RADA Electronic Industries of Netanya to install an advanced debriefing system on the 'entire fleet' of A-4 and TA-4s. RADA's initial press release talked of "all fifty" A-4s, agreeing with the 'Military Balance' estimate, although one aircraft crashed in February 2004. Installation of the new debriefing system, which integrates GPS, INS, a data processor and a video recorder to give a synchronized three-dimensional record of each mission was planned for 2004/5 and the A-4 is expected to remain in Israeli service in the training role up to 2010. Units believed to still operate the A-4 in 2003 include 102 'Flying Tiger' Squadron at Hatzerim, which pools its aircraft with the Flying Training School (also known as 252 Squadron) and 116 'Flying Wing' Squadrons at Nevatim.

From about 1989 about a dozen A-4Es were stored in anticipation of their sale to Argentina at Tel Aviv's Ben Gurion Airport. Under British pressure not to help Argentina replace its 1982 losses, the USA would not allow the sale. When the political situation eased, the US sold Argentina some of its (much more capable) A-4Ms and OA-4Ms, and the A-4Es were mostly sent to desert storage at Ovda or passed to the Hatzerim Museum.

The Israeli Air Force Museum has quite a large collection of (mostly unrestored) Skyhawks. About ten A-4s including E, F, H and N models are stored or preserved at the Hatzerim museum or elsewhere on the base. A further half-dozen are displayed at other bases or are known to be in use as ground instructional airframes.

In 2000 and 2001, seventeen ex-Israeli Skyhawks joined the US civil aircraft register. Ten A-4Ns and three TA-4Js were delivered to Advanced Training Systems International (ATSI) in Arizona for contract work, and in a separate deal, four A-4Ns were upgraded and sold to BAE Systems for use as target tugs at Wittmund in Germany. Further A-4Ns (including 333 and 358) have been seen at Israel Aircraft Industries' facility at Ben Gurion under rework for 'a customer' not believed to be either ATSI or BAE.

Israeli secrecy is notoriously tight, and no official listing of IDF/AF Skyhawks has ever appeared. The following represents the best attempt to match Bureau Numbers of aircraft delivered to Israel with individual IDF serials or side numbers, a process complicated by the fact the side numbers changed at least once for many aircraft and twice in some cases. For example, ninety A-4H models were produced for Israel. Initially they had two-digit serials such as '07' until 1971 when the surviving aircraft were given three digit serials starting with '1' (thus '07' became '107'). From 1974 they were reserialled in the '200' range.

Until Singapore acquired KC-130 tankers, their A-4Ss were often seen without IFR probes, as seen on this 142 Squadron example. The A-4S and TA-4S were the only models with 30-mm Aden cannons. TRH Pictures

Singapore (Republic of Singapore Air Force)

The Singapore government ordered fifty ex-US Navy A-4Bs and TA-4Bs in 1973 for the Singapore Air Defence Command (SADC), these being supplied from storage at Davis-Monthan Air Force Base, Arizona. A small number of these aircraft had seen Vietnam service in the anti-submarine fighter role with VSF-3 or detachments of other units on ASW carriers. Lockheed Aircraft Services at Ontario, California instituted an upgrade programme that saw over 100 changes made to update the A-4s for further service. After rework, the Skyhawks were known as the A-4S and TA-4S. After nine were completed by Lockheed and eight delivered to Lemoore for initial training of pilots and groundcrews with VA-127, the modification line was transferred to the Singapore Aerospace Maintenance Company (SAMCO) in 1977. Three of the A-4Bs were sacrificed for spares and finally forty-seven emerged, seven of which were two-seaters, three converted by Lockheed and four by SAMCO from additional ex-US airframes.

The first of the A-4s equipped two squadrons (Nos. 142 'Gryphon' and 143 'Phoenix' at Tengah and Changi, respectively) and were mainly tasked with the ground attack role. The SADC was renamed the Republic of Singapore Air Force (RSAF) in 1975.

In 1977 the RSAF decided to buy a further seventy airframes, this time a mix of A-4Bs and A-4Cs.These were delivered to Singapore in 1980 and the A-4Cs were refurbished by SAMCO to create the A4S-1. The Bs were used for spares reclamation. Initially entering service in 1982 as attrition replacements, the new aircraft allowed

A TA-4SU of No. 150 Squadron at Cazaux, France. At one time this was A-4B 142936 with VMA-134.

Republic of Singapore Air Force (RSAF) A-4S

BuNo	c/n	Was	RSAF	Units	Fate/notes
142850	11912	A-4B	00/600		USA training. Preserved Singapore Discovery Centre.
142832	11894	A-4B	01/601	142	USA training
142771	11833	A-4B	02/602	142	USA training
142908	11970	A-4B	03/603		USA training
142131	11385	A-4B	04/604	142	USA training
144874	12120	A-4B	05/605	142	USA training
144980	12226	A-4B	06/606		USA training
142778	11840	A-4B	'606'		Old RSAF Museum, Changi. Scrapped by 2003
145013	12259	A-4B	07/607	142	USA training. Singapore AF Museum, Paya Lebar.
142101	11355	A-4B	616	142	
142119	11373	A-4B	617	142	
			618		
142125	11379	A-4B	619	142	
			620	142	To Celtrad Metal Industries
142711	11773	A-4B	621	143	To Celtrad Metal Industries
			622		Preserved SAFTECH
			623		
			629	143	
142774	11836	A-4B	630		
142746	11808	A-4B	631	142	To Celtrad Metal Industries
142751	11813	A-4B	632	142	To Celtrad Metal Industries
142770	11832	A-4B	633	142	
142800	11862	A-4B	634	143	
			635	142	
142819	11881	A-4B	636	142	W/o in collision with Mirage IIIO A3-69 30 Mar 83
1m S					Tengah. Pilot ejected
142840	11902	A-4B	643		
142865	11927	A-4B	644	142	
142870	11932	A-4B	645	142	To Celtrad Metal Industries
142876	11938	A-4B	646	143	
142882	11944	A-4B	647	143	
142900	11962	A-4B	648	142, 143	
			649		
142942	12004	A-4B	650	142	
145043	12289	A-4B	653		Prototype for A-4SU.
144926	12172	A-4B	656	143	
144956	12202	A-4B	657	143	Preserved Tengah HQ as '28'
			658		

formation in 1984 of a third Skyhawk unit, No 145 'Hornet' Squadron, also based at Tengah. Purchase of a further sixteen A-4Bs in 1983 resulted in the creation of eight TA4S-1s. Apart from being based on the A-4C airframe, the S-1s differed in retaining 20-mm cannon rather than the 30-mm guns of the A-4S.

Equipped with Sidewinder missiles, the Skyhawks supplemented the RSAF's Northrop F-5Es in the air defence role as well as having a significant ground attack

BuNo	c/n	Was	RSAF	Units	Fate/notes
144971	12217	A-4B	659	143	To Celtrad Metal Industries
144974	12220	A-4B	660	143	
			661		
			672		Damaged Darwin 1984
145030	12276	A-4B	679	142, 143	To Celtrad Metal Industries
145038	12284	A-4B	680		
145046	12292	A-4B	681	143	To Celtrad Metal Industries
145056	12302	A-4B	682	143	To Celtrad Metal Industries
145059	12305	A-4B	683		Aeronautical Engineering Training Institute (AETI), Paya Lebar Air Base
			684		Noted Paya Lebar Feb 04

These aircraft are not known to have been delivered to Singapore but have been noted at Celtrad Metal Industries yard in Jurong:
A-4B 144960, A-4Cs 147792, 148598, 149544
A-4B 142860 dismantled at ST Aerospace, Seletar

capability. Frequent deployments were made to Malaysia, Indonesia and Australia for training and exercises. On 19 December 1979, a flight of RSAF Skyhawks, possibly comprising three A-4Ss and a TA-4S, flew into a mountain in the Philippines during an exercise to train pilots to fly in mountainous regions in cloud. Four pilots were killed, but one additional Skyhawk, flown by Tsu Way Ming, had returned to base with mechanical problems.

One unidentified TA-4S was lost on 2 February 1978 and another in a 1981 take-off crash that resulted in the death of the student. The pilot in the latter accident was Tsu Way Ming. After leaving the RSAF his pilot was to be the captain of the Silkair Airbus that crashed in mysterious circumstances in December 1987, eighteen years to the day after the Philippines tragedy.

By 1985, the age of the A-4S airframes and in particular the J65 engine, some of which had probably originated with 1950s-era F-84 Thunderstreaks, was causing increasing concern among the RSAF staff. In a period of a few months four Skyhawks

A-4S 636, seen here in 142 Squadron colours collided with a RAAF Mirage near Tengah in March 1983. The two pilots ejected but falling debris killed one person. TRH Pictures

Republic of Singapore Air Force TA-4S

BuNo	c/n	Was	RSAF	Units	Fate/notes
145047	12293	A-4B	651	142	USA training. Nose preserved, Paya Lebar
144937	12183	A-4B	652	142	
145043	12289	A-4B	653	143	
144894	12140	A-4B	687	141	Possibly crashed 11/79 Philippines
		A-4B	688		
		A-4B	689		
144979	12225	A-4B	690	141	Preserved Singapore Armed Forces Training Institute*

Three TA-4Ss are believed to have been written off in accidents. The nose at Paya Lebar may be from one of them.

Photographed with a range of weapons including dumb bombs, cluster bombs, Maverics and Sidewinders, this A-4SU was in service at Tengah in 2004.
Alan Warnes, 'Air Forces Monthly'

The RSAF A-4s have participated in many regional exercises. These aircraft were seen at Cope Tiger 2002 at Korat, Thailand. Note the degree of bulging on the rear canopy of the TA-4SU in the foreground.
USAF

were lost in accidents, mainly because of engine failures. The serviceability of the rest of the fleet was also low. This so-called 'Skyhawk crisis' was a major factor in the RSAF's decision to instigate a programme to re-engine and upgrade the surviving aircraft. Technical details of the A-4SU Super Skyhawk rework programme can be found in chapter two, but to date fifty-six single-seat A-4SU and twenty-two TA-4SU trainers have been noted, all fitted with the F404-GE-100 turbofan and modernized avionics systems. The RSAF's own website gives a total of sixty-four A-4SU and sixteen TA-4SUs. The new versions entered service in 1988, initially with No. 145 Squadron, and all the A-4S/TA-4S models were retired by 1993.

Black Knights

The RSAF's 'Black Knights' are the only aerobatic team currently flying the A-4, and one of only two teams to have worn a special colour scheme, the other being the USN 'Blue Angels'. Formed in 1974 with Hawker Hunters, and later equipped briefly with Northrop F-5Es, the 'Black Knights' made their debut at the 1990 Asian Aerospace show in Singapore with a team of six A-4SUs, all painted in a scheme of overall white with large areas of red trim. The team reappeared at the 1994 show, but only solo A-4s flew in 1996 and 1998. The team reappeared in 2000, this time as a four-ship of Skyhawks joined by a pair of F-16A Fighting Falcons. The team's aircraft and pilots are drawn from 143 Squadron at Tengah.

The team's show consists of a dozen formation manoeuvres, including such local specialities as the 'Bonsai' and the 'Way of the Dragon'. The 'Black Knights' aircraft wear their special scheme when carrying out their regular squadron duties, but have performed very infrequently over the years, mainly at Asian Aerospace.

For a number of years the RSAF has conducted much of its training in other countries

A 142 Squadron A-4S is seen perhaps twenty years before the picture shown opposite top. Note the reliance on unguided rockets of various types.

TRH Pictures

Known Republic of Singapore Air Force A4S-1/A-4SUs

BuNo	c/n	Was	RSAF	Units	Fate/notes
			914	145	
149587	12912	A-4C	915	142, 145	
148605	12798	A-4C	917	145	
148304	12614	A-4C	918	142, 145	In service 2003
147835	12519	A-4C	919	142, 145	F404 engine prototype
			923		
148528	12721	A-4C	924		
			925		
148458	12651	A-4C	926	142,145 BK	In service 2002. 'Black Knights 2'
147779	12543	A-4C	927	145, 150	AJT Detachment, Cazaux 2004
147797	12561	A-4C	928	145, 150	AJT Detachment, Cazaux 2004
145073	12319		929	142, 145	In service 2004
149522	12847	A-4C	936	143, 142, 145	In service 2003
			937		
147823	12587	A-4C	938	150	AJT Detachment, Cazaux 2004
145063	12309	A-4B	939	150	AJT Detachment, Cazaux 2004
			940	150	
145071	12317	A-4B	941	145	
148462	12655	A-4C	942	150	AJT Detachment, Cazaux 2004
			943	142, 145	In service 2002
145106	12352	A-4C	944		In service 2003
145110	12356	A-4C	945	142	
			946		In service 2003
			947		
			948		
148591	12784	A-4C	955		In service 2003
			956		
147809	12573	A-4C	957	150	AJT Detachment, Cazaux 2004
149588	12913	A-4C	958		In service 2002
			959		In service 2002
147785	12549	A-4C	960		In service 2003
			961		
148482	12675	A-4C	967	142	In service 2003
149628	12953	A-4C	969		In service 2002
149537	12862	A-4C	970		In service 2002
147743	12507	A-4C	971	145	In service 2003
148464	12657	A-4C	972	145	In service 2002
			973	143	In service 2002. Noted with LST nose
			974		In service 2002
149493	12818	A-4C	975		In service 2001
			976		In service 2001
147752	12516	A-4C	977	142, 145	In service 2003
			978		
			979		
147731	12495	A-4C	980	BK	Black Knights No. 2
			981		In service 2001

BuNo	c/n	Was	RSAF	Units	Fate/notes
			982		
145108	12354	A-4C	983		In service 2001
147841	12605	A-4C	984		In service 2003
			985		In service 2001
147821	12585	A-4C	986		In service 2002
149498	12823	A-4C	991	142	
148521	12714	A-4C	992	142	In service 2002
148526	12719	A-4C	993	150	
148603	12796	A-4C	994		
			999		
149617	12942	A-4C	?	BK	Black Knights No.4

BK=Black Knights demonstration team

because of the limited airspace around Singapore. Detachments were established in Australia and the USA to provide the majority of training for helicopter and F-16 pilots. In October1998, after considering several options in Australia, the Singapore government signed an agreement with France to set up an Advanced Jet Training (AJT) detachment at Cazaux, near Bordeaux in south-west France. No. 143 Squadron disbanded in 1997 and a new unit, No. 150 'Hornet' Squadron was established. In March

Known Republic of Singapore Air Force TA4S-1/TA-4SU

BuNo	c/n	Was	RSAF	units	Fate
147742	12506	A-4C	900	142	In service 2003
148311	12621	A-4C	901	142	
148483	12676	A-4C	902	150	AJT Detachment, Cazaux 04
148493	12686	A-4C	903	142	In service 2003
148525	12718	A-4C	904	141, 150	AJT Detachment, Cazaux 04
148529	12722	A-4C	905	142, 150	AJT Detachment, Cazaux 04
144916	12162	A-4B	906	142, 150	AJT Detachment, Cazaux 04
145041	12267	A-4B	907	141, 150	AJT Detachment, Cazaux 04
142881	11943	A-4B	908	150	AJT Detachment, Cazaux 04
145021	12267	A-4B	909	150	AJT Detachment, Cazaux 04
			910	142, 145	
142814	11876	A-4B	911	145	In service 2001
144966	12211	A-4B	912	143, 145	In service 2002
			913		
			930		In service 2002
			931		In service 2002
142936	11998	A-4B	932		AJT Detachment, Cazaux 04
144977	12223	A-4B	933		AJT Detachment, Cazaux 04
145033	12279	A-4B	950		AJT Detachment, Cazaux 04
142839	11909	A-4B	951		In service 2004
			952		In service 2001
			953		In service 2002

The A-4PTMs were modified from A-4Cs and Ls with modernized avionics and provision for precision weapons such as the AGM-65 Maverick missile.

1999, the first ten of eighteen Super Skyhawks were despatched by sea to France and joined 200 personnel and 140 family members. The second batch (all A-4SUs) followed later, The much less restricted airspace and extensive weapons ranges near Cazaux allow conversion training to be completed much faster than it could be in Singapore. Budgets for the AJT are limited, and the A-4s usually do not roam far from Cazaux to visit other airfields, but the RSAF has sent groups of six aircraft to participate in the French-led exercises ODAX and Opera. The RSAF's agreement with France covers a period of twenty years and it is likely that whatever type succeeds the A-4 will appear at Cazaux in the future. The A-4s will not be returned to Singapore but will either be scrapped or offered to museums.

Weapons employed by the Super Skyhawks include Mk 80 series unguided bombs, AGM-65 Maverick ASMs, Matra 68-mm unguided rockets and the GBU-12 Paveway smart bomb. In 1999 the use of the GEC-Marconi ATLANTIC (Airborne Targeting Low-Altitude Navigation Thermal Imaging and Cueing) FLIR pod was noted on 142 Squadron TA-4SUs used in exercise Pitch Black in Australia. This slim pod repackages the FLIR as used on AV-8B and GR.7 Harriers to allow night and bad weather navigation and targeting. One of the roles of the A-4SU is maritime attack, using the Maverick as the main anti-shipping weapon. A single photograph was published in the RSAF's 35th anniversary publication in 2003 showing A-4SU 973 fitted with a laser spot tracker unit in the extreme nose. Nothing further is known about this installation, although the picture appears to be fairly recent.

Each RSAF fighter squadron whether it flies F-16s, F-5s or A-4s takes over the air defence alert role on a rotating weekly basis. In August 2003, a wayward American civilian pilot on a round-the-world flight found himself escorted into Singapore by a pair of Super Skyhawks.

At time of writing, Singapore was expected to choose a new aircraft to replace the A-4 during 2005. Although the RSAF is coy about whether the new aircraft will be optimized for air defence or the long range strike mission, the Boeing F-15T Eagle,

Dassault Rafale and Eurofighter Typhoon were shortlisted in October 2003. For the time being the RSAF is operating about thirty aircraft in Singapore itself, probably pooled between between Nos. 142 and 145 Squadrons. Attempts are being made to husband the airframe hours of the A-4s to keep them even across the fleet until retirement.

Malaysia (Tentara Udara Diraja Malaysia)

In 1979 the Malaysian government obtained twenty-five A-4Cs and sixty-three A-4Ls from storage at Davis-Monthan AFB, Arizona with the intent of upgrading the majority for service with the Tentara Udara Diraja Malaysia (TUDM) or Royal Malaysian Air Force. This was part of the 'Perista' development programme, intended to provide the TUDM with strength in numbers against potential aggressors. Although the original plan called for fifty-four to be rebuilt as single-seaters and fourteen as two-seaters, Budgetary problems because of inflation scaled the programme back to where only forty aircraft were upgraded by Grumman at St. Augustine, Florida, emerging as thirty-four A-4PTM single-seaters and six TA-4PTM two-seaters. PTM is usually said to stand for 'Peculiar To Malaysia' but more correctly stands for Persekutan Tanah Melayu, or Federation of Malay States.

The US$120 million contract to upgrade the elderly A-4C and L airframes for Malaysian service was awarded in December 1982 to Grumman Aerospace and undertaken at their facility at St. Augustine, Florida. The package included modification and refurbishment of fifty-two additional J65 engines by Singapore Aerospace Maintenance Co (SAMCO).

Avionics were updated as outlined in chapter two. General remedial work included replacement of the wiring harness, corrosion repair, and overhaul of the hydraulic, pneumatic and environmental control systems and rebuild of the landing gear. The aircraft were by then around twenty years old and had seen hard service with the USN and/or USMC, including Vietnam combat in many cases, before further use with the Reserve squadrons.

The PTMs were given the provision to carry AGM-65A Mavericks and AIM-9J Sidewinders on all pylons, which were increased to five, each rated at 1,000lb (454kg) carrying capacity.

The first A-4PTM flew on 12 April 1984, and the first TA-4PTM on 28 August.

A fairly rare in-service picture of A-4PTMs of No.6 Squadron RMAF. During their fairly brief career they were repainted in this dark camouflage scheme. TRH Pictures

TUDM A-4PTM/TA-4PTM Skyhawks

BuNo	c/n	Was	Converted	TUDM	Units	Fate
149630	12700	A-4L	TA-4PTM	M32-01	6	Stored Kuantan
150593	13004	A-4L	TA-4PTM	M32-02	6	Stored Kuantan
145065	12311	A-4L	TA-4PTM	M32-03	6	W/o 1992 Wreck Kuantan
149626	12951	A-4L	TA-4PTM	M32-04	6	Stored Kuantan
147802	12566	A-4L	TA-4PTM	M32-05	6	Crashed Pohang State 1992, crew OK**
145103	12349	A-4L	TA-4PTM	M32-06	6	Technical College, Alor Setar
149594	12919	A-4L	A-4PTM	M32-07	6	Stored Kuantan
145101	12347	A-4L	A-4PTM	M32-08	6	Stored Kuantan
148479	12672	A-4L	A-4PTM	M32-09	9	Stored Kuantan
149531	12856	A-4L	A-4PTM	M32-10		
148306	12616	A-4L	A-4PTM	M32-11	6	Stored Kuantan
148588	12781	A-4L	A-4PTM	M32-12		
149506	12831	A-4L	A-4PTM	M32-13	6	Stored Kuantan
145141	12387	A-4L	A-4PTM	M32-14	6	Stored Kuantan
149551	12876	A-4L	A-4PTM	M32-15	6	Stored Kuantan
149633	12958	A-4L	A-4PTM	M32-16		
149518	12843	A-4L	A-4PTM	M32-17	9	
149607	12932	A-4L	A-4PTM	M32-18	6	Stored Kuantan
148611	12804	A-4L	A-4PTM	M32-19		
145092	12338	A-4L	A-4PTM	M32-20		
147798	12562	A-4L	A-4PTM	M32-21	9	Stored Kuantan
147780	12544	A-4C	A-4PTM	M32-22	6, 9	Stored Kuantan
148555	12748	A-4C	A-4PTM	M32-23		Stored Kuantan
148436	12629	A-4C	A-4PTM	M32-24	6	
145119	12365	A-4L	A-4PTM	M32-25		
149536	12861	A-4L	A-4PTM	M32-26		
145121	12367	A-4L	A-4PTM	M32-27		Stored Kuantan
147706	12470	A-4L	A-4PTM	M32-28		Stored Kuantan
147827	12591	A-4L	A-4PTM	M32-29	6, 9	
149573	12898	A-4L	A-4PTM	M32-30		Pres. TUDM museum
145078	12324	A-4L	A-4PTM	M32-31		Stored Kuantan
147796	12560	A-4L	A-4PTM	M32-32		
147736	12500	A-4L	A-4PTM	M32-33		Stored Kuantan
149497	12822	A-4L	A-4PTM	M32-34	9	Stored Kuantan
149583	12908	A-4L	A-4PTM	M32-35	9	Stored Kuantan
145114	12360	A-4L	A-4PTM	M32-36	6	Stored Kuantan
147782	12546	A-4L	A-4PTM	M32-37		
147703	12467	A-4L	A-4PTM	M32-38		Stored Kuantan
147807	12571	A-4L	A-4PTM	M32-39		
149608	12933	A-4L	A-4PTM	M32-40	6	Stored Kuantan

** Assumption made about identity of loss as other 1992 TA-4 loss is noted extant as a 'wreck' and this one was probably totally destroyed.

One unknown A-4PTM wreck stored at TUDM Museum.

One unknown A-4PTM is preserved inside the gate at Kuantan.

Pres=preserved

A-4s stored for Malaysia but not delivered

The remaining forty-eight A-4s purchased by Malaysia remained in the Arizona desert. Surprisingly, thirty-four of them were registered in November 1997 to Aviation Technologies Ltd of Sparks, Nevada. The aircraft remain stored at Dross Metal Industries' (DMI) yard on the edge of Davis Monthan AFB, and for what purpose they have been registered is unknown. In early 2004 they were all re-registered to new owners in four states.

BuNo	Reg.	BuNo	Reg.	BuNo.	Reg.
145064*	N128AT	147836	N154AT	149540*	N220AT
145076	N129AT	148307	N156AT	149550*	N224AT
145128*	N132AT	148316	N157AT	149555	N225AT
147669	N135AT	148500*	N159AT	149575	N226AT
147671	N142AT	148502*	N203AT	149581	N227AT
147690	N143AT	148509*	N204AT	149591	N228AT
147696*	N144AT	148573*	N205AT	149595	N229AT
147754	N145AT	148581*	N207AT	149620	N233AT
147761	N146AT	148597*	N214AT	149636	N230AT
147768	N147AT	148602	N215AT	150581	N235AT
147793	N148AT	149500	N218AT		
147815	N153AT	149502	N219AT,		

*A-4C. All others A-4L

Deliveries of the PTMs took place in 1984 and 1985. The delivery route was unusual in that the Skyhawks flew eastbound with stops that included Willow Grove, Pennsylvania, Iceland, various bases in the United Kingdom, and Sigonella, Sicily. One group, which included some of the TA-4s was seen at RAF Alconbury in March 1985, and the last deliveries went through Mildenhall in December that year. No.6 Naga (Dragon) Squadron initiated the Skyhawk into TUDM service in 1985 and No.9 Jebat (Hawk) Squadron formed with Skyhawks in 1986. Both units were based at Kuantan on the east coast of Peninsular Malaysia. No.6 Squadron acted as the operational conversion unit (OCU) and operated all the TA-4PTMs as well as some of the single-seaters.

Malaysian A-4 service was relatively brief, and apart from their high attrition rate,

This is one of the A-4Ls intended for Malaysia but never converted. Seen in faded VC-2 colours at the DMI Aviation yard in October 1994 it was registered N145AT in 1997 and sold to Ace Aerospace in Jacksonville, Florida in early 2004. Graham Robson

little is known about their actual use, although they took part in exercises under the Five-Power Defence Arrangement (FPDA) with Singapore, the UK, Australia and New Zealand. Many of these involved the Integrated Air Defence System (IADS) centred at Butterworth, Malaysia and saw operations with the Skyhawks of Australia, New Zealand and Singapore.

In the late 1980s, Argentina reportedly showed an interest in Malaysia's A-4s as attrition replacements for those lost in the Falklands War. An offer was made to supply some IAI Pampa trainers and armoured vehicles to Malaysia in return for the A-4s but nothing came of this offer.

The Skyhawks proved hard to maintain and suffered from spares shortages in TUDM service. At least nine of the A-4PTMs and two TA-4PTMs are known to have been written off in TUDM service. Identities of the lost aircraft are not known, but the dates for the A-4PTM losses are 23 September 1985, 15 March 1988, 24 June 1988, 8 September 1988 (two, presumably in a collision), 3 October 1988, 29 October 1988, 14 August 1990 and 9 July 1993. This last aircraft crashed shortly after take-off from Kuantan, the pilot ejecting safely. The TA-4s were both lost in 1992, on 30 July and 21 August.

In 1989 it was announced that Malaysia would replace its Skyhawks by1995 with British Aerospace Hawk Mk 208s, and most of the A-4s were withdrawn by 1994. Six A-4PTMs were retained for use as tankers with the D-704 refuelling pod for a few more years, until approximately 1997. As an aside, the Hawk 208 carries less useable load over a shorter distance than the A-4 can and at a slightly lower speed.

After retirement, Malaysia's surviving A-4s were towed to a corner of Kuantan Air

With everything hanging, An AF-1 comes aboard the São Paulo. *The 'hook to ramp' distance as the Skyhawk crosses the stern of the Brazilian carrier is smaller than most US-naval aviators are used to.* Corné Rodenburg

The AF-1 is used in the fighter role with AIM-9L Sidewinders by the Marinha do Brasil's VF-1 'Falcões'.

Base and put into outdoor storage. Only some of the aircraft had covers over their canopies or forward fuselage when photographed in 1999, and the jungle was beginning to reclaim their parking area. Having been exposed to the humid environment it is unlikely that they could be made airworthy again.

Despite having retired its own Skyhawks, Malaysia was said to have been interested in obtaining the RNZAF's T/A-4Ks, which became available in early 2002. Instead, in 2003 they announced an intention to purchase the New Zealand fleet of Aermacchi MB.339CBs for use as trainers.

Força Aeronaval da Marinha do Brasil AF-1 and AF-1A

BuNo	C/n	KAF	Marinha
160180	14558	801	N1001
160181	14559	802	N1002
160183	14551	804	N1003
160186	14554	807	N1004
160188	14556	809	N1005
160189	14557	810	N1006
160190	14558	811	N1007
160192	14560	813	N1008
160193	14561	814	N1009
160195	14563	816	N1010
160196	14564	817	N1011
160197	14565	818	N1012
160198	14566	819	N1013
160199	14567	820	N1014
160201	14569	822	N1015
160202	14570	823	N1016
160203	14571	824	N1017
160204	14572	825	N1018
160205	14573	826	N1019
160206	14574	827	N1020
TA-4KU	**AF-1A**		
160212	14580	883	N1021
160213	14581	884	N1022
160215	14583	886	N1023

Brazil (Marinha do Brasil)

In the late 1990s, Brazil became the newest military operator of the Skyhawk, and to the delight of many took the A-4 back to sea for the first time in a combat role since the retirement of Argentina's carrier a decade earlier.

As a result of inter-service rivalries, the Brazilian Navy or Marinha do Brasil had been forbidden from operating fixed-wing aircraft in 1965. The Navy utilized a variety of helicopters, but the carrier-borne S-2 Tracker ASW aircraft were owned and operated by the Força Aérea Brasilia until they were retired in 1996.

Since 1956 Brazil's only aircraft carrier had been the Navio Aérodromo Ligeiro (NaeL) (light aircraft carrier) *Minas Gerais*, a British-built 'Colossus'-class ship, which was commissioned in 1945 as HMS *Vengeance* (R71) and sold to Brazil in 1956. *Minas Gerais* (A11) was 702ft 5in (214.1m) long with a maximum width of 119ft 6in (36.5m),

Like all earlier carrier-based Skyhawks, the AF-1 uses a bridle system for launch. A holdback cable takes the strain of full engine power until the catapult fires. Corné Rodenburg

and a crew of 1,000 plus 300 air wing personnel.

In the 1990s, the Marinha do Brasil convinced the government of its requirement for a naval air defence and ground attack capability to support Navy and Marine actions and protect Brazil's long coastline and assets such as oil rigs. Consideration was given to obtaining a surplus 'Forrestal'-class carrier from the US, but this was rejected for several reasons. For one thing, such a large ship would be too large for Brazil's needs, and too expensive to operate, requiring a much larger crew.

Acquisition of former US Navy single-seat Skyhawks was considered, but inspection of aircraft at AMARC in 1997 showed that they all had very high flight hours and would have needed extensive reworking for carrier operations. Instead Brazil was able to purchase twenty-three A-4KUs and TA-4KUs from Kuwait for about US$79 million. The aircraft had an average of 1,700 flight hours at the conclusion of their Kuwaiti service and were generally in very good condition.

Brazil's constitution needed to be amended to allow the operation of fixed-wing aircraft by the Navy and this was done in presidential decree on 8 April 1998. On 30 April a purchase agreement was signed with Kuwait for the purchase of twenty A-4KU and three TA-4KU Skyhawks as well as nineteen spare J52-P408 engines and many other spare parts and weapons, including 217 AIM-9H Sidewinders.

The aircraft were prepared for shipping by Boeing and arrived at Rio de Janeiro on 7 September 1998 before being delivered by road the final 100 miles (160km) to the airbase at São Pedro da Aldeia, south of the city. Boeing supervised an overhaul of the Skyhawks, although they were not significantly modified from their original configuration. The A-4KUs were redesignated AF-1 and the TA-4KUs became AF-1As under the Brazilian system.

The Skyhawks were issued to Primeiro Esquadrão de Aviões de Interceptãçao e

Ataque, or the First Interception and Attack Squadron, known by its US-style designation VF-1 and the name 'Falcões' (Falcons). This unit was established on 2 October 1998 at a ceremony at São Pedro although at that time had no airworthy aircraft.

The first AF-1 to be flown by a Brazilian pilot took to the air on 26 May 2000. The pilot was Lieutenant Jose Vicente de Alvarenga, who had been the last Naval Aviator to be awarded his wings after training with VT-7 in 1999.

In September 2000 the first touch-and-go landings were made on *Minas Gerais*, and on 18 January 2001, four of the Brazilian Skyhawks conducted the Marinha's first fixed-wing flight operations of the modern era, when they went aboard in the South Atlantic. Carrier qualifications were assisted by a US Naval Reserve flight instructor and a retired USN landing signal officer (LSO) employed by private firm Kay & Associates of Illinois to help the Brazilians create a carrier-based air combat capability almost from scratch.

In mid-2001, Brazil announced purchase of the French Navy's carrier FNS *Foch* (R99) which was commissioned in 1963. The price for the ship, which was stripped of its defensive armament was a very low US$12.5 million, although a figure of $50 million had previously been asked for by the French defence department.

The *Foch* sailed from Brest to Rio in February 2001 and was refitted for Brazilian service as the NAE *São Paulo* (A12). It was officially decommissioned from the French Navy and accepted by Brazil on 15 November 2001. The *São Paulo* is longer and wider than its predecessor, with a total length of 869ft 5in (265m) and beam of 150ft (45.72m). The crew is approximately 1,200 plus air wing personnel. The *Minas Gerais* was retired in October 2001. In late 2003 it was offered on the auction website eBay with a starting bid of US$6.5 million.

The Brazilian Skyhawks are perhaps the only aircraft with braking parachutes to regularly operate from carriers (excluding occasional USMC A-4M deployments), although this is not used for shipboard operations. In June 2004 several AF-1s visited the USS *Ronald Reagan*, which was sailing around South America on route to its new home port of San Diego. The Skyhawks could only make approaches and wave-offs as the *Reagan* lacks the bridles needed to launch them. The AF-1A two-seaters are not used for shipboard training as their heavier weight and lower fuel capacity limits the number of practice landings possible in one session. It is possible that TA-4Js will be acquired from the US for this mission.

To date the *São Paulo* has conducted operations only in Brazilian waters. VF-1 currently only has about eight carrier qualified pilots, and no more than six Skyhawks have been embarked at one time. The Sidewinders and cannon are the only armaments employed by Brazil's Skyhawks.

Proposals for improving the Brazilian A-4's capabilities include a new Head Up Display, new navigation and weapons delivery system, a RWR and a multi-mode radar. A forward-looking infrared (FLIR) system is one The outdated AIM-9H missiles will need replacement, perhaps by the locally-designed MAA-1 Piranha, and air-to-ground weapons integrated with the AF-1.

Once operated by the US Navy's VA-93 Det Q, A-4P C-226 is seen on its last mission, against the British landings at Fitzroy on 8 June 1982, piloted by Teniente J. J. Arraras. It was shot down over Falkland Sound by an AIM-9L fired by Flight Lieutenant Dave Morgan in Sea Harrier ZA177 and Arraras was killed. Three of the four pilots of 'Mazo' flight fell to the Sea Harriers that afternoon.

TRH Pictures

CHAPTER FIVE

Export Skyhawks at War

As well as the United States' extensive use of A-4s in combat in Vietnam, the Skyhawk saw action with Israel, Argentina, Kuwait and Indonesia. Israel was the biggest export user, taking about as many A-4s as all other foreign operators combined. They also lost more aircraft in combat than most nations purchased. Argentina's Skyhawks saw an intense period of combat over a few weeks in the autumn of 1982, and Kuwait's fought during the invasion of their country in 1990 and its liberation in 1991. Indonesia used their A-4Es periodically against separatist rebels throughout the 1980s and 1990s.

Argentine A-4s in combat

Argentina was the first export customer for the Skyhawk. Between 1966 and 1970, the Fuerza Aérea Argentina took delivery of fifty refurbished A-4Bs and A-4Cs from the USA. Argentina's naval air arm, Comando de la Aviación Naval Argentina (CANA) acquired sixteen A-4Qs for use from the aircraft-carrier ARA *25 de Mayo* (ex-HMS *Venerable*). When not embarked, they were based at Naval Air Base (BAN) Comandante Espora, Bahía Blanca.

South American politics being what they are, the first action seen by Argentine Skyhawks was not made against an external aggressor. In December 1975 Navy Skyhawks of 3 Escuadrilla de Caza y Ataque (3a Esc) made one strike against rebels in Buenos Aries during an internal revolt within the Air Force. During a 1978 dispute with neighbouring Chile over the Beagle Channel at the southern tip of South America, CANA's A-4Qs flew CAP sorties from *25 de Mayo*, which sailed to the region as part of Operation Tronador. Although combat was not joined, there were several interceptions of Chilean Navy aircraft and a Skyhawk was nearly cleared to shoot down a Chilean CASA C.212 Aviocar.

The FAA's Skyhawks were operated by Grupo 5 de Caza at BAM (air base) Villa Reynolds and Grupo 4 at BAM El Plumerillo. These aircraft were designated A-4P by the US government and the manufacturer, but were usually known as A-4Bs in Argentine service. In 1976 twenty-five more A-4s, this time C models, were imported for the FAA. Like the B/Ps these had been reworked and updated with many A-4F features.

In the late 1970s, both services were desperate to acquire more Skyhawks and other modern weapons, but a US arms embargo against the ruling Argentine military junta prevented this. By March 1982, when Argentina launched an invasion of the British territory of the Falkland Islands (known to them as las Islas Malvinas) approximately thirty-six A-4s remained in FAA service, and ten more could be made ready for action by CANA. The latter, embarked on *25 de Mayo*, supported the initial amphibious landings near Port Stanley, and one was operated from the airfield there to test its suitability for A-4s. Fortunately for the British, the airfield was not regarded as safe for operations with a combat load, and for the rest of the war the Skyhawks were operating at maximum range from shore bases on the mainland, a distance of at least 380 nautical miles (705km).

In mid-April, the CANA A-4s were readied for attacks on the British fleet then arriving in Falklands waters, but the loss of the cruiser *Belgrano* to the British submarine HMS *Conqueror* forced *25 de Mayo* back to port to avoid a similar fate. From then on, the A-4Qs operated from Rio Grande. Although the A-4Qs were Sidewinder capable, they operated with bombs only during the war.

The first full engagement between the FAA Skyhawks and the British task force on 12 May saw HMS *Glasgow* badly damaged and four A-4s shot down by SAMs and AAA. After this, air force operations fell into a pattern of high-level transit with a refuelling from a KC-130 tanker and a low-level attack run with 500lb Mk 82 'Snake eye', 750lb M-117 or 1,000lb British-made bombs. The A-4Cs had been modified to mount five weapons pylons so could carry two additional Mk 82s in addition to up to three on the centreline. Israeli-made Shafrir I AAMs had been seen on A-4Cs in 1978, but were probably only fitted for publicity purposes during the tensions with Chile, and were not properly integrated with the Skyhawks until after the Falklands War.

Incorrect fusing and the ultra-low-level height from which they were dropped prevented many Argentine bombs from exploding. This was fortunate for the British, as four more ships would have probably been lost had all bombs detonated on impact. Other 'duds' fell close to British command posts on land. The bravery of the Argentine A-4 pilots cannot be questioned – the majority of their aircraft did not have a remotely modern navigation system, none had radar, radar warning, ECM or guided weapons of

The FAA deployed most of its Skyhawks to San Julian and Rio Gallegos in the far south of Argentina in April 1982. Facilities at the civilian airport at San Julian were very austere and communications particularly poor. These were improved by the end of the month before conflict was joined with the British task force.

TRH Pictures

The KC-130 was vital in allowing the A-4s to reach targets in the Falklands with a useable warload.
TRH Pictures

any kind, and they had just enough fuel for a single pass on the target, which was defended by guns, ship- and ground-launched SAMs and Sea Harriers with all-aspect AAMs. Against the Sea Harrier, the A-4s were effectively defenceless, with no missiles of their own and only an unreliable cannon. Accordingly they suffered eight losses to 'La Meurta Negra' (The Black Death).

The battles of 21 May

One of the heaviest days of air combat was 21 May 1982, the day the British task force began its landings at San Carlos Water in Falkland Sound. Following reconnaissance sorties and some attacks by aircraft from Port Stanley, and by FAA IAI Daggers from the mainland, FAA and CANA Skyhawks were launched against the landings.

First to arrive over the Falklands were two flights of three A-4Bs of Grupo 5, each armed with a single British-made 1,000lb (454kg) bomb. Coming across the 'Leander'-class frigate HMS *Argonaut* (F56), which was sailing unescorted, they struck it with two bombs at 1230 hours. Neither bomb exploded, but the ship was badly damaged by explosions of its own Seacat missiles and was out of action for five days.

A second flight of Grupo 5 A-4Bs was already refuelling from a KC-130 as the first mission returned. One of the four Skyhawks was unable to take on fuel and dropped out, followed by another for technical reasons. A third bombed an abandoned Argentine freighter by mistake, leaving Capitán Carballo to attack the Type 21 frigate HMS *Ardent* (F174) alone. Carballo's bomb was a near miss and he escaped the scene, but his attack attracted the attention of a combat air patrol of two Sea Harriers, flown by Lieutenant Commanders Mike Blissett and Neil Thomas of No. 800 Squadron from HMS *Hermes* (R12).

Thomas recalled: 'We were at about 1,000 feet halfway down Falkland Sound, and [the Type 22 frigate HMS] *Brilliant* vectored us off West Falkland after a contact they'd got.' This was Carballo's Skyhawk, making good its escape. 'We headed off at a fair old rate of knots, and were approaching Chartres [Settlement] when we picked up four A-4s coming over the ridge'.

A-4C C-207 was based at San Julian during the Falklands conflict. It was credited with the destruction of HMS Coventry. *The other silhouette represents an attack on HMS* Brilliant. *Built in 1958 and retired in 1999, this veteran A-4C is preserved at Argentina's National Aeronautical Museum.*
TRH Picture

This was a Grupo 4 attack, intended to be co-ordinated with one by Grupo 5, but which had the misfortune to arrive just as the defences were at their most alert. The tracks of the attacking and defending aircraft crossed at right angles, and as the Sea Harriers broke to starboard to get behind them the A-4s also broke into a hard 180-degree turn to starboard.

'As soon as they saw us the A-4s turned tail, jettisoned their bombs and headed off to the south'. Thomas and Blissett pulled harder into their turn, wheeling at full throttle through a 270-degree turn which placed them directly in the Skyhawks' six o'clock position.

'They must have lost a lot of speed, because we ended up about a mile and a half astern. Mike was nearer than myself, and fired; I couldn't see him until then. He got the man on the left, and having picked Mike up reasonably well to my left, about 40 degrees off, I got a very good growl from the target, so I just shot the missile and it went straight to it. The other two A-4s broke to starboard, with Mike close astern of them. I got a growl from my second Sidewinder but couldn't fire, because I didn't know where Mike was. So we missed the other two'. In fact, Mike Blissett damaged one of the other A-4s with cannon fire, although it returned safely to base. The two Skyhawks came down within a hundred metres of each other. Both pilots, Teniente (Lieutenant) Nestor Lopez and Primer Teniente (1st Lieutenant) Daniel Manzotti being killed.

Although a morning mission by CANA A-4s had been ordered to turn back, in the afternoon the same six A-4Qs were launched with different pilots in two divisions; the first led by Capitán de Corbeta (Lieutenant Commander) Alberto Philippi, and the second by Teniente de Navio (Lieutenant) Benito Rotolo. Each aircraft was armed with four 500lb snakeye bombs and 200 rounds of cannon ammunition and carried two 300-gallon tanks. Forty-two minutes after take-off from Rio Grande, Philippi's division descended to 100ft and then to 50ft as it crossed Falkland Sound, having failed to find its briefed target, a British frigate acting as a radar picket. Rotolo's three Skyhawks were about twenty minutes behind the first flight.

Since the earlier FAA A-4 attack, *Ardent* had been damaged by two bombs from a Grupo 6 Dagger and was making its way to the safety of a group of British ships when Philippi's A-4s approached in battle formation at 450kts (833km/h). Adjusting his flight path to make a diagonal attack, Philippi fired his cannon, which promptly jammed, and dropped his bombs at the preset 250-millisecond interval as the ship launched two Corvus chaff/flare rockets. Electronic countermeasures had no effect on the A-4s or their 'dumb' weapons, and several of the retarded bombs hit *Ardent* in the stern, as did those of his wingman, Teniente de Navio José Arca.

Arca describes his attack and the aftermath: 'When I started the bomb run against the frigate as the No. 2, I had only seven or ten seconds of separation between myself and the aircraft of Capitán Philippi when I needed nineteen seconds to avoid the bomb explosions. I could not adopt the correct position because when we started the bomb run a curtain of fire formed between the ship and us. The ricochets and the explosions were too close to our aircraft. I remember that I saw a missile launch from the ship and I broke

The Argentine Navy's small fleet of Skyhawks saw intense combat from land bases during the war. A-4Q 3-A-314 was shot down by the cannon fire in the encounter described here, Gustavo Márquez being killed. Another aircraft is preserved at Batán in these markings as a memorial.

TRH Pictures

The Type 21 frigate HMS Ardent *was attacked by FAA Skyhawks and Daggers and CANA Skyhawks on 21 May 1982. Hit by several bombs, it was abandoned and sank the next day, but this success cost Argentina five A-4s, all brought down by Sea Harriers.*

TRH Pictures

right to avoid it and then I returned to course. Because of the small separation between the planes our manoeuvres to line up for bomb launch were almost simultaneous and I saw the launch of the four bombs of Capt. Philippi and the bomb tails open. At this moment I hoped that he missed the target so as not to give me problems with the explosions, but the fourth bomb made a direct hit on the stern. The explosion was immense and I had no choice but to pass through the fireball at the same time that I said to the leader "one on the stern" and dropped my bombs. After that I heard [No. 3 Teniente de Fragata (Sub-Lieutenant) Marcello] Márquez saying 'another on the stern'. After we left the target parallel to the shore I identified my leader at 1000 metres to the left and Márquez at 1000 or 1500 metres to the right. No more than fifteen seconds after that Márquez said "here come the Sea Harriers" and at that moment I saw a Sea Harrier firing a Sidewinder that after a short flight went up the exhaust nozzle of Philippi's plane. I looked to the right and didn't see Márquez but a Sea Harrier instead and almost at the same time I received the first 30mm shell hits on the right wing. Flying at only three metres altitude I almost hit the water and I tried to control the airplane and go for the one that attacked me to break his aim, but I received more hits on the left wing. I prepared to eject because the hydraulic system was totally destroyed and I had lost the electrical system and oxygen. At 480 knots I turned to manual control (although the NATOPS manual said that the top speed for this was 250 knots) and I tried to turn to face one of the Harriers. The combat lasted for about 40 seconds and they left me, maybe because they don't have fuel or ammunition. I headed to Puerto Argentino [Port Stanley] over the coast, trying to avoid Goose Green, at low altitude and 500 knots and watching the fuel quantity indicator, because I now had only 100lbs, which was going very fast because of the holes, six on the left wing and four on the right.

'Close to the runway I tried to put down the landing gear but only the right and the front wheels went down. The indicator said the left one was not secured. I told that to the operations command and he said "the left landing gear is missing, I can see the sky through the holes you have, go and eject over the bay". I had no choice. Climbing to 2500 feet I went to the ejection point. I held my oxygen mask and with the right hand I pulled the ejection handle. After a powerful explosion and having the sensation of tumbling I found myself descending by parachute. The aircraft continued flying in a spiral towards me, like he was trying to hit me, refusing to let me abandon him. He passed close to me and made another circuit before the anti-aircraft artillery, watchful of the danger, shot him down'.

José Arca landed in the water and was rescued by an Argentine Army UH-1 helicopter. His colleagues were not as lucky, Philippi was shot down by a Sidewinder fired by Lieutenant Clive Morrell of No. 800 Squadron, who had inflicted the damage on Arca. Philippi also ejected safely, but spent three days evading capture before reaching an isolated cottage. He was returned to Rio Grande on 30 May. Márquez's A-4 had been hit by cannon fire from the Sea Harrier of Flight Lieutenant John Leeming, an RAF

The Sea Harrier was the nemesis of the Skyhawk in the Falklands War, destroying eight Air Force and Navy A-4s. Although it scored no kills over Skyhawks, FRS.1 XZ455 of No. 800 Squadron shot down two Argentine Daggers with AIM-9Ls in May 1982.

Author's collection

Many of the Argentine A-4Cs adopted these unusual colours before the 1982 conflict. During the war they added yellow tactical markings. Argentina's A-4Bs and Cs had the outer wing pylons as first introduced on the A-4E. TRH Pictures

exchange pilot, and had disintegrated, killing him instantly.

Ardent was attacked by Rotolo's A-4s fifteen minutes after the first CANA attack. No further hits were scored and the three A-4s escaped with minor shrapnel damage. The frigate had suffered mortal damage and had to be abandoned, listing and on fire. She sank the following evening.

In the final accounting, FAA Skyhawks flew 219 combat sorties during the conflict, sinking four Royal Navy warships and damaging many others. Against this must be balanced the loss of nineteen aircraft and seventeen pilots. CANA Skyhawks flew thirty-four sorties. Losses were three A-4s and two pilots, with fatal damage claimed on two warships – results hotly debated between the two services. Whatever the actual balance, the A-4 was the most successful Argentine aircraft in the Falklands/Malvinas conflict.

The war led to a collapse of the military junta in Argentina and an eventual return to democracy, but it was not until 1994 that the USA lifted the arms embargo and agreed to the supply of late-model A-4s to the FAA. The new FAA Skyhawks, designated A-4AR (A-4M) and TA-4AR (OA-4M) achieved initial operating capability (IOC) in mid-2000.

Israel's *Ayits* in action

Israel's first Skyhawk unit, No. 109 'Valley' Squadron, formed at Hatzor in January 1968. The first combat missions came during the following month when they attacked Jordanian artillery and Palestinian bases along the Israel-Jordan border following attacks

The A-4N was developed specifically for Israel using many features of the A-4M plus locally-developed avionics. The prototype first flew in June 1972. About thirty Ns had been delivered by October 1973. No. 140 'Golden Eagle' Squadron, one of whose A-4Ns is seen here at the end of its landing run, was active with A-4s from 1973 to 1986, mainly at Etzion. *IDF/AF*

on Israeli settlements. The proximity of the target to the A-4's base meant that all five pylons could be used for carrying bombs, which at the time were 250lb and 500lb French weapons. Syrian MiGs were encountered during missions against PLO bases near Damascus a year later.

War of Attrition – the Skyhawk ace

In March 1969 Egypt's President Nasser announced a 'War of Attrition' against Israel. This largely involved the shelling of Israeli positions in the Sinai until Israel retaliated with air attacks on Egyptian missile sites in July. A-4s were often in action in this period during fighting around the Suez Canal. In a planned operation on 6 February 1970 the IDF/AF attacked the Egyptian port of Gardaka, and Skyhawks struck a minelayer, which attempted to escape into open waters but was eventually sunk with rockets and bombs by 102 Squadron.

Although there have been no 'ace' Skyhawk pilots in the traditional sense of scoring five aerial victories in the same aircraft type, one Israeli pilot achieved 'acehood' in the Ayit by adding a pair of MiGs to three earlier kills scored in the Mirage III.

Ezra Dotan was one of the most experienced jet pilots in the IDF/AF. An early incident in his career was the ejection from a Mystère IV that went into a spin on a November 1961 training flight. By June 1967, Dotan was a Major and a Mirage IIICJ pilot with No. 117 Squadron at Ramat David. On the 7th of that month he flew a mission to H-3 airfield in western Iraq in search of a downed pilot and his aircraft was hit by an AA-2 'Atoll' AAM fired by a MiG. During the battle, he managed to destroy an Iraqi Hawker Hunter. Nursing his aircraft back to Israeli airspace, he was urged to eject, but reportedly replied 'Babban doesn't go down that easily', and managed to make a fiery landing at an airstrip at Megido.

Earlier in 1967, Dotan had downed two Syrian MiGs with the Mirage, a MiG-17 on 7 April, and a MiG-21 on 5 June. This latter kill was achieved with 30mm cannon after a long chase at low level. On 12 May 1970, Lieutenant Colonel Dotan, now commander of the IDF/AF's No. 109 'Valley' squadron of A-4H Skyhawks set off from Hatzor air base on a search-and-destroy mission against Syrian armour around Mt Hermon on the Lebanese border. He and his wingman were armed with five nineteen-shot pods loaded

A young Israeli airman reloads the 20mm cannon of an A-4H as the end of a ninety-day ceasefire approached during the War of Attrition in November 1970. This is A-4H 796, probably of 102 Squadron. The bombs are of French design.

Author's collection

with 2.75in folding-fin rockets. While circling the area, Dotan's wingman spotted a pair of Syrian MiG-17 'Fresco C's far below and began chase. US restrictions on technology transfer meant that the A-4H had a gunsight suitable only for air-to-ground use and no provision for AAMs, but the two Skyhawk pilots were determined to use the tools at their disposal to destroy the MiGs.

The wingman fired his cannons at one MiG but missed. Dotan closed to 130 metres behind the second MiG and salvoed two rocket pods at it. These fell below the target, so Dotan raised the nose and fired again, hitting the MiG with most of the thirty-eight rockets and blowing it to pieces. Suddenly the two Skyhawk pilots realized that they were in the midst of a formation of MiGs, as cannon fire swept past their cockpits. The MiG behind Dotan overshot and the Israeli pilot lined up on it but found himself menaced by another and dived for safety. Spotting yet another MiG-17 in afterburner far below him, Dotan gave chase, and had to eject his empty rocket pods to reduce drag so that he could pull up before hitting Mount Hermon.

Dotan's A-4H Skyhawk, coded '03' was one of the first four Israeli Skyhawks and the first to actually fly in Israel, on 1 January 1968. More importantly, by May 1970 it was the first and at that time only one to be fitted with 30mm DEFA cannon in place of the original 20mm Colt Mk 12s. Dotan came out of the dive at treetop level and followed the

MiG over the farmland, between the hills and houses. A pair of Mirage IIIs came on the scene, but Dotan told them to 'go find their own MiG'. However, Dotan lost sight of 'his' MiG for a time among the hills. When he acquired the MiG again he was going too fast (570 knots/1,057km/h) to intercept and had to chop the throttle, open the airbrakes and even lower the flaps to stay behind. He later said that if he could have stuck his ears outside the cockpit, he would have. He got so close behind the MiG that he could not lower the nose to bring his guns to bear. The MiG was evading wildly, but the A-4 hung on until the Syrian fighter broke hard and climbed, filling the gunsight. Dotan gave the MiG a long burst of 30mm, which tore through its left wing, which ripped off, sending the 'Fresco' spinning into the ground below, where it exploded. On return to base, Dotan buzzed the tower and then did two victory rolls. He, his wingman and groundcrews celebrated with cake and champagne.

For his combat accomplishments in the A-4 and his leadership of the first Ayit squadron, Ezra Dotan was known as 'Mr Skyhawk' within the IDF/AF. He died in October 1990.

Although the range of weapons supplied by the USA to Israel was initially limited and did not include cluster bombs or napalm, most of the American inventory of conventional weapons was eventually made available to Israel. Weapons used by IDF/AF A-4s included US and French-made bombs, Zuni rockets, AGM-45 Shrike anti-radiation missiles, AGM-62 Walleye II electro-optically guided bombs, GBU-8 HOBO TV-guided bombs Paveway I LGBs. Air-to-air missiles included Rafael Shafrir II and AIM-9D Sidewinders.

1973 – the Yom Kippur War

By 1973, Iraq, Egypt and Jordan were all well equipped with SA-2, SA-3, SA-6 and SA-7 SAMs. The latter two types were new to the region, and the hand-held SA-7 'Grail' caused particular difficulties for Israel. During the Yom Kippur war that broke out in

102 Squadron A-4H 272 was credited with sinking an Egyptian minelayer in the port of Gardaka in February 1970 during the War of Attrition. Seen in 1977, it was later upgraded to A-4N standard. TRH Pictures

The TA-4H and J had a combat role as forward air control platforms, tankers and occasionally as bombers. Significant numbers remain in service. IDF/AF

October, the six Skyhawk squadrons flew more attack sorties than all the other types combined and the SAMs took a heavy toll of A-4s, of which 181 were in Israeli service at that time, constituting forty-three per cent of the IDF's combat aircraft. It has been said that thirty A-4s were lost in a single day during the conflict in frantic ground attack and close support missions to stem the Egyptian and Syrian advances. This worst day was probably 7 October when eight pilots were recorded killed and one missing. In all, over fifty A-4s failed to return to their bases in the Yom Kippur fighting, with many others damaged.

Although the vast majority of losses were caused by SAMs, there were two air-to-air losses acknowledged in 1973, both on 8 October to a MiG-17F, said to be flown by a Syrian pilot named el-Giri. The wreckage of a 109 Squadron A-4E shot down near the Suez Canal on the 7th and photographed by Egyptian troops was said to have been the victim of an EAF MiG-21MF. Following a desperate appeal from Israeli Prime Minister Golda Meir to US President Richard Nixon the US transferred forty-six A-4Es from USN stocks to make good some of the losses. The first of these arrived on 17 October and were able to participate in the main period of fighting, flying eighty-five combat missions. The remainder saw action against Syrian forces on Mt Hermon after the cease-fire with Egypt. The A-4Es needed overhaul before use because of corrosion of landing

This A-4H displays the Chavit tailpipe extension introduced after the Yom Kippur War, and the Skyhawk's characteristic forward-retracting undercarriage. Author's Collection

gear and deterioration of rubber seals caused by their use in a salt-water environment.

To counter radar-guided SAMs, the A-4s' speedbrakes were filled with radar-deceiving 'chaff' (foil strips cut to the wavelength of the radar). Inexperienced pilots had a tendency to open the brakes and release all their chaff at the first warning of a SAM launch. The temporary solution to the IR-guided SA-7 was to equip one A-4 in each flight of four with as many flare pods as possible, which were released over the target area just before the bombers struck. TA-4s flew behind the forward line of Israeli troops with the backseater observing and calling out SAM launches to other aircraft. Later in the war, the A-4s used toss-bombing techniques to lob cluster bombs onto Egyptian AAA positions. Five A-4s were lost on these missions on 17 and 18 October.

The Israelis later modified their A-4s with added ECM, chaff/flare dispensers and extended jet pipes to cool the exhaust flow. This latter modification came about when it was found that the J52-engined 'Sa'ar' (Dassault Super Mystère) was suffering a lower proportion of losses. The engine of the Sa'ar was buried more deeply in the fuselage and the jet pipe extended beyond the tail surfaces. Many A-4s were lost through shrapnel damage to the tail controls, and a tail extension was developed and tested, and approved for production in November 1973.

On 7 October, Israel launched Operation Tagar (Skirmish) a counter-attack against Egypt's air assets, including attacks by A-4s and F-4s on air bases and SAM sites. This was abandoned when it was realized the Egyptians were better prepared than expected with well-defended airbases, dispersal of aircraft and quick repair of damage. More importantly, the greater threat from Syrian forces in the north had been recognized.

A new operation dubbed Dugman (Mannequin) 5 was launched against batteries of Syrian SA-6 missiles. Although full of confidence and expecting the mission to be 'a piece of cake' according to one F-4 Phantom squadron commander, the photographic coverage of the missile sites was out of date and the SAMs were not where they were expected to be. The result was a 'colossal failure'. Seven Israeli jets were shot down, four of them A-4s.

The famous MiG-killing A-4H '03' was lost on 18 October 1973 when it flew into a barrage of 23mm AAA and SA-6 and SA-7 mobile SAMs while pulling out from an attack on fixed SA-2 and SA-3 missile sites at Kantara. Damaged by an explosion, the Skyhawk, flown by 109 Squadron pilot Jacob Kubik, managed to leave the area but was

A No. 116 Squadron A-4N lands at an Israeli airfield. The 'Flying Wing' Squadron was based at Tel Nof and later Nevatim. IDF/AF

hit again by gunfire. With the engine rapidly losing power, Kubik ejected as the Skyhawk fell through 10,000 feet (3048m). Landing in no-man's land, Kubik walked towards friendly lines until he was caught in a firefight between Egyptian and Israeli forces, but was rescued by his own troops. In total six Skyhawks were lost with one pilot killed and seven aircrew made prisoner (as TA-4Hs were used as bombers alongside single-seaters) in several attacks against the Kantara SAM sites.

A ceasefire finally came into play on 24 October although sporadic fighting continued into 1974 and beyond. The war was considered a marginal victory for Israel, although losses of men and equipment were extremely heavy. Revelation of the Nickel Grass airlift of war materiel precipitated the OPEC oil embargo and the first of the 1970s 'oil shocks' which caused economic effects far beyond the Middle East. Annual US military aid to Israel went up tenfold by 1975.

The accepted figure for losses in October 1973 is fifty-four A-4s out of total losses of 103 aircraft of all types. At least ten A-4s were shot down on the 7th alone. 102 Squadron flew 992 sorties and lost seventeen aircraft over 832 missions (Israeli combat units were large by US standards, with a complement of around twenty-five aircraft). No. 109 Squadron lost sixteen A-4s and seven pilots killed, five others becoming prisoners. No. 115 was down to three operational Skyhawks after five days of fighting.

Skyhawk in Air Combat

There are only two reliable claims for aerial victories scored by Israeli A-4 pilots, both scored by Ezra Dotan in 1970. On the other side of the ledger, Egyptian Air Force MiG-21 pilots (including at least one Russian) claimed three A-4Es destroyed and one damaged during the War of Attrition. One lost and one damaged A-4 correspond with air-to-air claims in this period.

In October 1973 IAI technicians worked feverishly to repair damaged aircraft and return them to service. A-4 tail sections that couldn't be fixed were replaced by new units delivered in US transport aircraft and the hybrid aircraft flown straight into battle. TRH Pictures

An A-4 streaks to give support as Israeli APCs advance through the Golan Heights. This photo was issued on 10 October 1973, a day when at least two Skyhawks were lost to Syrian SAMs. TRH Pictures

On 6 October 1973, a Syrian MiG-21MF pilot claimed an A-4E in combat, an event which tallies with an Israeli loss. On the 7th Syrian 'Fishbeds' claimed four A-4s, Iraqi MiG-21 pilots claimed two and an Iraqi Hunter pilot one. Israel lost six Skyhawks that day which were not attributed to the ground defences. A Further six Yom Kippur War claims can not be matched against available IDF/AF loss records. A true accounting of the air combat career of the A-4 will have to wait until the day if and when Israel opens its records to objective enquiry and the same happens with its Arab neighbours.

Israel's A-4s saw action on several occasions after 1973, notably leading up to and during the 1982 invasion of Lebanon. Israel's fighters made many claims in this period, and the figure of eighty-two aerial victories for no losses is often made. The exact truth may never be known, but Syrian MiG-21 pilots submitted claims for a pair of A-4Hs on 8 June 1982 among sixteen claims made during that month, some of which (such as an E-2C Hawkeye) clearly have little basis in fact. Another pair of IDF/AF A-4Es are said to have been shot down on 26 April 1981 by a Syrian MiG-21MF and a MiG-23MS. Israeli data that has become available only records one combat loss in this period, a Skyhawk of unknown model that was shot down by Palestinian ground fire on 6 June 1982, the pilot, Aharon Ahiaz being made prisoner. This was the first IDF/AF aircraft brought down since 1973. Improvements to the A-4's survivability, such as the extended exhaust pipe and better ECM, and the use of RPVs to locate mobile SAMs and aircraft (including some A-4s) in the SAM-suppression or 'Wild Weasel' role certainly kept Israeli Skyhawk losses to a minimum in 1982.

The A-4 was widely used for close air support over Lebanon, at which time five squadrons were operational. Notably they was used alongside F-4E Phantoms to designate and attack Syrian tanks at night with Mk 82 and Mk 83 laser-guided bombs following daytime battles between Israeli and Syrian armoured forces. From 1982 until July 2000, when Israel finally withdrew, the A-4 was continuously involved in armed patrols and bombing missions over Lebanon. Two periods of particular action against Hizbollah guerrillas were called 'Accountability' in 1993 and 'Grapes of Wrath' in 1996.

After 1982, a few of Israel's A-4Ns adopted the Hughes Angle Rate Bombing System (ARBS) as used on the USMC A-4M. This improved conventional and glide-bombing accuracy as well as allowing use of the Paveway I series of LGBs.

Despite the induction of large numbers of F-16s into the inventory, one A-4 squadron remains in active service as does a training unit. Substantial numbers of A-4s are believed stored as a war reserve.

Kuwaiti A-4s in Desert Storm

In the early morning of 2 August 1990 Iraqi forces crossed the Kuwaiti border and headed for Kuwait City and the country's main military bases. Details of the chaos that followed and the valiant efforts of the defenders to hold back the Iraqis have received little recognition. More air combat took place during the invasion than is usually appreciated. Although the Kuwaiti military were not on a state of alert, many of the Air Force's jets managed to get airborne and encountered Iraqi helicopters at low level over Kuwait City. The pilots of six Mirage F1CK fighters (flown by Nos 18 and 61 Squadrons) claimed the destruction of thirteen Iraqi helicopters between them, mainly Mi-8 'Hip' and SA.330 Puma transports. Using R.550 Magic missiles and 30mm

A Free Kuwait Air Force A-4KU, armed with 500lb 'Snakeye' bombs.

Loaded down with Snakeye bombs, an A-4KU (now N-1020 with the Brazilian Navy) awaits a mission for the Free Kuwait Air Force in early 1991.
TRH Pictures

cannon, they shot down some of the heavily laden helicopters as they tried to evade between the buildings and others that tried to escape having dropped off their contingents of special forces troops. One source also says that they also destroyed one MiG-21 and an Il-76 jet transport. The A-4s and the Hawk Mk.61 trainers of No.12 Squadron attacked Iraq's armed helicopters (Mi-8s, but possibly also Mi-25 'Hinds') over the city with cannon, and the Skyhawks claimed five kills. Three of these were confirmed, the victorious pilots being Hassan al-Qattan, Ala'a al-Sayegh and Adnan Abdul Rasool. Stories have circulated since 1990 that Skyhawks destroyed airborne Iraqi helicopters with cannon, Sidewinders and even a 500lb bomb. The use of bombs in the air-to-air role is known to have been discussed with the KAF's American advisors before the war.

Later in the day A-4KUs encountered Iraqi Mig-29s and Mirage F1s, which appeared

The Free Kuwait Air Force was an air force in exile. During Operation Desert Storm, flying nearly 1,400 sorties for one loss. Most of their missions were over Kuwait itself.
TRH Pictures

too late to protect the assault helicopters, but there was no aerial combat between them. Subsequently the A-4s attacked columns of advancing Iraqi troops by day and by night until al-Jabr was overrun. Some missions were said to have been flown from the highway beside the base, which was so narrow that at least two A-4s ran off into the desert while landing but were recovered without damage. It is more likely that the location was the al Abdaliyah highway strip situated to the north west of al-Jabr. Eventually, out of ammunition and low on fuel, the surviving Skyhawks flew to Bahrain on 4 August.

During the Desert Shield build-up to the Gulf War itself, the surviving A-4s and the Mirages were reorganized as the 'Free Kuwait Air Force' and based at Dhahran, Saudi Arabia, where they were maintained by US civilian contractors.

The A-4KUs were notionally Maverick capable but were never equipped with these missiles in service. Known weapons used include Mk 7 cluster bomb dispensers and Mk 82 500lb Snakeye bombs with and without 'daisy cutter' fuse extenders. Patriotic slogans such as 'To Saddam With Love' and 'Remember Kuwait' were sometimes painted on the bombs and dispensers in Arabic. At least one was seen with TERs on the outer pylons carrying ADSID (Air-Delivered Seismic Intrusion Detectors) sensors, as well as a load of Mk 82s on the centreline. ADSID consisted of spike-shaped devices that were dropped in an area where enemy forces might infiltrate. They would transmit a signal when they detected the noise or vibration caused by troops and vehicles. ADSID was used on the A-4s at the request of the US Marines, whose nearest ADSID-capable aircraft were

Honouring a time-old tradition, the Kuwaitis and the US contract personnel marked their bombs with suitable slogans during the campaign to liberate Kuwait.

TRH Pictures

Harriers based in Bahrain, but who wanted to monitor an area of Kuwait.

By the end of September 1990, the airworthy Kuwaiti A-4s were gathered at Khamis Mushait AB in Southern Saudi Arabia for a period of training. In November they were sent to Dharhan alongside other coalition aircraft, including RAF Tornadoes. In the period of Operation Desert Shield up to 16 January 1991, the Kuwaiti A-4s flew a total of 258 'operational' and 427 support sorties – although what the former were and the actual distinction between the two is unclear.

Lieutenant Colonel Muhammed Mubarak was the commander of 9 Squadron and led the first Free Kuwait Air Force mission of the Gulf War. He was shot down by an Iraqi SAM and captured. US Department of Defense/TRH

The Free Kuwait A-4s flew their first mission against Iraqi forces on the morning of 17 January 1991, the first day of operation Desert Storm. The mission went badly and it is said that ten of the eleven A-4s involved dropped their bombs on Saudi territory in error. The eleventh, flown by the squadron commander, Lieutenant Colonel Muhammed Sultan Mubarak, was shot down at 1030 local time twenty-five nautical miles south of Kuwait City by a radar-guided SAM. The location suggests he was attacking his own former base at al-Jabr. Mubarak ejected and was made a prisoner of war and appeared on Iraqi TV three days later. He was not released by 6 March 1991 with the bulk of Coalition prisoners, but is believed to have been freed later.

Published figures say that the twenty-four Free Kuwait A-4s flew 651 missions or 1,361 individual sorties during Desert Storm. After the liberation of Kuwait in February 1991, the A-4s were put into storage pending the delivery of F/A-18Cs and Ds that had been ordered prior to August 1990. Eventually the majority were sold to Brazil.

Indonesian A-4s in combat

The Indonesian Air Force (Tentara Nasional Indonesia-Angkatan Udara, or TNI-AU) received thirty A-4Es and two TA-4Hs from surplus Israeli stocks in 1977 and 1985. They were used mainly in the ground attack and reconnaissance roles, with a secondary air-to-air role. Air-to-ground weapons included locally-built bombs and 2.75in (70mm) rockets. For the reconnaissance role, the A-4s used the Minipan or Vicon 70 cameras and AIM-9s and 30mm DEFA cannon for air combat.

The Skyhawks were used, alongside Rockwell OV-10F Broncos (supplied in 1976 without weapons), in attacks on separatist forces in the territory of East Timor, which was invaded by Indonesia in 1975, and West Papua (also known as Irian Jaya). The Broncos were adapted to use Soviet weapons, and this may be true of the Skyhawks as well, although Indonesia later made its own copies of US bombs and rocket pods. According to leaders of the East Timor resistance, the Skyhawks and Broncos were used in 'ceaseless attacks'. Outside groups opposed to the occupation of East Timor talked of the use of napalm and 1,000lb (454kg) bombs against rebel camps.

Little information is available on Indonesian combat operations, but it is known that the TNI-AU A-4Es and OV-10 Broncos were the aircraft most commonly used in attacks on rebels fighting for independence in the territories of East Timor and Irian Jaya (West Papua). During 1998, Indonesia took delivery of two ex-USN TA-4Js which were refurbished by SAFE Air in New Zealand. This contract was controversial because of the Indonesian military's role in East Timor.

When the East Timor independence referendum took place in 1999 and the related Australian-led Interfet (International Force for East Timor) peacekeeping operation was initiated, Indonesian A-4s and F-16s were said to have been forward deployed to be within striking distance of the territory, as was a KC-130 tanker to support the Skyhawks.

At the time of greatest tension a group of eight RNZAF A-4Ks were in Malaysia preparing to return from a training deployment to South-East Asia. They were put on standby in case the conflict escalated. The Indonesian government made a veiled threat to shoot down any reconnaissance flights by RAAF F-111s that crossed into Indonesian airspace. Australian F/A-18 Hornets were deployed to Darwin. The most serious threat was that of an attack on the ships carrying peacekeepers between Darwin and East Timor. Ironically, the RNZAF A-4s had just been training with the Royal Australian Navy for

The Indonesian A-4Es retained the tailpipe extension from their Israeli service but adopted a striking three-tone colour scheme and colourful markings. They were heavily used in attacks against seperatist rebels.
TRH Pictures

Seen at the 'last chance' area of their home base of Hasanuddin in July 1999 are a TA-4H and two A-4Es in the later toned-down camouflage and markings. They nearly saw combat with Australia and New Zealand over East Timor that year.

Alan Warnes, 'Air Forces Monthly'

just such a potential scenario. After six weeks the RNZAF aircraft went to RAAF Amberley, in Queensland, Australia by a circuitous route that avoided Indonesia. After a further period of standby, the Kiwi Skyhawks returned to New Zealand. It may never be known how close Australia and New Zealand came to war with Indonesia, including the possibility of Skyhawks seeing combat on both sides.

CHAPTER SIX

Post-War US Operations

The Skyhawk was beginning to vanish from the Navy's active fleet by 1973. Soon the majority of single-seaters were passed to Naval Reserve squadrons, with many single- and two-seaters going to adversary and support units. The Naval Fighter Weapons School (or 'Topgun') was established before the end of major US involvement in Vietnam and gave the A-4 a whole new lease of life. Training against A-4 'bandits' helped the US Navy wrest the balance of air combat victories and losses back in their favour. Having replaced the TF-9J Cougar in 1969, the TA-4J continued to provide advanced jet training for student naval aviators for thirty years, until finally phased out in late 1999.

In the Marine Corps the A-4M and OA-4M, versions developed specifically to USMC requirements were in their heyday throughout the 1970s and '80s, although they were never to see combat. As well as close air support and light attack, Marine A-4Ms had a secondary nuclear role, using the new generation of compact weapons such as the B-43 and B-61 bombs.

A-4 'Mike'

The A-4M was a version designed solely for the Marines. It was chosen largely because it was cheaper and better able to operate from forward airstrips than was the more sophisticated A-7. Although delivered to the first USMC squadron (VMA-324 at Yuma) almost two years before a Marine A-4 dropped the last bomb in Vietnam, the M never saw combat.

The 'Mike' served with seven active-duty Marine squadrons as well as four reserve and two training squadrons. A small number of Ms also served with Navy squadrons in the adversary role and with test and evaluation units.

As delivered, the first A-4Ms were equipped to a similar standard as the USMC A-4Fs, and distinguishing photographs of the two variants can be tricky from some angles. More equipment was added in service and for later deliveries, such as the ALR-45 radar warning receiver with its distinctive 'hot dog' tail antenna and blister fairings around the nose. This was also retrofitted to many Fs. The most significant capability improvement came with installation of the Hughes ASB-19 angle-rate bombing system (ARBS), which was fitted to many, but not all A-4Ms. The ARBS was first flown on an A-4M in 1977 but production sets were not ready for installation until 1981.

On those A-4Ms fitted with ARBS, a nose seeker window contained a TV camera adapted from that in the Walleye missile and a laser-spot tracker (LST). The image from the TV camera appeared on a screen on the left side of the instrument panel and its boresight point was projected on the head-up display. As with the Walleye, the nose

VT-25 'Cougars' flew the TA-4J from 1972 until 1992. The alphanumeric tailcode system later gave way to single letter codes. McDonnell Douglas via Mike Hooks

camera could be locked onto the contrast between parts of the target, whereas the LST locked on to a point marked by a ground-based or airborne laser such as the Pave Penny system. Either method would give the pilot a steering point to aim for to reach the release point for his LGBs.

ARBS had the advantage of being a passive system and could not be jammed nor give away the Skyhawk's position, unlike radar. The small size and especially the minimal frontal area of the A-4 contributed to its stealthiness.

The Marines added AGM-65 Maverick missile capability to the Skyhawk with carriage and compatibility tests taking place in 1979 and the first live launch from an A-4M occurring at China Lake in June 1980. This was also the firing by a Marine aircraft or pilot of this weapon, which has since become a staple of USMC Hornet and Harrier squadrons. Several foreign users also later adopted the Maverick for their A-4s.

A memorable cruise

Through the 1970s and '80s, With the A-4E and F and later the A-4M and OA-4M, the Marine light attack squadrons made regular 'cruises' to the WestPac area, deploying to US bases in the Philippines and Japan and participating in exercises with friendly nations. When in the Pacific, A-4 squadrons were assigned to the Twelfth Marine Aircraft Group (MAG-12) of the First Marine Aircraft Wing (MAW-1), headquartered at MCAS Iwakuni.

One WestPac cruise by VMA-223 was particularly memorable, mainly for the wrong reasons. The 'Bulldogs' deployed on a six-month WestPac in May 1981. On 9 September, A-4M BuNo 158151 crashed near Japan. As the official accident summary tersely put it: PILOT EJECTED AFTER ACFT DEPARTED CONTROLLED FLT. MINOR INJURY. In the equally succinct words of one squadron pilot: 'Tojo had a slat departure and ejected just west of Iwakuni'. The squadron then deployed to the Philippines, and on 19 October, BuNo 160241 was lost during aerial gunnery practice. AIRCRAFT CRASHED INTO SEA FOLLOWING EXPLOSIONS. PILOT EJECTED was the official version. Unofficially it was: 'Toni' had his jet blow up in the gun pattern off the Philippines. Speculation was that 'Betty' shot him down, being out of position in the gun pattern'.

On 3 November, the squadron began to return to Japan with three aircraft making the first leg from Cubi Point to Kadena, Okinawa. There one of the A-4Ms, BuNo 158421, flown by a First Lieutenant known as 'Ragu' had a starting problem and remained behind, joining a further flight of three that was to leave two days later. One of these aircraft was 'downed' by a faulty gyro, delaying the remainder of the flight's departure until it was nearing sunset. About forty-five minutes after take-off the flight encountered icing in cloud and Ragu reported that he had lost his airspeed indicator. The flight leader called on Ragu to fly in close formation so the two aircraft could make a section precision approach to Iwakuni. The leader would make a missed approach and drop the disabled A-4 off when the 'meatball' landing aid was sighted. By now it was dark with light rain and fog near the airfield. Just after the two aircraft lowered flaps and landing gear at approximately 3,500ft altitude, they became separated.

What happened next is not entirely clear, but it is possible Ragu mistook the lights on some nearby fishing boats for those of his flight leader and tried to formate on them. The next thing that he was aware of was water surrounding his legs as the aircraft sank into approximately 90 feet (27m) of water. Reaching the surface, he was quickly rescued by

The Marines operated the TA-4F in the fast forward air control role until the more specialized OA-4M was developed. These rarely seen markings appeared on an H&MS-31 TA-4F, which was later converted to OA-4M standard and then sold to Argentina as TA-4AR C-902. TRH Pictures

A line-up of 'Wake Island Avengers' A-4Es at Iwakuni. Marine Skyhawks were a common sight in Japan from the 1960s to the 1990s. Author's collection

the MCAS Iwakuni SAR helicopter, suffering only from mild hypothermia. When the aircraft was recovered from the water, nine nautical miles (17km) south of Iwakuni's main runway, the canopy was found behind the aircraft, but the release mechanism was intact and the ejection system had not been initiated. On 14 November the A-4M was raised from the bottom and transported by barge to Iwakuni where it was inspected by the mishap board and a McDonnell Douglas technical representative. The main landing gear and lower part of the nose gear had been stripped off by the impact, as had the slats, and the nose section forward of the main pressure bulkhead was missing. Other than that the Skyhawk had suffered remarkably little damage and consideration was actually given to repairing it for future service. Corrosion from saltwater immersion had caused a lot of harm, however and it was estimated that in excess of 30,000 man-hours would be needed to effect the necessary repairs. For that reason the aircraft was stricken from the inventory. Ragu himself fared better and today commands a Marine Air Wing.

Awaiting the application of squadron markings over its new tactical paint scheme, A-4M 158421 served with VMA-223 from 1978 until it flew into the sea near Iwakuni as related in the text. Author's collection

The OA-4Ms almost all appeared in the low-visibility grey TPS paint scheme that replaced the gull grey and white colours in use since the 1950s. TRH Pictures

Marine training aircraft of the 1970s are illustrated in this Harry Gann photograph, including an A-4M and a TA-4F of VMAT-102 'Hawks'. Harry S Gann, McDonnell Douglas

The mishap investigation board was unable to establish the exact cause of the accident but found the aircraft had been flying with an inoperative radar altimeter, in violation of squadron procedure, and this was likely a contributing factor. The pilot's life preserver had been actuated by salt water immersion as designed, but the method of canopy separation and the 'mishap pilot's cockpit egress evolution' (how exactly he escaped) could not be established.

The nature of the accident had convinced the other pilots that it had been fatal until word of the rescue got back to the Operations shack. A 'Ragu is Alive' party was immediately held at which a possibly excessive amount of champagne was consumed. Things got slightly out of hand and it was here that the worst injury of the entire incident was suffered, when a nurse had her nose broken by the elbow of one squadron member who was drawing back to hit someone else.

Of the 158 production A-4Ms, approximately thirty-six of them were destroyed in accidents, three of them by the 'Bulldogs' in late 1981. 'So that is the sad story of one of our WestPac deployments' ends our informant.

The last active duty Marine A-4 attack unit was VMA-211 'Avengers', who passed their A-4Ms to reserve unit VMA-133 'Dragons' in February 1990. The very last Marine Corps Reserve Skyhawk squadron was VMA-131 'Diamondbacks' at Willow Grove, Pennsylvania, who formally retired the A-4M in August 1994.

OA-4M

One of the most specialized Skyhawk versions was the OA-4M, a version of the TA-4F optimized for the Marines. The OA-4M's primary role was Tactical Co-ordinator (Airborne) or TAC(A) and Forward Air Controller (Airborne) or FAC(A). The TAC(A) role was essentially to reconnoitre the enemy's positions along the front line and pass the information to friendly troops. The FAC(A) mission was to direct close air support (CAS) aircraft to the target.Subsidiary roles included relay of communication between troops on the ground and CAS aircraft, dumping chaff ahead of a strike, target towing and proficiency flying for air group staff pilots.

The twenty-three OA-4Ms were operated by four different Headquarters and Maintenance Squadrons (H&MS, later designated Marine Air Logistics Squadrons (MALS)). These were H&MS-11 'Playboys' based at El Toro, California; H&MS-12 'Outlaws' at Iwakuni, Japan; H&MS-13 at Yuma, Arizona and H&MS-32 'Bandits' at Cherry Point, North Carolina. Only one OA-4M, an H&MS-13 aircraft (154624) was lost in a flying accident, crashing at Yuma in March 1986 following an engine flameout. Both crew ejected. Another (154336 of H&MS-32) was destroyed by a crashing AV-8A Harrier at Cherry Point in May 1980.

The last active Marine Corps Skyhawks were the OA-4Ms of MALS-12, part of MAG-12 at Iwakuni Japan. A final four-plane flypast on 16 July 1990 marked the end of the active duty Skyhawk and a decade of OA-4M operations from Iwakuni. Although not immediately available, the far more sophisticated F/A-18D Hornet was to replace the OA-4M and was integrated into fighter-attack (VMFA) units in the TAC(A) and FAC(A) roles rather than issued to separate headquarters units.

Once retired from active service, some OA-4Ms went to the Naval Air Test Center at Patuxent River, one was put on display in Japan and the remainder were sent to Davis-Monthan AFB for storage. Four were refurbished in the late 1990s for sale to Argentina.

An A-4M of VMA-223 circa 1981. This aircraft later went to Argentina and flies today as C-935.

Skyhawk display teams

The famous 'Blue Angels' demonstration squadron were not the first display team to fly the Skyhawk. In 1957 Commander R. L. 'Zeke' Cormier, whose previous posting had been as leader of the 'Blue Angels', then flying F9F Panthers and Cougars took command of VA-113 'Stingers' at Miramar. Very quickly he began organising a squadron demonstration team using A4D-1s, which became known as the 'Albino Angels'. The part-time display team used the normal gull grey and white colour scheme with the addition of trim in metallic blue edged in black during its short existence, which was not blessed with official approval.

By 1973, the 'Blue Angels' had operated the powerful, spectacular and noisy F-4J Phantom for four years. The Phantom was also maintenance intensive and fuel thirsty, and this was the period when the oil crises forced by events in the Middle East increased prices and restricted supply for the US consumer (and taxpayer).. Several accidents and incidents with the F-4 contributed to official discussions as to whether the team should be disbanded or suspended. Fortunately, at this time the light attack squadrons were in

An OA-4M of H&MS-12 'Outlaws' based at MCAS Iwakuni, Japan circa 1985.

The 'Blue Angels' TA-4Js retained the moveable wing slats, unlike their A-4Fs.
TRH Pictures

the process of relinquishing their A-4s, and the availability of the more fuel efficient and lower maintenance 'Scooter' saw the team re-equip with the A-4F and fly them successfully for thirteen years. The A-4 had actually been seriously considered for the 'Blues' as early as 1967 (along with the F-8 Crusader and F-5 Freedom Fighter) but had been rejected because of the need for A-4s in Vietnam. A batch of early F-4Js, which had been delivered without radar was available and so the Phantom was chosen instead at that time.

'Blue Angels' Skyhawks

The eight A-4Fs that were selected were modified at Palmdale to make them suitable for aerobatic demonstrations. The rework programme was similar to that used to create the 'Super Fox' model for the adversary squadrons in that the P-8 engine was replaced by the P-408, the avionics hump and armament were removed and the slats were bolted into the retracted position. The reason for this was so that they did not deploy during close formation manoeuvres, something that could prove disastrous if it happened asymmetrically on one aircraft or if they

The 'Blue Angels' are seen during winter training at El Centro, California.
Harry S Gann, McDonnell Douglas

Following a formation take-off, the number four 'Blue Angels' Skyhawk manoeuvres into the 'slot' at the beginning of another airshow display.

Frank Mormillo via 'Aeroplane'

One of company artist R. G. Smith's many Skyhawk paintings captures the excitement of a 'Blue Angels' display at an American air show.

McDonnell Douglas, via Mike Hooks

deployed at different times to individual aircraft in a formation. Additionally, an improved fuel pump allowed inverted flight for an extra thirty seconds, the tailplane was adjusted to give three degrees nose-down trim because the team's manoeuvres required a constant stick push force in level flight, and an integral folding boarding ladder was fitted in the port gun bay. A smoke oil system and a braking parachute were added. After rework, the aircraft were marked in the famous blue and yellow colours with the legend 'McDonnell Douglas Skyhawk II' on the tailfin. A TA-4J was also acquired and went through many of the same modifications.

With the arrival of the A-4 the team achieved squadron status as the Naval Flight Demonstration Squadron. In all, eighteen different A-4Fs were used from 1974 to 1986. One TA-4J served with the team as Number 7 during this period, but was supplemented by at least three others borrowed from Training Command when down for maintenance. These borrowed TA-4s were usually overall white with partial team markings and known as 'Caspars' after the cartoon ghost.

At least four of the 'Blue Angels' A-4s were lost in accidents, with two fatalities, one of which occurred in a collision at Niagara Airport, New York in 1985. Another aircraft loss occurred at NS Roosevelt Roads, Puerto Rico during a 1980 airshow. The two solo aircraft crossed over the runway and observers saw a big belch of fire blow off the lead solo's ventral engine access ('hell hole') door. The pilot made an immediate landing and went screaming down the runway at over 200 knots before going off the end and into an adjacent mangrove swamp. When one observer arrived with the crash crews, the pilot (Lieutenant Ross) was standing up dazed in the cockpit and everyone was screaming at him to jump off the burning aircraft (which he did). The cause was attributed to a very small hole in a fuel line, which caused a fine mist to spray into the engine bay, causing an explosive build up of vapours.

By 1985, the team's A-4s had expended a lot of their fatigue life and were competing for spare parts with the Adversary A-4 squadrons. A programme to replace the Skyhawk for the 'Blue Angels' was begun, and after considering and rejecting the T-45 Goshawk, the FA/-18 Hornet was selected and was ready for use for the 1987 display season. The thirteen-year era that the Skyhawk served the 'Blue Angels' was the longest of any team aircraft until the Hornet surpassed this mark in 2001.

At least eighteen single-seat Skyhawks are preserved in 'Blue Angels' colours in the United States, although the majority of them never served with the team. The displayed aircraft range from A-4As to a late-model A-4M complete with hump and ECM antennas! Meanwhile three genuine 'Blues' aircraft hang alongside one impostor (an A-4E) in the atrium of the National Museum of Naval Aviation at Pensacola. The team's main TA-4 is preserved aboard the USS *Lexington* in H&MS-13 colours.

Training Command

For thirty years the TA-4 took the student naval aviator from the intermediate training phase to the advanced phase, through carrier qualifications and eventually to the coveted Wings of Gold. Although initially designed as a combat-capable two-seater for the Marines, the TA-4 Skyhawk was a natural to replace the elderly TF-9J and TAF-9J Cougar in the advanced training role within the US Navy Training Command. The TA-4 came at just the right time for McDonnell Douglas, who were facing the end of single-seat A-4 production. Large orders for the TA-4F and TA-4J allowed development

The tailcode 'C' represented Training Wing Three in the coding system introduced in the 1980s. The commander of VT-25 was assigned this TA-4J when it was seen in October 1984. Graham Robson

Many adversary units passed on their TA-4s to Training Command, and they retained their unique camouflage schemes until they passed through depot maintenance. This former VA-127 TA-4J was seen with VT-7 in October 1993. Graham Robson

VT-23 conducts carquals with its Skyhawks, the rite of passage for over 11,000 Naval Aviators over 30 years. Note the hot refuelling operation going on at left.

US Navy/TRH Pictures

for two seaters for export and eventually 555 dual control Skyhawks were built, nearly one-fifth of total production.

The Skyhawk joined Training Command on 6 June 1969 when the first seven TA-4Js were delivered to VT-21 'Red Hawks' at NAS Kingsville, Texas. By 30 June this huge squadron had received nineteen TA-4Js, but also operated thirty-four TF-9J and nineteen TAF-9J Cougars, the latter being single-seaters used in the weapons instruction role. The Cougar was finally retired in 1974, and eventually nine Training Command (TraCom) squadrons were equipped with Skyhawks, although not all simultaneously. The complement of the squadrons varied, but they were large units by any standard. In 1988, VT-7 'Eagles' at Meridian, Mississippi had fifty-eight TA-4Js. That same year the squadron returned the A-4E to TraCom. The E, which was then otherwise used only by some adversary and test units was utilized by VT-7s instructor pilots to lead multiple aircraft formation training missions. These Es retained their avionics humps and wore the full white with red trim colours of TraCom's TA-4s. In September 1988 several instructors took the opportunity to make touch-and-go and arrested landings aboard the training carrier USS *Lexington*, taking the A-4E back to sea for the first time in eighteen years.

Earning the 'Wings of Gold'

TA-4s were used in the training of Student Naval Aviators (SNA), including both pilots and Naval Flight Officers (NFOs) for the Navy and Marine Corps as well as many foreign students. The syllabus for the SNA pilot varied over the years, but the following is typical of the Advanced Strike portion used in the last years of the TA-4 in TraCom.

Having successfully completed the basic flight training portion of the course, flying such aircraft as the T-2 Buckeye, T-34 Turbo Mentor and (for prospective NFOs) the T-47 Citation II or T-39 Sabreliner, the SNA arrived at one of the bases in the American South. The A-4s were based at one time or another were: Meridian, Mississippi, home of Training Wing One (TW-1); Kingsville, Texas (TW-2); Beeville, Texas; and Pensacola, Florida (TW-6).

Advanced Strike Training consisted of twelve stages that totalled 105 flight hours in the Skyhawk. The programme started with instrument training including Basic Instrument, Radio Instrument, and Airways Navigation. Simulators were used for around sixty-five hours to refine instrument flight and emergency procedures. Civil and military rules and regulations were taught, as was coping with assorted emergencies in instrument conditions, systems knowledge and emergency procedures. The phase culminated with a navigation check flight, passing of which resulted in an FAA instrument rating and qualification to take the Skyhawk on an instrument cross-country solo.

The next phase was FAMS (familiarisation flights), flown with the student in the front seat. Here the performance limits of the A-4 were investigated for the first time, including aerobatics, stalls, spins and spin recovery and high speed flight. Field carrier landing practice (FCLP) and various types of precautionary and emergency approach were practiced on most flights, often at outlying fields. The Fresnel landing system (meatball) was used on every landing back at the main base.

Having proved his or her competence as a Skyhawk pilot, the SNA then had to learn to employ his skills tactically, beginning with formation flying. Basic 'form' flights were followed by aerobatics in formation, formation approaches and night formation, in either two plane sections or four plane divisions.

The weapons instruction phase was one of the most popular parts of the course. Originally conducted at a variety of ranges near the training bases, from the 1980s this was mainly done by regular detachments to El Centro, California. Here the SNAs learned the basics of the basics of bomb dropping and strafing. Weapons accuracy was graded by instrumentation on the range. Competition was fierce to achieve the best bombing

The TA-4 was also used for training Naval Flight Officers or NFOs. This VT-7 TA-4J is readied for a carrier launch with the backseater 'under the hood' for instrument training.

Author's collection

TA-4Js of VT-22, Training Wing Two at Kingsville, Texas on a 1979 formation flight.

US Navy

scores, not least because the student with the lowest accuracy on the day's bombing was expected to carry a pink-painted practice bomb with him or her for the rest of the day.

The next stage was a series of Operational Navigation flights or ONAVS. These required the student to fly a predetermined route at 500 feet and anywhere from 300 to 450 knots. Using terrain features and prominent landmarks to navigate, ONAVS taught the prospective naval fighter/attack pilot terrain masking for ingress and egress to and from a target to avoid radar detection. The route was planned and flown with the object of putting bombs on target within a ten-second window.

The student by now should have gained the confidence to succeed at the next phase, air combat manoeuvring or ACM. This taught the basic principles of guns dogfighting as used since the beginning of air warfare. Initial ACM setups had the student in an offensive position, trying hard to keep on the tail of the instructor, but later flights were

TA-4J 'Top Quality' seen here in 1970s VT-4 markings crashed while landing at Pensacola in February 1985. The solo pilot ejected

Author's Collection

An A-4L of Naval Reserve squadron VC-13 'Saints'. This particular aircraft is preserved at the Mid-America Air Museum in Liberal, Kansas.

more 'anything goes' to bring the guns to bear and often saw the A-4 literally 'go ballistic', needing immediate corrective inputs to return to wing-borne flight.

The finale of the ACM stage was 2 v 1 combat where two students would gang up on an instructor, learning the basics of mutual support in a tactical role.

Finally, the student was ready for the part of the syllabus that marked the difference between the naval aviator and all others – carrier qualification or CQ. The phase began with each class spending two weeks of 'bouncing' at a practice field with a landing signal officer (LSO) grading every pass. Half of the nearly eighty practice landings were made at night to further increase confidence. The successful completion of this period meant the SNA was ready to be sent to the 'boat'.

The actual CQ or carqual period would begin with a flight of three students led by an instructor flying out to a carrier in the Gulf of Mexico. From 1962 until 1991 this was usually the USS *Lexington* (AVT-16), an 'Essex'-class ship first commissioned in 1943. Certainly not a large carrier by modern standards, the 'Lady Lex' was perfectly adequate for the Skyhawk. Nevertheless students were always surprised at how small the ship looked from pattern altitude. 'Like a postage stamp' was a common impression. Breaking into the circuit overhead the ship at 300 knots and 800 feet, the Skyhawk was slowed to on-speed (130 knots) and landing gear, flaps and hook were lowered. At about a mile abeam of the ship, the student's first carrier approach proper began, leading, if all went well, to an arrested landing on the deck of that 'postage stamp'.

The exhilaration and relief of the first 'trap' was often so great that the SNA would

This unusually-painted A-4M (BuNo 160245) served all its career with Navy test units. When photographed in 1979 it was with the Naval Weapons Evaluation Facility at Kirtland AFB, New Mexico. TRH Pictures

forget to raise the tailhook and cut the throttle and had to be signalled to do so by deck crew before being directed forward to the catapult for their first cat shot.

If anything, the first cat shot was an even more memorable experience than the arrested landing. The TA-4 was the last US Navy aircraft to require a bridle system for launch which connected hooks in the wheel wells to the shuttle in the catapult track. Once hooked up securely, the student put the throttle fully forward, grabbed the catapult grip, saluted the cat officer and 'squeezed the black juice out of the stick' as 16,000lb of steam pressure kicked them in the rear and accelerated the Skyhawk from zero to 130 knots in two seconds. As one pilot said; 'the first time it forces the air out of your lungs and the natural reaction is to scream. I screamed on all ten of my first cat shots'

After the student's mind caught up with the seat of his pants and the whole caught up with his mount, he would climb to pattern altitude, turn downwind, and do it again. Usually ten arrested landings and cat shots were made before the SNA was 'qualled' and ready to be 'winged' – the culmination of eighteen months training and 270 flight hours.

Thirty years of TraCom Scooters

The first VT-21 students completed their wings course by becoming carrier qualified on the TA-4J aboard USS *Wasp* (CVS-18) in September 1969. Exactly thirty years later the last group from VT-7 qualified aboard Washington (CVN-73) in September 1999.

VT-7 had received its first Skyhawks in August 1971 and was unique among the A-4-equipped VT squadrons in training students from friendly foreign nations as well as US aviators. By 1997 the 'Eagles' had trained 157 French, Spanish, Italian, Kuwaiti, Thai, Brazilian and Singaporean students as well as 2,941 US Navy and Marine aviators.

After a long gestation, the British Aerospace/McDonnell Douglas T-45A Goshawk began to replace the Skyhawk with Training Command in 1992, when it began to be issued to VT-21. The intended production numbers were cut back and squadrons re-equipped at a slow rate, but the Goshawk (which was only the airframe part of the T-45 Training System) was a much more modern aircraft, offering – particularly in latest T-45C form – with many of the cockpit features of the latest aircraft such as the F/A-18C Hornet.

By mid-1999 the Training Command TA-4 fleet as a whole had accumulated

Very different in appearance from when it served with VF-164 in 1973 as the last 'Lady Jessie', BuNo 158022 is seen on its arrival at AMARC in April 1994 in the markings of adversary squadron VFC-12. Graham Robson

2,004,100 flight hours on 1,629,100 sorties. Over 71,100 carrier arrested landings were recorded. In total, over 11,370 pilots and 5,080 NFOs won their Wings of Gold on the TA-4. On 26 June that year a ceremony was held at the National Museum of Naval Aviation at Pensacola to mark the retirement of the Skyhawk from Training Command. Organized by the Chief of Naval Air Training with associated events put on by the Skyhawk Association, the event saw many attendees from the forty-five year history of the A-4, including test pilots, attack pilots, adversary pilots, instructors, students, ex-Vietnam PoWs, representatives of VT-7 and VC-8, the two remaining Skyhawk squadrons, and many who were just friends of the 'Scooter'. Sadly Ed Heinemann and Robert Rahn were among those from the Skyhawk's genesis who were no longer around to see the conclusion of its career. The official retirement ceremony culminated with a missing man flypast by four aircraft of VT-7. The doors of the museum's atrium rolled up to reveal a manned TA-4J parked outside, beacons flashing. As a Navy piper played a single note, the speaker called 'Skyhawk departing' and the aviator secured the aircraft systems, climbed out and closed the canopy. At that moment the formation flew overhead and one Skyhawk pulled up vertically, visible through the glass ceiling of the atrium between the diamond of 'Blue Angels' A-4s as it climbed into the overcast.

Although the Training Command A-4s were 'retired', the last class of Skyhawk students was still to graduate, and the last session of carrier qualifications took place in September 1999 aboard the USS *George Washington*. Eight pilots qualified, including five Marines, one Reservist and one foreign student. To mark the retirement of the 'clockwork' Skyhawk, which lacked the Head-Up Display of the T-45, a feature of all frontline Navy jets, the students wore a patch proclaiming them 'The Last Studs Without HUDs'. The very last Skyhawk student to win his wings was Brazilian Lieutenant José Vicente de Alvarenga, who was to go on to help introduce the A-4 to a new nation and return it to regular carrier operations.

The final US Navy Skyhawk catapult shot was made from the *Washington* by the commanding officer of VT-7, Commander Jim 'Spot' Galanie on 30 September 1999. A week later, this Skyhawk left Meridian for the last time to join most of the rest of VT-7's A-4s in storage at Davis-Monthan Air Force Base, Arizona.

Safety Record

Over its long career, the Skyhawk had one of the safest records in naval aviation, particularly for a single-engined aircraft. Nonetheless at least fifty-six of the 165 A4D-1s were destroyed in accidents or stricken after mishap damage for a thirty-four per cent loss rate. At the other end of the production run, thirty-six of the 158 production A-4Ms, or twenty-three per cent were destroyed, albeit over a much longer service period. Neither version saw combat, but the A4D-1 probably saw more carrier operations than the M, which only made periodic shipboard deployments.

The details of the first A-4 lost in Navy service are unclear, but the first successful ejection occurred on 29 March 1957, the pilot being a Lieutenant Commander P. F. Cunningham. The first available accident statistics are for the 1963 calendar year, the loss rate in land-based operations (including bombing practice and all-weather day and night flying) was one A-4 per 10,000 flight hours. In a published comparison with five other carrier jet aircraft that had been serving for at least five years (unspecified, but presumably the F-3 Demon, F-6 Skyray, F-8 Crusader, A-3 Skywarrior and A-5

VA-127 were known as the 'Batmen' when this all-white TA-4J was photographed in the early 1970s. Later known as the 'Clylons', the squadron adopted the nickname 'Desert Bogeys' when they took on the adversary role in the late 1980s.
Author's collection

Vigilante), this was twice as good as the next safest, and four-and-a-half times better than the most accident-prone.

In general, the Navy's accident rates dropped in spectacular fashion in the late 1950s and early1960s. In 1954, the Navy lost 776 aircraft, or over two per day. The introduction of the angled-deck carrier caused the most dramatic plunge, as carrier aircraft now had the option of going around from a missed approach without winding up 'in the pack' of aircraft spotted forward on the deck, or engaging the barrier, which was often very damaging. The mirror landing system and later the Fresnel lens replaced the batsman's hand signals, which were increasingly hard to see and act on at jet speeds. The slower response speed of jet engines necessitated the instant feedback at greater distance that the 'meatball' could give.

Unreliable equipment and the Cold War imperative to conduct carrier operations at night and in all weathers contributed to the high accident rate. Ironically, Pat Patrick was the beneficiary of another pilot's misfortune in the early days of the A-4. 'I can remember one night off Cape Hatteras when I had to bring my wingman down because he had no gyro and no radio transmitter. Just before we pushed over from 28,000 [feet] and entered the clag (solid from 28,000 down to 2,000) my gyro rolled over dead and I had to fly a partial panel approach to drop off my wingman on the ball then turn downwind and shoot a no gyro CCA [carrier controlled approach] to get myself aboard on a black ass night with no horizon at all and in and out of rain squalls (with no rain removal system of any kind).

When we were about 8 miles out on a CCA final an F3H-1 Demon hit the ramp of the USS FDR and lit up the sky. The fire and the search lights looking for the pilot (Andy Anderson, an Air Force exchange pilot) gave us a VFR approach until the deck was cleared and we got aboard with the aide of the search lights). Andy was as good as they come as a stick and throttle guy so I am convinced that he had either an engine or electrical failure just short of the ramp. Except for Andy's bad luck, I am not at all sure that I could have kept the concentration for that long on a partial panel flight.'

The improvement in safety from the mid 1950s was also partly because of improvements in aircraft and ground-based navigation equipment including radar, better weather prediction and improved reliability of jet engines. The Naval Safety Center was established in the mid-1950s and contributed to the fall in accidents. Prior to this time, details of mishaps were often not disseminated throughout the Navy in a systematic way. One of the major functions of the NSC has been to publish 'Approach', a monthly journal of instructive but often entertaining accounts of disaster and near disaster from which others can learn.

Also important was the major change in culture resulting from the adoption of NATOPS (Naval Aviation Training and Operational Procedures Standardization) in 1961. Although the introduction of NATOPS was followed by a brief rise in the accident rate, the trend ever since has been a decline towards the current stable state. In 2000 twenty-two US Navy aircraft were lost in mishaps.

Prior to NATOPS, many practices and regulations were established at a Fleet, Wing, or even Squadron level. NATOPS called for standardized training and operating procedures for each type of aircraft as well as across the different communities and commands. It covered every aspect of training and operation, and generated stacks of thick manuals. Eventually each unit assigned an aviator to the job of NATOPS Officer, with the job of keeping the various publications up to date and administering NATOPS tests at briefings and other times.

NATOPS gave aircrews from different communities and units a baseline from which to proceed, although it was sometimes jokingly referred to as 'Not Applicable To Our Present Situation' or 'Never Attempt To Operate Plane Safely'. An average of the first few years of Skyhawk operations gave a loss rate of six A-4s per 100,000 flight hours, and is worth comparison with some other contemporary and current aircraft and for the Navy as a whole. In 1950, the Navy overall had fifty-four accidents per 100,000 flight hours, but in 1999, the figure for the Navy and Marine Corps combined was 1.9. A four-year average for the late 1990s was 2.4. It should be noted that there are far fewer aircraft flying today than fifty years ago, but that in general they are each flying longer missions.

The stripped-down adversary A-4 could still teach the highly manoeuvrable Hornet and other 1970s and 1980s fighters a few tricks. This A-4F of East-Coast adversery unit VFC-12 rides shotgun with a VFA-106 F/A-18B M. LeFavor/TRH Pictures

VF-126 at Miramar operated many A-4s in a wide variety of pseudo-Soviet colour schemes. These 'bandits' are stripped down A-4F 'Super Fox' models with the J52-P408 engine. US Navy/TRH

The F-8 Crusader's mishap rate was 14.3 per 100,000 flight hours, over twice that of the Skyhawk. The F/A-18 E/F Super Hornet's mishap rate was stated as 3.0 prior to the loss of two aircraft in a November 2002 collision, although these were the first to be completely destroyed. The definition of accident or write-off has changed over the years. The Navy today refers to various degrees of mishap, in which a 'Class-A' mishap involves damage greater than $1 million, or loss of life. The poorest-performing aircraft today is the AV-8B Harrier, with a Class-A mishap rate of 11.4. The AV-8A was far worse at 31.8 mishaps per 100,000 flight hours. Unlike other types, two-thirds of Harrier mishaps are mechanically related rather than caused by human factors alone. The Harrier's hovering capability is blamed for placing extra stress on the engines and other components.

Official statistical analysis for the A-4's later years is not available, but the author's brief analysis of the NSC data for all A-4s in the period 1980 to June 2002 shows 127 Class-A mishaps, in which 129 Skyhawks (models A-4E, F, M, TA-4F, EA-4F, TA-4J and OA-4M) were written off.

Twenty-eight incidents involved fires; there were five aerial collisions, nine

This A-4F 'Super Fox' of VFA-127 seen in 1989 is a former 'Blue Angels' aircraft Graham Robson

explosions (without preceding fires), nineteen engine failures or flameouts without fire or explosion and seventeen departures from controlled flight. Four aircraft failed to return for unknown reasons, seventeen flew into the ground in controlled flight (even so, at least four pilots successfully ejected after initial impact), ten flew into water, six were destroyed in ground collisions or runway departures and two aircraft were lost after bird strikes. One chase aircraft crashed after it was struck by a weapons rack jettisoned by an F/A-18, and an OA-4M had an AV-8A Harrier crash on top of it. Only four of the losses seem to have directly involved carrier operations.

Eighty-eight accidents or incidents involved ejection. Five of these were unsuccessful. In all accidents, thirty single-person fatalities and two double fatalities were recorded. In several cases, more than one A-4 was lost in a mishap and there were several fatal and serious non-fatal incidents in which the Skyhawk was later repaired. The author has flown in a TA-4 from which the crew ejected on the runway some fourteen years previously. Sometimes a mishap is downgraded after a damaged aircraft is surveyed; a procedure which pleases squadron bosses no end.

An example of a lucky (or unlucky, depending on one's point of view) Skyhawk is TA-

Ed Heinemann's only A-4 flight was on 5 June 1974 when Lieutenant Bill Mocock of VF-126 took the designer of the Skyhawk on a trip up the California coast and aaround Catalina Island. in TA-4J 152855. US Navy

4J BuNo 158085. This VT-21 Skyhawk was rolling out after landing at Pensacola In November 1989 when it struck another aircraft that crossed the runway and suffered Class B damage. The following September it departed the Pensacola runway after a failed arrested landing and the pilot ejected. The custodian at this time was the Naval Aviation Depot (NADEP), who it would seem had only recently finished repairs from the previous incident. Class B damage was inflicted again as a result of this event. In April 1992, '085 suffered Class C damage in an unspecified mishap at Kingsville, Texas when on the books of Training Wing 2 (CTW-2). Finally, and now with VT-22, the hapless Skyhawk departed the Kingsville runway on rollout on June 14 1993 and turned over. Although damage was once again assessed as Class B, the TA-4 was this time stricken from the inventory, and no doubt robbed for spare parts, much to the relief of many, one assumes.

In a 1980 incident, a TA-4J pilot from VC-10 spent thirty-eight hours in the sea following an ejection made necessary by engine failure. The incident occurred near the Bahamas, so the pilot was at little risk of exposure, although sunstroke and dehydration were both serious threats. These days aviation survival school classes are told that rescue should arrive on average within fourteen minutes of a landing in the water.

Although a few Class B and C accidents such as gear-up landings occurred later, the last total loss of a US Skyhawk was probably 153498 of VT-22, which suffered an inflight fire on 25 June 1993. Facing imminent control loss, the crew successfully ejected.

Topgun

By1968 the US Navy began to realise that it had serious deficiencies in the operational training of its aviators. Although adept at interceptions and long-range missile engagements, the art of dogfighting had become all but lost. In combat with

'Topgun' A-4E 149990 is seen at Miramar in an Israeli-style colour scheme in 1970. Some sources say that, after service with VA-81, it was actually issued to Israel as '887' in October 1973,

Author's collection

A-4M 160245, seen in a low visibility colour scheme in 1983 had a long career at China Lake, and made a guest appearance in the film 'The Right Stuff' in more colourful markings.
China Lake via Gary Verver

North Vietnam's agile MiG fighters, the Navy's Phantoms and Crusaders were losing an aircraft for every 3.7 that they themselves claimed. Despite the promise of powerful radars and sophisticated guided missiles, the rules of engagement and operating conditions in South-East Asia meant that the medium-range AIM-7 Sparrow often could not be used because of the need to achieve positive visual identification of the target. When fired they often failed to guide because of damage from humidity and rough handling aboard ship.

The opportunity was taken during the 'bombing halt' that began in 1968 to establish a graduate level air combat training programme for the best aviators from the Navy's fighter squadrons, who would return to their units and impart their new knowledge to their colleagues. The first class of the new programme was begun in March 1969 as a department of VF-121, the West Coast F-4 Phantom RAG. This became a separate command of its own in 1972, named the Naval Fighter Weapons School (NFWS), usually known as 'Topgun'. Use of A-4 Skyhawks as adversary aircraft dated back to at least 1967 when attack squadron VA-126 at Miramar, California was redesignated VF-126 and

VC-1 'Unique Antiquers' at Barber's Point, Hawaii provided fleet adversary support, target towing and other services for over thirty years. The KC-130R giving a top up here is from VMGR-352
US Navy

One of the last Skyhawks in US service, VC-8 TA-4J 158137 was put on display aboard the USS Hornet *at Alameda in April 2003.*

began to provide 'bandit' aircraft for dissimilar air combat training (DACT). Frequently confused with Topgun, VF-126 was more of a day-to-day adversary unit rather than a structured 'schoolhouse'. The A-4 was chosen for these units for several reasons, chief among them the small visual signature (including lack of a smoke trail) and performance and manoeuvrability similar to that of the MiG-17. The NFWS and other adversary units also adopted the F-5E/F Tiger II as a MiG-21 simulator. Stripped down and often fitted with the P408 engine and associated wider intakes, the adversary A-4Es and Fs were sometimes called the 'Mongoose' or 'Super Echo' (E) or 'Super Fox' (F). Usually flown clean without pylons or external fuel, the lightweight and high-powered adversary Skyhawks could boast a thrust-to-weight ratio of greater than unity. An amazing array of pseudo Soviet colour schemes appeared over the years, few of them ever closely replicating real patterns found on Eastern Bloc fighters. Soviet-style 'bort' or tactical numbers appeared on aircraft noses and red stars on the tails. In latter years, small flags were sometimes painted on the fins in place of the Soviet star. Examples of the Iranian, Iraqi, Yugoslav, Chinese and Russian Federation flags were noted on A-4s.

The Topgun programme proved extremely successful in improving the Navy's kill/loss ratio to around 13:1 when air combat resumed in earnest in 1972. The walls of the NFWS

A flight of VC-8 TA-4Js cross the Overseas Highway en route to NAS Key West from Oceana. VC-8 were based at Roosevelt Roads, Puerto Rico but made frequent detachments to the mainland to support the workups of the Atlantic Fleet carrier battle groups.

Author

The NATC and Naval Test Pilots School at Pax River used this TA-4J, seen here with an ALQ-167 threat simulator pod. Retired in 1994, it is under restoration for the Collings Foundation as N524CF and will be operated in the colours of an H&MS-11 'Playboys' TA-4F.

TRH Pictures

hangar at Miramar were soon decorated with silhouettes of MiGs shot down by Topgun graduates. Only a few aircrew could participate in the Topgun programme every year, but as part of the USN's greater emphasis on ACM, further A-4 adversary squadrons were established, including VF-43 and VFC-13 at Oceana, VA-127 at Lemoore and Fallon, VF-45 and detachments of VF-171 and VF-101 at Key West.

Composite Units

Before, during and after Vietnam, the US Navy operated squadrons in a utility or fleet support role. Initially known as VU (Utility) units, by the time the Skyhawk joined them, it appears they had all become VC (Composite) squadrons. Two were later designated VFC (Composite Fighter) squadrons. Under the VC banner, many tasks were carried out, and usually more than one aircraft type was operated. As well as A-4s, these were such machines as DF-8F Crusaders, US-2C Trackers, QF-9 Panthers, DT-28B Trojans, DP-2E Neptunes and UH-34E Sea Horses, to name a few. Most of these were involved in launch, guidance or recovery of various types of drone for surface-to-air and air-to-air gunnery. The 'mission statement' of a typical VC unit explains some of their roles: 'to train aircraft controllers and ship gun crews; provide flights to assist in the completion of functional radar tests for Atlantic Fleet and NATO naval units; conduct of transition training in the squadron aircraft for newly designated aviators; and aerial combat manoeuvring flights in conjunction with fleet fighter squadron combat readiness training'.

As for the last of these missions, at least in the mid-1960s, Walt Fink, who flew with VC-1 says: 'Our adversary role was really tame. Boring, even. We were the "bad guys" for the Hawaiian Air Defense Command and also for the Carrier Air Groups passing through the area on their way to Vietnam and getting their ORIs [operational readiness inspections). This entailed flying out several hundred miles, dropping down to assigned altitude, and turning inbound to the ship (or Oahu, if we were flying against Hawaiian Air Defense Command). Sometimes we had ECM pods, some of the S-2's carried chaff etc, but we got to do no ACM at all. In fact, we were instructed to take NO evasive action when intercepted by the fighters. We just turned on our anti-collision beacons and transponders and continued the flight. Toward the end of the week-long ORIs, the VF boys would get pretty testy with long hours (and harassment by the COMFAIRHAWAII observers and raid aircraft as well) and their intercepts were lots more than just flying alongside and waving at us. Sometimes they'd make supersonic runs on us (a sonic boom close aboard is damned loud) or would pull up in front of us with the burners cooking. At night that was pretty spectacular – and turbulent'.

The Composite squadrons were generally located near the Navy's main training areas. VC-2 was based at Oceana, with a detachment at Cecil Field, Florida. VC-4, not usually known as a Skyhawk unit, also had an A-4 det. at Cecil at one time. VC-5 were based at Atsugi, Japan and Cubi Point in the Philippines; VC-7 were at Miramar, California; and VC-8 made Roosevelt Roads, Puerto Rico their home for over forty years. VC-10 was also based in the Caribbean, at Guantanamo Bay, Cuba. VC-12 and VC-13 later became VFC-12 and -13 and were to be found at Oceana and Miramar, respectively.

The Skyhawk was retired for the first time in June 1999 when Training Command held a 'Farewell Skyhawk' ceremony at Pensacola, attended by many A-4 aviators past and present. VC-8 was to continue to operate the Skyhawk until 2003. Author

After the disestablishment of several VC units in 1992-3, it fell to VC-8 'Redtails' to carry on the US Navy Skyhawk story away fromTraining Command. When VT-7 stood down in 1999, they became the very last US users, operating six TA-4Js alongside an equal number of UH-3H Sea Kings.

VC-8 had first received A-4B Skyhawks in 1965 to launch the AQM-37 supersonic target drone. Over time, the Skyhawk with the AQM-37 and BQM-34 drones replaced a mixture of Panthers, Furies, Crusaders, Neptunes and other aircraft for the traditional VC roles of drone launch, ship radar and weapons operator training and target towing. TA-4s replaced single-seat Skyhawks in the early 1970s. From 1997 the squadron was assigned the Fleet Adversary mission and began training pilots to fly the A-4 as an air-to-air fighter as well as an anti-ship and ground attack platform. These were much more stringent missions than those flown by the Vietnam era Composite squadrons, involving the full range of single– and multiple aircraft tactics against air and surface units wanting the most training value out of every expensive sortie.

As well as supporting naval operations in the Caribbean, the A-4s frequently deployed to Key West, Oceana and Fallon to offer adversary training to other units. For a number of years they were the only non-Reserve unit in the Navy to offer a dissimilar aircraft to the Hornets and Tomcats flown by USN fighter squadrons.

VC-8 also conducted training for FACs, dropping inert bombs at the direction of ground-based controllers from all the US armed forces. Although not common, it was still possible in the Skyhawk's last years to see a TA-4 fully bombed up with up to ten 500lb BDU-45 'blue bombs' for FAC training.

The April 2003 announcement of closure of the Navy's controversial bombing and gunnery range on the island of Vieques spelt the end of VC-8, which had been based at 'Roosey Roads' since 1959. Although a Hornet squadron was officially the last unit to

Accepted by the Navy in July 1967 TA-4J 153525 is seen climbing out from Oceana in August 2001 when with VC-8, with which it served since August 1994. After nearly thirty-six years of service, it was retired to the Glenn Martin Museum near Baltimore in May 2003. Author

With the achievement of full Adversary qualification, VC-8 repainted its TA-4s in suitable colour schemes. Half of the last six Skyhawks were blue and half were brown, as seen over the Virginia coast in August 2001.

Author

use the Vieques range, after they had departed back to the US, VC-8 loaded one 250lb bomb on an A-4 and did the honours.

On 3 May 2003, TA-4J 154649, the last Skyhawk in US military service, was delivered to the Palm Springs Air Museum by VC-8 pilot Lieutenant Rob 'Woodsy' Woods. It was 'the saddest day in history' as another squadron pilot put it. An official A-4 retirement and squadron disestablishment ceremony was held at Oceana on 23 August, by which time all the VC-8 Skyhawks had been donated to museums or put into desert storage. This marked the end of forty-five years of squadron history and thirty-eight with the A-4.

Outlining the A-4's and VC-8's history for the official retirement programme, an anonymous squadron member summed up; 'With the disestablishment of VC-8, an era ends. For the first time in nearly fifty years, ships will deploy and air wings will enter harm's way without the benefit of the Skyhawk as either friend or foe'.

The early Skyhawks were a joy to fly in daylight and clear weather. This this early A4D-2 without a refuelling probe is carrying an external navigation package, which made up for some of the deficiencies of its own avionics.

Douglas

CHAPTER SEVEN

Flying and Fixing the Skyhawk

'Every pilot I know loved to fly all models of the A-4, even when they were killing us off at a terrible rate.' The words of one pilot who flew all the Navy's single-seat Skyhawk models sum up the joy of flight and the dangers of military aviation. As the A-4 was developed, it got heavier and was expected to carry more, but also benefited from extra thrust and better systems as well as better shipboard equipment and standardized operating procedures.

Looking at the different versions, 'Pat' Patrick says: 'the A model was a crude daylight VFR bomber only. In a clear air mass it was a fun aircraft to fly, but it was a miserable aircraft to fly when there was no visible horizon either day or night. The B model added the AOA indexer, in-flight refuelling, a fuel-flow gauge and a slightly more reliable engine. It was still only safe in daylight VFR'.

The C model added a radar and most importantly a very reliable and easy to read AJB-3 all attitude indicator to replace the pull-to-cage gyro. It also added a radar altimeter that prevented some of the common accidents where the A-4 just flew into the water at night on in the clag. More importantly, perhaps it added a pilot's relief tube, which became more necessary as inflight refuelling and larger external fuel tanks permitted longer missions. The A could stay airborne for 1.5 to 2.0 hours, but the B's refuelling probe and 300 gallon tanks meant double cycles of 3.5 to 4.5 hours.

The E model kept the radar and improved instruments of the C and added a far more reliable and higher thrust engine, which reduced losses to below pre-war levels. The J65-engined models had become less nimble as they got heavier with only small thrust increases.

'The F model was the real winner, says Patrick. It had all of the best features of the previous models and was back to very close to the same thrust to weight of the A-4A (which was awesome). It had a much better weapons system, better ECM, good instrumentation and a great engine.

On a sunny day, if the engine kept running, the A-4A was probably the most enjoyable to fly of the early Skyhawks. With a stripped down adversary A-4F powered by the P408 engine, the pilot had the added comfort of reliability and better instrumentation, navigation equipment, and ECM. 'The F model brought back the fun'.

With only 8,100lb (3678kg) dry weight and 7,700 lb of thrust, an A-4A climbed like a rocket at light weights, such as when making the escape manoeuvre as it lofted a nuclear 'shape' towards a practice target. In the case of a load of one 2,025lb (919kg store and internal fuel only, at this point the A-4 might have about 3,600lb (1634kg) of fuel remaining. From 100ft (30m) to 40,000ft (12192m) could take less than six minutes. At this high altitude it was a fuel-efficient cruise back to the carrier, landing after a flight

A Marine Corps aviator poses with his VMA-211 'Wake Island Avengers' A-4E in Japan in the 1970s. The candy striped refuelling probe mirrored the squadron's red and white rudder markings.

Author's collection

of about 48 minutes with about 1,060lb (481kg) fuel remaining.

This was just one attack scenario studied, tested and practised for in the Cold War. Whether it was realistic against a defended target and from a carrier close to the enemy's coast, in range of bombers, surface and submarine forces is debatable. Early Skyhawk pilots joked of their 'one pilot, one shot, one way nuclear bomber'. The bad weather or night capability of the A4D-1 or -2 by itself was nil, although 'buddy bombing' techniques were tested where an A4D flew wing with an A3D Skywarrior, relying on that aircraft's navigation and radar systems until the IP (initial point) and then carrying on alone using the LABS system. After that it was 'find your own way home' in whatever conditions prevailed. The A4D-1 and many A4D-2s lacked any kind of windscreen

A neat diamond of A4D-2s of VA-81 'Sunliners' circa 1961 illustrates the planform of the Skyhawk. VA-81 was one of the squadrons that stood nuclear alert off Cuba in 1962.

US Navy

clearing device, although a wiper was introduced during A4D-2 production.

Walt Ohlrich, later to command a Skyhawk squadron in Vietnam, had a contrary view of the A4D-1, saying 'No one liked the Dash-One – it was an unstable little beast'.

Prior to the introduction of programmes such as NATOPS, Skyhawk instrumentation was often non-standard, even within a squadron. It was not uncommon for there to be two kinds of altimeters and three kinds of gyros in one unit's aircraft. This was not just true with Skyhawks, but common across Navy aircraft, partially explaining the terrible safety statistics of the time.

Aboard ship, some squadrons had loss rates that would not have disgraced a Japanese Kamikaze outfit. A 1959 cruise by VA-172 on the USS *Franklin D. Roosevelt* saw six of twelve aircraft lost, along with four of sixteen pilots. VA-86 lost twelve aircraft and six pilots from *Independence* on a Mediterranean cruise the same year. The small, badly lit carrier decks, unreliable hydraulic catapults, poor cockpit instruments (also badly lit), short-lifed engines and lack of navigation aids contributed to the appalling accident rate, as did inadequate and unstructured training, unauthorized low flying ('flat-hatting') and ad hoc dogfighting ('hassling'). It was cured over time by standardization of training and equipment, diagnostic cockpit systems and bigger ships with steam catapults, better lighting and TACAN homing and other precision approach equipment. Perhaps most importantly, jet engine reliability improved, from 25 to 360 hour mean time between failures (MTBF) in the 1950s to 1,000 hours plus MTBF today. Even the 1950s-

The Hughes Mk 11 gun pod, seen here on the centreline pylon of an A-4B, contained a twin-barrelled 20mm cannon with a rate of fire of 4,000 rounds per minute. It was not very widely used by US Skyhawks.
TRH Pictures

generation J52-P408 as still used in the EA-6B Prowler has a MTBF of 1,100 hours.

Even before the Skyhawk entered service, Douglas and the Navy were developing its conventional attack potential. All conventional weapons in the inventory were trialled on the A4D-1, including mines and torpedoes. One of the weapons trialled but not adopted was the ASM-N-8 Corvus, a supersonic air-to-surface missile designed to be launched against heavily defended targets, including surface ships and radar installations. Drawings exist of the Skyhawk carrying two of these large weapons, which were initially intended to have a nuclear warhead but later proposed in conventional form. The Corvus was launched for the first time from a Skyhawk at Point Mugu in July 1959. Despite the success of trials, the weapon was cancelled in 1960 after $80 million (over $550 million in today's money) had been spent.

An interesting hybrid weapon tested on the Skyhawk at China Lake was the Bombwinder, which was essentially a 3,000lb M118 bomb with an AIM-9's forward fins and seeker for guidance. As tested on the centreline of an A-4C in 1967, the bomb had minimal ground clearance. A very gentle rotation was needed for take-off (the pilot had

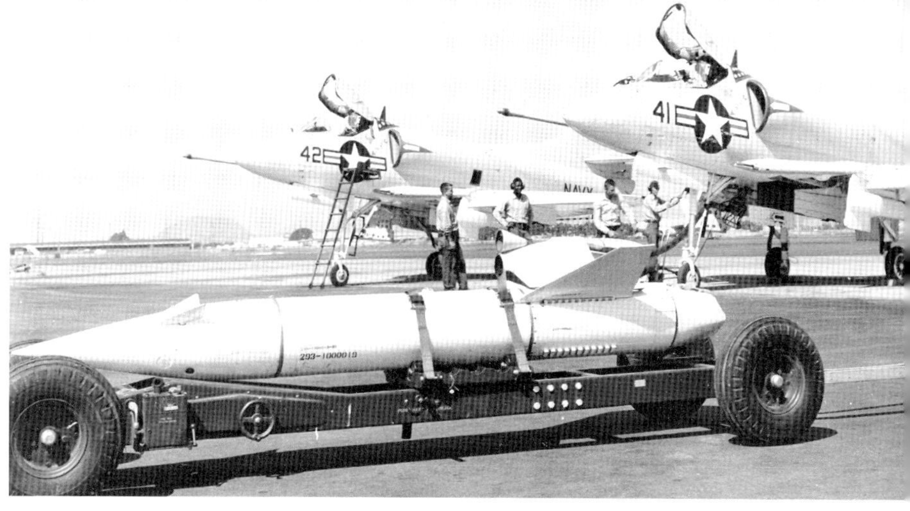

The AGM-12 Bullpup was an important early Skyhawk weapon. Seen here in 1958 with VX-5 A4D-2s, the Bullpup A model was at this time designated ASM-N-7A.

Martin via Gary Verver

a photo of the aircraft and bomb on his instrument panel to remind him of the possibility of scraping the rear fins on the runway). Landing with the bomb (which contained a large spotting charge) attached was not permitted. The concept of an infrared-guided freefall bomb appears to have been a technological dead end.

As used in combat, the Skyhawk primarily dropped the Mk 80 series of 'slick' and snakeye bombs, various types of cluster bombs and napalm (firebombs). Bombing accuracy improved during Vietnam from a CEP (circular error probable – a measure of miss distance) of 400 feet (122 metres) using the basic manual gunsight to about 130ft (40m) on those aircraft with the CP-741 toss bombing computer, which was part of the avionics package in the hump on the A-4F. The poor manual bombing accuracy was made up for to some degree by using cluster bombs. The earlier CBU-24 and - 29 had a notable 'doughnut' bomblet pattern, which sometimes left the target unharmed in the centre. The later Mk 20 Rockeye weapon filled in this hole.

When fitted with multiple ejector racks (MERs) on three pylons, the A-4E/F could carry a theoretical load of twenty 250lb bombs (six on each MER and two on the outboard pylons). However, when down, the main landing gear doors interfered with the forward inboard positions on the MERs and these slots were usually left empty. In Vietnam the Marines sometimes found a way around this by physically holding the doors closed until the MERs were loaded and then letting the door rest on the bombs. Not a 'legal' or advisable solution, but sometimes a necessary one when the situation called for maximum air support. The Navy would sometimes do a similar thing with the triple ejector rack (TER) by loading a 250lb Mk 81 bomb on the inboard position with the door resting on it and 500lb Mk 82s on the other spots. At least seven A-4s were lost in Vietnam because of premature detonation of their own bombs, and another four were fatally damaged by ingesting their own rocket debris.

Cannon

Where the fixed cannon was fitted to US Skyhawks, it was the Colt Mk 12, a weapon also used in a quad installation on the F7U Cutlass and the F-8 Crusader and in a pair in the Mk 11 gun pod sometimes carried by A-4s. The number of 20mm rounds carried on the A-4 varied from 75 to 200 rounds per gun, depending on model and on the amount of ECM gear fitted in the wing roots. Training Command TA-4s normally had only the starboard gun fitted.

'The Mk 12 was very *g* sensitive' remembers VT-25 instructor John Alger. 'It was an almost guaranteed jam if you tried to arm it with anything but one *g* on the bird. When it jammed, you were done shooting for the day. Since you turned the arming switch off after every strafing pass, you had quite a few chances to mess it up. The A-4 was never intended to be an air-to-air machine. There was a gunsight setting (15 or 20 mils comes to mind) for air-air shooting, but was not a lead-computing sight so it would have taken some pretty good Kentucky windage to hit anything'.

Nevertheless, the guns were used widely in Vietnam for CAS and rescue combat air patrol (RESCAP) missions. They were the best answer when troops were in very close contact and when the enemy was closing in on a downed pilot. They were accurate enough at point-blank range to fire at the enemy within tens of metres of the downed pilot.

Start up

Starting the A-4 varied by model and engine, but on the A-4M, with its jet fuel starter (JFS) unit, the procedure followed this sequence. Once the pilot gave the 'turn' signal and the plane captain returned the 'clear' signal, the start switch was turned on and the T-handle on the right of the instrument panel was pulled up. This released the hydraulic accumulator pressure to turn the JFS. A 'start' light came on the annunciator panel as the JFS kicked in, then the handle was pulled down. At 5 per cent RPM the throttle was moved to strike the ignitors. At 15 per cent the throttle was moved 'around the horn' to introduce fuel flow and spool the engine up to idle revolutions. At 20 per cent the engine should light off, if not then you have a 'wet start'. This could happen if the pilot did not hit the ignitors or they were not working. If so, he had to shut fuel off by replacing the throttle in the idle detent, taking care not to hit the ignitors on the way back, which could cause an explosion. The pilot monitored fuel flow, RPM and oil pressure and kept his eye on the plane captain in case he spotted anything wrong, such as fire.

The start light went out at 45 per cent RPM and the start switch

Fire bombs or napalm were a common US Skyhawk weapon. A-4Bs of VA-163 are seen making a low-level napalm run at a June 1963 China Lake firepower demonstration. China Lake via Gary Verver

A close-up of the starboard Mk 12 cannon muzzle on an A-4SU. The original A-4S had a 30mm Aden cannon. Author

was turned off. RPM was increased to 52 per cent and engine gas temperature (EGT) rose to 320 degrees Celsius (608F). When EGT was stable at this figure, all electrical power was brought up and the main systems (HUD, TACAN and radios) are checked for proper functioning. If EGT exceeded 455 degrees C (851F), this was a 'hot start' and the pilot needed to shut off the fuel but continue to run the engine until temperature decreased to 320 degrees. All being well, the pilot checked in with his wingman and was ready to taxi. Increasing throttle to 65 per cent was about right to get moving depending on outside air temperature, but less would maintain a slow taxi speed. Care had to be taken not to allow forward speed plus any headwind to exceed 60 knots (111km/h) with the canopy open to avoid damaging it.

The starting procedure on A-4s without the JFS required an external air supply or 'huffer', and hand signals for the plane captain (PC). As former Marine A-4M and current BAE Systems A-4N pilot Dennis Pratt puts it: 'To start you need external power and you give the PC one finger for power. When ready to start and the huffer is attached give PC two fingers for air (blow me). At 45 per cent give the PC three fingers to stop air (stop blowing me). When established at idle give the PC four fingers to put the switch by the electrical connection to internal so the aircraft generator can power the aircraft and then disconnect electrical power'. From then starting continues as above.

A live GBU-16 1,000lb bomb is seen under an RNZAF A-4K. Author

A Douglas publicity photo illustrates the theoretical maximum load of the A-4E. The approximate combined weight of 18 Mk 81 250lb bombs (actual weight 270lb) and two AGM-12C Bullpups at 1,800lb each added 8460lb (3841kg) to the A-4E's basic empty weight of 9,853lb (4469kg).
Douglas Via Mike Hooks

On an operational land-based mission, the Skyhawk taxied to the arming ('last chance') area where the safety pins were removed from the bombs, the breech plugs pulled from the guns and a round cycled through each. A voltage check would be made on any rocket pods carried.

Take-off

Compared to a shore landing (see below), take-off in the A-4 was simplicity itself. There was no problem with over-rotation and nosewheel lift-off occurred at practically the same moment as the mainwheels left the ground. Test pilot Drury Wood said that the only comment he could make about the take-off was to say 'take off'. In reality it was slightly more complicated than that.

This RNZAF TA-4K is carrying a TGM-65 training version of the Maverick. The image from Maverick's seeker head could be displayed on the MFD screens in either cockpit of the Kahu T-bird'. New Zealand bought the AGM-65B Scene Mag TV-guided and AGM-65G IR-guided versions.
Author

Royal Air Force Squadron Leader Peter Harris poses with one of the first A-4Ms equipped with the Angle Rate Bombing System (ARBS) at China Lake in 1981. ARBS was later adopted for the RAF's Harrier GR.7 as well as the Marine Corps AV-8B.
Hughes/TRH

The actual pre-take-off procedure was to set tailplane trim to four units up for a take-off with half or full flaps and two units for a no flaps take-off. This should be done before starting to taxi and correct setting confirmed by an external check by the plane captain. Having obtained clearance to take off, the A-4 was taxied onto the runway hold and from there it goes as follows: hold brakes and advance throttle to maximum without sliding on the locked wheels, check instruments, release brakes, advance throttle to Military power and begin take-off run. Until the rudder becomes effective at about 70 knots indicated air speed (IAS), direction can be adjusted by slight pressure or gentle taps on the brakes. At about 115 kts the nose wheel should be lifted well off the runway to increase

A-4M 160245 was the first Skyhawk and the first Marine aircraft to fire the Maverick, initially in AGM-65E laser-guided form.
Hughes/TRH

aerodynamic lift and the aircraft should become airborne at 120 kts. at least for an early model Skyhawk. A heavier aircraft such as the A-4F would need more like 145 kts. A lightly-loaded A-4 was in some danger of overrunning its safe gear down speed just after take-off.

A minimum-run take-off required full nose-up trim (6 units) and full flaps. The nose could be lifted at 105 kts and take-off effected at 110 kts. As the aircraft climbed out in this condition, almost constant re-trimming could be needed to achieve the desired climb-out angle.

Pulling the nose up hard at this point was likely to result in a stall because of the high induced drag of the delta wing at high AOA. The best climb speed was above 300 kts, so the nose should be held steady against the horizon to allow a gradual climb at first. The alternative 'Blue Angels' method was to hold the aircraft in ground effect until reaching 250-300 kts (over a long runway!) and then pull into a 2-3 *g* climb at 45 degrees or so.

JATO

To reduce take-off roll on a short runway, or more often to allow a greater weight of ordnance and fuel to be carried, most Skyhawks could make use of jet-assisted take-off or JATO. The JATO system actually used liquid-fuelled rocket bottles affixed to the airbrakes, hence the alternative acronym RATO. A JATO take-off began with pre-flight calculations of the aircraft weight, air temperature and wind speed to allow the correct firing delay time to be established. It was important to time the firing of the rockets so that they burned out just after lift-off. Firing too early or too late would give a longer roll than desired, which might be critical if at near maximum weight on a short strip. For example, an A-4E taking off on a 90 degree F (32C) day with full internal fuel and a load of six Mk 82 bombs would begin its take-off roll as normal and the pilot would fire the

The forward-retracting undercarriage of the Skyhawk, as seen on this A-4K, saved weight and complexity as it was locked into place by air pressure as it extended, rather than with hydraulic power. Author

An A-4C of VMA-324 shows the boost given by JATO on take-off. The Marines were enthusiastic users of the system although it took careful planning and handling to get the best out of it. TRH Pictures

rockets after 600-700 feet (183-213m). This would give a total roll of under 2,000ft (610m).

Figures for an A-4M say that on an 86 degree F (30C day) with 2,000ft pressure altitude, and 10 knots (19km/h) headwind, a 20,000lb (9074kg) A-4M would use a 450ft (137m) firing delay, the ground roll would be 1,350ft (412m). and the distance to clear a 50ft (15m) obstacle would be 2,500ft (762m). Without JATO, the same A-4M would need 3,600ft (1097m) to clear 50ft.

The JATO firing switch was usually located on the catapult grip near the throttle and also functioned as the chaff and flare switch. The throttle lever also mounted the microphone switch. On at least one occasion a pilot inadvertently pushed the wrong button while asking the tower for take-off clearance while his engine was at less than full power. The resulting departure was marginal to say the least and even more spectacular than usual as the aircraft left a dust trail for a mile or so beyond the runway as it struggled for altitude.

The JATO propellant left thick trails of white smoke behind as the Skyhawk roared down the runway. If a squadron of twelve A-4s all left in a short period with no breeze, the airfield would essentially go into (rather smelly) IFR conditions. After take-off the bottles were jettisoned by retracting the thrust hooks and could be recovered for later use if not too damaged (or in the hands of the Viet Cong).

Landing

With its tall landing gear, the A-4 has always had unusual shore landing characteristics, especially in a crosswind. A 1957 'Approach' magazine article by Douglas test pilot Drury Wood was devoted to the subject. Imagining a typical A4D-1 or -2 flight to the fictional 'NAS Boondock', Wood recommended an approach at

The 'Blue Angels' showed how precisely the Skyhawk could be flown in formation.

Frank B. Mormillo via 'Aeroplane'

'reasonable' speed. 'I personally do not like to use over 250 knots. This allows a better opportunity to merge with other traffic, and no effort has to be made to drop to gear placard [maximum safe] speed'. Navy pilots tended to move faster than this in the pattern. VA-72 skipper Bob Hunt defined 'reasonable speed' as 250-300 knots in a separate 1957 piece for 'Approach'.

Following the break, flaps and landing gear would be lowered on the base leg, although not simultaneously as this prolonged the operation of both systems unnecessarily. By the ninety-degree point, a speed of 120-130 kts gave a comfortable approach speed with full flaps. This could drop to about to 110-115 kts over the threshold at which point power was cut. Use of the speedbrakes was not recommended as it added longitudinal buffet but did not materially contribute to placing the engine in a better acceleration range. That was the test pilot's viewpoint. In the early days, there were few standard manuals and squadrons largely adopted their own procedures.

Before the angle of attack (AOA) indexer became standard on fleet A-4s in about 1960-61, one squadron's procedure was to fly every approach at 125 kts regardless of stores configuration. The AOA indexer was fitted above the cowl or on the canopy frame and showed that the pilot was above, below or on the correct glidepath. Adoption and use of the indexer allowed the pilot to fly 'lineup, ball and AOA' without constant reference inside the cockpit. It also showed that the speed in the turn onto finals with two tanks and a buddy store should have been more like 138 kts to stay safely above the stall. Numerous unexplained accidents in which an aircraft simply fell into the sea at night as it turned onto the approach were probably caused by adhering to this sort of 'rule of thumb' speed. Pilots carrying a heavy load were flying 'near the ragged edge of the stall' without knowing it.

Standard procedure later became to fly the Skyhawk at a set AOA on the approach (19 units on the A-4B, 17.5 on the A-4C/E and 16.5 units on the TA-4J), with stall being around 27 units on the B/C/E and 22-23 units on the TA-4. A configuration of two 300-gallon external tanks is assumed in each case. The differing AOA units for each version gave the same approach speed and horizontal attitude for the same aircraft gross weight. Units of AOA are not degrees, but an arbitrary setting which varies by aircraft type.

On the ground

It was when the A-4 touched down that its landing characteristics differed from most jets. Because of its high landing gear and large keel area, the A-4 would not weathercock into the wind, but instead would yaw away from it. A crosswind landing was to be made on the upwind side of the runway to allow for drift. The nose gear could not be held off for any appreciable time to give aerodynamic braking, so was to be put down quickly, followed immediately by retracting the flaps and deploying the speedbrakes. Forward stick kept the nosewheel down and aileron was employed to keep the upwind wing down, but care was needed to keep both mainwheels on the deck, as a wheel under braking returning to earth would most likely suffer a burst tyre. Aileron trim could be used if necessary.

A normal stop could be made into 15 knots of wind in 2,700 feet (823m). With no wind as little as 2,200 feet (671m) was needed if the engine was throttled right back on touchdown. Drury Wood's advice to the pilot who found himself at an airfield where there was no runway into wind, nor one with less than a ninety-degree crosswind of fifteen knots was to 'land at another field'.

As a result of the somewhat tricky shore landing characteristics of the A-4, almost all export customers specified or added braking parachutes and spoilers, (as did the Marines to the A-4M). The exception was Australia, whose A-4Gs had no chutes until they were sold to and refurbished by New Zealand. Many foreign users did not have the luxury of multiple runways to choose from at even their biggest bases, so they needed some way of damping the Skyhawk's speed and anti-weathercocking tendencies on the runway, such as lift spoilers as fitted to A-4Fs and later models. If selected, the spoilers were armed in flight and actuated by a 'weight on wheels' switch when the main landing gear was compressed and power was below eighty per cent. Despite this, there were known incidents of the spoilers inadvertently deploying in flight. In such cases, the aircraft could be kept flying and landed with application of almost full power.

Carrier landings

Until the mid-1960s there were no two-seat high-performance jet trainer aircraft in the Navy, precluding the opportunity for advice and training from an instructor pilot. There were no landing simulators until the introduction of the Night Carrier Landing Trainer or NCLT in the late 1960s. 'With no two-seat aircraft and no NCLT, a pilot's first

Lieutenant John Hamilton RAN, one of many pilots to have flown 155069 over the years in its various guises as an A-4F, G or K, seems to be enjoying his work. in this photo taken circa 1979-81. Laurie Hillier

Sidewinders have long been part of the A-4's armoury. This is a dummy AIM-9P on an A-4SU Super Skyhawk. Author

look at a night carrier landing was the real thing. Many pilots did not survive the experience' says Pat Patrick. One or two pilots were killed on average during most carrier qualification periods.

Before NATOPS, some squadrons' SOP (standard operating procedure) was to land with airbrakes in and others with them out. The J65-engined A-4s had a 'flat spot' at about 85 per cent power where acceleration was poor. If the airbrakes were out and power was set at 85 per cent, retraction of the brakes gave much better acceleration. When NATOPS was introduced, it became standard practice that all Navy jets would land with brakes out, whether on land or at sea. Soon afterwards the J52, which had no flat spot, was introduced, but the procedure remained. Use of the brakes cost a little more fuel per landing pass but allowed quicker acceleration in a wave-off or bolter situation.

Fuel System

The fuel control system needed careful handling on the early Skyhawks. The test programme that preceded the A4D's introduction to service was perhaps not extensive enough in some aspects. Long periods at high altitude super-cooled the JP-4 fuel in the tanks. The fuel control could only process the cold fuel at about 3,000lb (1361kg) per hour, which was sufficient for cruising flight but not enough to maintain a steady

Carrying practice bomb carriers after a session on the range, an A-4K comes in to Ohakea for a touch-and-go landing in April 2000. Author

An AF-1 slams down on the deck of the São Paulo *and pulls the arresting wire taught. The long nosewheel strut absorbs most of the shock to the pilot.* Corné Rodenburg

glideslope in dirty configuration. The 'cure' was to use a burst of extra power on the downwind leg and if full thrust was not forthcoming, then shift to manual fuel control. On several occasions in the 1960 time frame, the fuel control 'hung up' at the critical moment just before a carrier landing, resulting in a 'floating on' to the very end of the deck or at worst, a gear-down water landing a few feet further back. The reason this had not been picked up in earlier testing was probably because of the introduction of new fuel filters and the switch to 300 gallon tanks, which exposed more fuel to supercooling than the earlier 150 gallon tanks.

Cockpit

The single-seat cockpit was cramped to say the least. Pilots actually wore out the shoulders of their flight suits against the cockpit sides and some put felt patches on their helmets to avoid damaging the canopy. Visibility forwards and to the sides was good and

The view from the back of a TA-4 as it approaches Oceana. Navy pilots treat every field landing as a carrier landing and the rate of descent on final approach is high to say the least, up to 700 feet per minute Author

likened to 'riding in a convertable car'. The view to the rear was poor, although the three mirrors on the canopy bow helped a little. The manoeuvrability of the A-4 allowed the pilot to check around him by doing a quick roll, but 'checking six' was always a problem. The raised seat and larger 'blown' canopy on the A-4M, N and KU helped visibility to the rear to a degree, as well as that over the nose.

The TA-4 pilot had no such problem. As one veteran attack pilot put it 'the two-seater cockpit is like a motel room' compared to the single-seater. The all-round view is far superior from both seats despite the central frame down the centreline.

Roll rate

One of the distinctive flight characteristics of the A-4 was its extremely high roll rate, often quoted as up to 720 degrees per second without external stores. Rate of roll with the stick full over was so high that most pilots found it impossible to perform an exact 360-degree revolution, usually overbanking slightly when levelling out. Putting the stick hard over for a break before landing would likewise give more than the 60-80 degrees desired. The flight manual prohibited more than five consecutive rolls, but most pilots tried five at least once.

Stall characteristics were benign, aided by the automatic leading-edge slats. At a speed about fifteen per cent above the stall, increasing buffet gave warning of its impending onset. The slats themselves could catch out an unwary pilot if they moved unevenly. Standard USN procedure is to make a slat check, which was a series of turns at different speeds before performing aerobatics or air combat manoeuvres to ensure symmetric slat operation. The pilot's checklist states why: 'Exceeding 21 units AoA with a stuck slat will cause an abrupt departure from controlled flight. Roll rates into the failed slat can be expected to exceed 140 degrees per second with adverse yaw…depending on altitude at onset of departure, recovery and/or safe ejection may not be possible.' For this reason, the 'Blue Angels' A-4Fs and some adversary A-4s had their slats bolted shut to prevent asymmetric operation, which could cause a fatal loss of control at low level or in a tight formation.

Speed

The Skyhawk was certainly subsonic in straight and level flight, the A-4F being limited to 675mph (1086km/h), but could achieve Mach 1.2 in a dive. The procedure was to climb to 45,000ft (13716m) and then push over into a 70-degree dive. By 30,000ft (9144m) the aircraft was supersonic, but it took a further 18,000ft (5486m) with a constant 120lb (54kg) stick force to recover without exceeding 1.8*g* on the way down. The recovery altitude was the limiting factor to the top speed, not any structural consideration. Test pilot Bob Rahn said that the pullout (in the A4D-1) felt like a cowboy going over a cliff on his horse, shouting 'Whoa, whoa you son of a gun!' Typical for transonic aircraft, mild pitch-up would be encountered as the A-4 decelerated between Mach 0.95 and 0.85 in the dive. The powered elevators on the A4D-2 and later models reduced the pullout force required.

In level flight a Skyhawk with the J52-P-408 engine could outrun an F-4 Phantom at low level if the F-4 stayed out of afterburner. The smokeless nature of the -P-408 also reduced the range at which the A-4 could be detected or tracked visually.

Strength

Ed Heinemann attributed some of the success of the A-4 to it having been built stronger than the Navy's specification. 'The Navy wanted a load factor of, I think 6.5 *g*'- I gave them 7.5' he told 'Flight International' magazine in 1979. 'The reason I did that was as it became overloaded, as they knew it would, it would still have enough strength'. One incident in the Skyhawk's early years illustrates the inherent strength of the design. In 1966 Walt Fink was assigned to 'the Navy's smallest squadron', a three-pilot detachment at NAS Atsugi, Japan, delivering repaired aircraft to the Philippines and returning battle damaged but flyable aircraft to Japan. On 5 March 1966, a BOAC Boeing 707 (G-APFE) flew into an extremely strong lee wave over Mt. Fuji, Japan. It was said that the pilot was trying to give his passengers a closer view of the mountain on a very clear day. Unfortunately the airliner was unable to handle the invisible, but terrifically violent airstream rolling over the mountain. A violent gust caused the tail fin to collapse, followed by the progressive disintegration of the rest of the airframe. Walt Fink takes up the story.

'I was scheduled to fly an A-4 test hop and right after take-off, Atsugi tower called to say they'd had a report of a plane crash seven miles south of the summit of Mt. Fuji, and asked if I'd check it out. I climbed up to altitude and headed west, and could see the plume of black smoke rising vertically, south of the mountain's summit well before I really got in the immediate vicinity. Once past the first range of hills/mountains, I started a descent to get a better look at the scene.

'I guess I was at about 2,500 feet above ground level (I emphasise I guess...the old memory dulls with age...but I recall that the radar altimeter had begun to unlock, which it did at that altitude) when Pow! that turbulence got me. The A-4 was really manoeuvrable, but this stuff rendered it (and me) relatively helpless. I can remember wiping out the whole cockpit with the stick just trying to get – and stay – right side up and the nose pointed more up than down. At six foot three, I didn't have a whole lot of room in the Scooter's cockpit anyhow, and was rapidly bangin' my head off the canopy from side to side. One fitting on my mask got jarred loose.

Eventually I exited the lee wave turbulence [at] about 11,000ft, I believe. The first thing I did was to check to see if the drop tanks were still hanging on the wings and the plane was OK. Everything appeared to be normal (except maybe my shorts) so I acted as a radio relay for the SAR helo from Atsugi. While orbiting overhead the scene, an F-105 came cruising by, having a look, and the helo came up on frequency saying he couldn't get into the scene either, because of the turbulence. The helo and I both returned to Atsugi for normal recoveries.

'The *g* meter registered something like plus ten and minus seven – or in that range – I forget exactly, and I wrote it up after landing. The ground inspection found nothing so the plane was returned to flying status'.

Of course the *g* forces in this incident were only transitory in nature rather than sustained. The danger to the A-4 was more that a corrective input could cause stresses which, when added to that turbulence would cause structural failure.

Walt concludes: 'My own opinion is that the A-4 is a pretty compact little beast and just plainly rode it out better than the 707, which got tossed around too but with its larger mass and inertia, couldn't ride with the punches. Stuff began to fail structurally with side loads the manufacturer never intended the bird to be subjected to'.

Skyhawk described

Over twenty-seven years of production and many in-service modifications, the Skyhawk remained recognisably the same aircraft from the prototype of 1954 to the last A-4M of 1979. This section describes the features common to all Skyhawks and some of the modifications that kept it a potent, if pocket-sized warplane throughout five decades of peace and war.

The A4D-1 set the pattern for the many models that followed and many of its features were common to all Skyhawks, but it had a few unique features compared to those that followed. A long instrumentation probe was faired into the otherwise blunt nosecone of the prototype, giving the suggestion of speed that the Skyhawk appearance otherwise lacked. The A4D-1 was well proportioned, certainly, but hardly sleek, especially with its stalky undercarriage and lumpish main landing gear doors down. The intakes were simple half-round shapes mounted midway up the fuselage behind the cockpit. The fuselage tapered towards a simple short exhaust at the base of the tail. The fin was connected to the upper fuselage by a long fillet, giving more than adequate keel area for stability.

Wing

The Skyhawk's wing differed little between versions and was a cropped delta featuring aerodynamically operated leading-edge slats. The upper wing skin was 0.064in (1.62-mm) thick and cut from a single sheet 28ft (12.7m) long by 186in (4.72m) wide and at the time the XA4D-1 was built was the largest thin-gauge sheet ever rolled. There were 55 oval inspection holes in the upper wing surface. Covered by fastened plates, in

An A-4G catches the fourth (of five) wires on HMAS Melbourne. *The RAN conducted cross-deck operations with HMS* Hermes *in 1968 and HMS* Eagle *in 1971 during which A-4Gs landed on the British carriers. Seen in the markings of VC724, this Skyhawk later became NZ6211 with the RNZAF.* Laurie Hillier

In clean configuration and with the big P408 engine, the A-4M and derivatives were highly manouevrable. Here an A-4AR cavorts for the camera on a pre-delivery test flight. Note the false canopy to confuse a dogfight opponent as to the aspect of the Skyhawk.

Denny Lombard, Lockheed Martin

This head-on view of an unpainted A-4AR emphasises the basically triangular fuselage cross-section of the Skyhawk and its minimal frontal area.
Denny Lombard, Lockheed Martin

forty-five degrees to it (five). On some early A4D-1s, vortex generators ran a short distance from the mid-wing up the mid-fuselage. The A4D-2 and subsequent models had a second row of twenty-two generators ahead of the ailerons. The outboard eleven ran towards the tip at an angle of about twelve degrees. These generators guided the airflow towards the aileron for greater control effectiveness.

Weapons stations amounted to a single centreline rack with a carrying ability of 3,575lb (1622kg) – the weight of the Mk 95 earth-penetrating nuclear bomb – and two wing pylons, each rated at 1,200lb (544kg) according to the aircraft manuals. This was the filled weight of the original 150 gallon fuel tank, and apparently the manuals were not changed to reflect the later 300 gallon tanks which weighed 2,239lb (1057kg) when full. The Bullpup 2 missile sometimes carried here weighed 2,345lb (1064kg). For the strike role, the Skyhawk would have carried the nuclear store on the centreline and two fuel tanks under the wings. For any sort of war mission, either wing or centreline tanks were necessary. The A4D-5 (A-4E) introduced two extra pylons, rated at nominally at 500lb (227kg) which were later retrofitted to some earlier export models such as Argentina's and Singapore's. On some of these, each outer pylon was rated at 1,000lb (454Kg). The actual weight of a Mk 82 '500lb' bomb with Snakeye fins was 565lb (256kg), and these were frequently carried on the outer pylons of A-4Es and Fs. Even a 'slick' Mk 82 weighed 530lb (240kg).

The airframe was mainly built from an aluminium alloy called Primary 70-75, or 7075-T6, a version of the common 75S alloy. Almost the whole airframe was fabricated from standard sheet, strip and extrusions, with very few forgings. One of the only forged pieces was the pivot point for the variable-incidence tailplane.

The centre wing spar and the front and rear spars (which formed the edges of the wing box) were made from 2 inch (5.8cm) thick alloy plate. The front spar was machined straight, but heated and bent to give the required thirty-five degree wing sweep.

The wing skin was stiffened with Z-section extrusions attached to the skin with NACA-type rivets for efficient sealing.

Photographs of operational A-4Ms with the laser spot tracker in the nose are comparatively rare. This VMA-211 aircraft was seen in 1989 and had received the ARBS fit sometime after late 1987.

Graham Robson

The wing box formed a fuel tank and so its sealing was critical. As rivets were added during construction, a miniature TV camera was used to check their seal. A sealing compound called PR-1422 was pumped in and heat cured, followed by a liquid soap compound. Pressurized air was used to create bubbles, which helped technicians to find leaks. The wing was taken to another site and 200 gallons (711 litres) more sealant was sloshed inside and the wing was rotated as if on a spit, ensuring an even coverage throughout. Leading edges and wing tips were attached to the wing box and did not contain fuel. The wing was attached to the main fuselage frames by ten steel tension bolts. These were located on the leading edge, front, intermediate and rear spars and the trailing edge channel section.

Tail

The horizontal stabiliser was swept at 33 degrees and combined an all-moving tailplane with conventional elevators. The electrically-operated stabiliser was the only powered control surface on the Skyhawk, except on the A4D-1, where it was manual.

The range of stabiliser trim movement on the A4D-1 was between twelve degrees nose up and one degree nose down. The actuator assembly was strengthened on the A4D-2 and movement range reduced from to eleven degrees up and one down. On the E, F, M and TA-4F/J, the range was adjusted again to give 12.25 degrees nose up and one degree down. The exception was the F model used by the 'Blue Angels' which was modified to have three degrees nose-down trim. Both fin and rudder had two spars. The upper tailplane skin was 0.125in (3.18mm) thickness and the lower was 0.160in (4.06mm). All control surfaces were constant chord

A close-up ot the refuelling probe of a VC-8 TA-4J. Although the 'cranked' probe was introduced in the 1960s, some A-4s retained the straight probe into the 2000s. Author

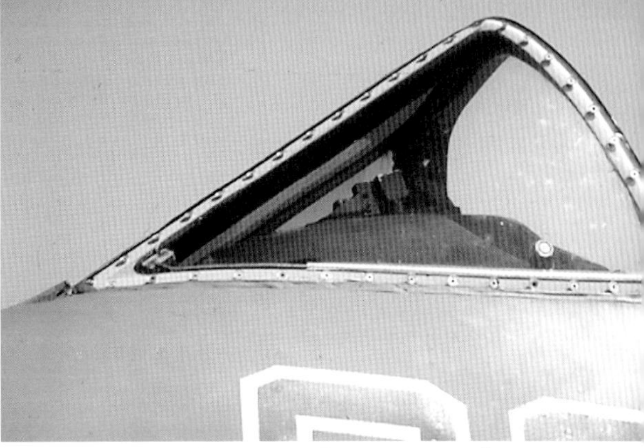

The TA-4SU windscreen (above left) retains the windscreen wiper found on the A-4C and many A-4Bs. The TA-4J (above right) had a square-framed central panel and side panels without external frames. Author

except the rudder, which tapered towards the top.

Putting it together

The Skyhawk had fewer than half the parts used in its predecessor, the AD Skyraider. Nevertheless, there were over 15,000 rivets in an A-4 and a late-model Skyhawk took nine months to build, coming together in the last three months at Palmdale from sub-assemblies built at Long Beach (wing and forward fuselage) and Tulsa (tail section and rear fuselage).

When the Skyhawk was designed, no self-starter for the engine was installed, being regarded as 'excess baggage' in the air by Heinemann's weight-obsessed design team. An external power source was required for engine starting on most A-4s. Douglas developed an ingenious portable air supply unit, designated the GTC-85 but universally known as the 'huffer'. The huffer was shaped like a miniature fuel tank and was capable of being carried on a pylon as an external store, giving the A-4 a self-deploying capability to bases and airports that didn't have compatible ground power units available. This capability was frequently used by the 'Blue Angels' in particular; who painted their huffers in team colours with numbers matched to each A-4. The huffer had recessed wheels for ground

The A-4M, N and KU had a larger canopy and windscreen than previous models, giving a superior view. McDonnell Douglas

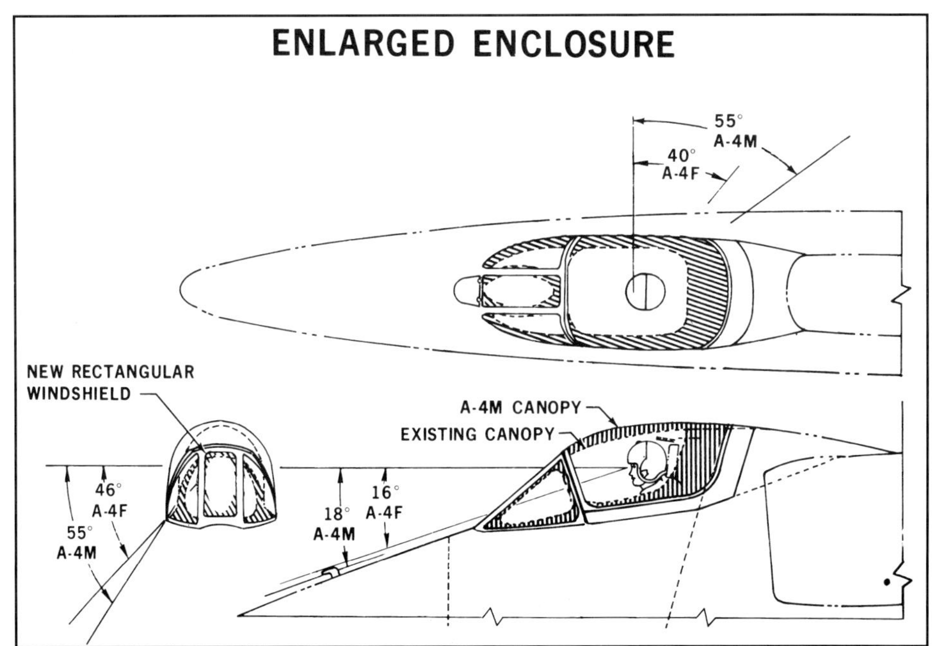

movement, which added little extra drag when carried externally. Only the A-4M and the related A-4KU and TA-4KU (later AF-1 and AF-1A) had self-starting capability. This was provided by a jet fuel starter (JFS), which exhausted from an outlet in the middle of the starboard fuselage side. This is a key recognition feature for the M and KU models, distinguishing them from the outwardly similar A-4N.

The square windscreen panel was introduced on the TA-4F and appeared on all factory-built two-seaters as well as the A-4M, N (seen here) and related models. Author

Cockpit

The instrument panel design of the A4D-1, –2 and –2N was an evenly-spaced collection of dials and gauges. On the early A4D-1, eight same-sized circular instruments displayed tailpipe temperature and RPM, Mach/airspeed, attitude, climb and dive rate, fuel quantity, gear and flap position, altitude, heading (compass), turn-and-bank, and rudder and elevator trim. A smaller *g*-meter and an eight-day clock flanked the bombsight. Addition of the low-altitude bombing system (LABS) and its controls on production A4D-1s saw the fire light and other warning captions moved from the top of the panel to the sides. Other instruments swapped position and changed in format during the production run of the A4D-1 and -2.

The engine gauge combined several functions in one. The left needle gave RPM and the right TPT (tail pipe temperature, also known as engine gas temperature or EGT). These were the only ones to show a continuous range of engine operation. Within this gauge were two 'flip-flop' type indicators; a fuel boost window that indicated only 'on' or 'off' and an oil indicator window that read 'Normal', 'High', 'Low', or 'Out'. There were no analogue oil pressure, oil quantity or fuel flow gauges. The only engine warning light in the A4D-1 read 'FIRE'. This light was frequently on in humid tropical conditions or in rain due to moisture in the system. Pilots would often cover it with tape to cut down

The rear seat in an ex-Israeli TA-4J. The yellow object in the centre of the headrest is the 'head-knocker' safety lever.

Author

the glare. A hydraulic system warning light was added on the A4D-2.

The A4D-1 and -2 had no low fuel warning light and a 'push-to-test' gauge system that required electrical power to work. If forgotten during the pre-flight checklist, and if the aircraft had not been refuelled between flights, a flame-out caused by fuel starvation might be the result. The gauge only measured internal fuel until the A-4C model introduced one that also allowed external fuel quantities to be tested.

The A-4C and subsequent versions had a radar altimeter as well as a standard pressure altimeter. The radar altimeter only worked between zero and 2,500 feet (762m) above ground level (AGL). Above 2,500 feet AGL the needle went behind a mask and stayed out of sight until the aircraft descended through that altitude again.

Angle of Attack (AOA) information on the A-4B and later models was presented by an indexer usually mounted on the left canopy bow and an indicator dial on the main panel. The indexer display consisted of three vertical lights. In the centre was a 'doughnut' or on-speed indicator; above it was a 'v' and below it a chevron (^). If the v or chevron was lit (in green) the AOA was too high or low, respectively. If lit up amber in conjunction with the doughnut, the aircraft was approaching or departing the correct condition. Input to the indexer was provided by a vane (also called a transducer) mounted below the cockpit on the port side of the fuselage. This airfoil-shaped device stayed 'pointed into the wind' while the wing AOA moved relative to it.

The A4D-1 had a very unreliable attitude-indicating gyro. It was so mistrusted that pilots flew at night with the cockpit lights as low as possible to improve the chances of being able to discern even a faint horizon. The gyro

This view of the front cockpit of a VC-8 TA-4J, shows the simple gunsight as used on most Skyhawks before the A-4M.

Author

The Kahu programme essentially squeezed the cockpit and avionics of the F-16 into the Skyhawk. The rear cockpit of the TA-4K (below) lacked the Ferranti 4510 wide-angle HUD but retained the two head-down displays and HoTaS controls of the single-seaters.

Author

was of the 'pull to cage' type and would often need resetting because of precession or because it just 'fell over'. This required lining the wings up with the horizon and pulling a knob to recage it. On a black night without the gyro, pilots had to fly a 'partial panel' approach using VSI, altimeter, heading indicator and airspeed, trusting that these added up to a wings-level approach. The A-4C added the much better AJB-3 attitude indicator and a radar altimeter, preventing many accidents.

The inadequacy of these instruments led to wholesale revision and replacement of the instrumentation on the A-4C, E and F models. The instrument panel underwent further revision on the A-4M and between early and late production examples of this model. Addition of a HUD saw the panel enlarged and an all-new weapons and ECM panel on the top portion flanking the HUD control unit.

Eection Seat

The original Douglas NAMC Type II ejection seat seat fitted to the A4D-1 and -2 had only eighty parts and weighed only 40lb (18kg). A contemporary North American Aviation seat had 240 parts and weighed 98lbs (44.5kg). Heinemann's design team had started from scratch and eliminated unnecessary features such as footrests. Lightness helped improve the seat's performance, although early models were not 'zero-zero' capable, being propelled by a 37mm cannon cartridge. Its only method of operation was by pulling on the face curtain handle above the pilot's head. This handle was broadly rectangular and smaller than on later seats.

The Douglas ESCAPAC-1 seat was fitted in the A-4C and retrofitted to many earlier aircraft. Generally similar to the NAMC seat, it had a broader headbox which contained a safety handle in the centre of the two-part headrest. This was known as the 'headknocker' because it stuck out when the seat was safe and bumped the back of the pilot's helmet. By reaching behind their head, and pulling the upper part of the lever forward, the pilot released the headknocker to swing upwards into the seat armed position. Most importantly, an alternate or secondary ejection handle was situated on the

The rear fuselage and original smooth-surfaced rudder of one of the first A4D-1s are seen here on the production line. Although the 'tadpole' rudder proved the solution for rudder 'buzz' problems, all production A4D-1s had the original design.

Douglas via 'Aeroplane'

lower part of the seat. This was introduced after it was realized that pilots were often unable to initiate ejection with the upper handle because of *g* forces or a need to keep a grip on the control column until the very last moment. The handles were usually rubber.

On the right-hand side of the lower part of the seat was the harness release handle, which was mounted within a metal guard. This handle disconnected the pilot from the seat if it did not happen automatically after ejection. A handle on the forward right side of the lower seat pack separated the pilot from the cushion, which contained the life-raft and survival kit. This unit dropped below the pilot as he descended and was retained by a long lanyard.

The 1G-3 version of the ESCAPAC seat used on the A-4F and later models had an 'earburner' rocket on the left side of the headrest. This was a small rocket that was angled at the top and which rotated the seat away from the pilot for seat-man separation. Earlier seats had bladders under the seatpan and behind the parachute to execute separation. A system called DART (Directional Automatic Realignment of Trajectory) on later seats was essentially a cable attached to the bottom of the seat, which stabilized its trajectory as it went up the rail. Zero-zero capability was given by the parachute ballistic spreader, a pyrotechnic device which lived within the chute, looked something like a hand grenade and worked like one during ejection. It had weights attached to the parachute that deployed the canopy even if there was no air flow to open it, as might be the case if the aircraft was stopped on the runway.

Variants of the ESCAPAC-1, with rocket assistance on later models, were used in all Skyhawks from the A-4C onwards and also in the A-7 Corsair II, B-57 Canberra, S-3 Viking, early A-10 Thunderbolts and F-15 Eagles as well as the earliest F-111s and the prototype F-16s. Thus the lightweight seat for the Skyhawk provided Douglas with an extra source of income for many years, even from the sales of its competitors' aircraft.

The integrated flight suit and harness as worn by early A-4D pilots incorporated the anti-g suit, parachute harness and survival vest. This allowed the parachute itself to be installed in the seat as the back cushion. Although this added slightly to the equipped weight of the aircraft it made the pilot's task in getting to, pre-flighting and climbing aboard his aircraft much simpler, particularly on a crowded carrier deck. The integrated harness concept was adopted for all USN tactical aircraft and later by the USAF for most of its jet aircraft, although the *g*-suit and survival vest/harness later became separate items.

Fuselage

The fuselage structure was conventional in comparison to that of the wing. There were ten fuselage frames and a nose bulkhead. The middle and strongest of the three main fuselage frames was inline with the middle spar of the wing. The engine was attached to this frame, which also mounted the attachment points for the rear fuselage. The keel began as a sheet metal angle in the cockpit area, changing to a channel extrusion up to the fuselage break point.

Heavier skins around the cockpit (up to 0.1in (2.5mm) thickness) provided ballistic protection for the pilot and obviated the need for space-consuming structural strengtheners, thus maximising internal volume for a minimum external shape. The A-4SU rebuild project in Singapore saw additional cockpit side protection added to those aircraft.

Skyhawk tails and their differences. Clockwise from top left: A-4N with square fin tip and 'Chavit' tailpipe extension, TA-4J with standard curved leading edge;A-4M with ALR 45 antenna and A-4K with square fin and ILS antenna. Author (3). Graham Robson, bottom right.

The cockpit floor was made of a 0.40in (10.1mm) web with 1in by 1in stiffeners. Under the cockpit floor was a depleted uranium (DU) bob weight, which was used to balance the elevator control system, providing 'feel' for the pilot and preventing overstress by too rapid an application of aft elevator. There was another weight (either DU or lead) fitted in the aft fuselage to maintain the centre of gravity.

From the A4D-5/A-4E onwards, a pair of gun gas deflector plates were added to the forward fuselage with one either side just below and ahead of the intakes. This prevented gas from the cannon entering the intake and causing a possible flame-out, and also

Skyhawk powerplants compared

Engine	Length	Diameter	Weight
J65-W-16A	121.9in (310cm)	37.5in (95.3cm)	2,750lb (1247kg)
J52-P6A	117.0in (297cm)	30in (76.2cm)	2,056lb (932kg)
J52-P408A	118.9in (302cm)	38in (96.5cm)	2,381lb (1080kg)
F404-100D	89.0in (226cm)	35in (88.9cm)	1,820lb (826kg)

Engine	Thrust	TtW	PR	SFC
J65-W-16A	7,700lb (35.71kN)	2.80 to 1	7.0:1	0.91lb/lbf/hr
J52-P6A	8,500lb (37.81kN)	4.13 to 1	13.0:1	0.79lb/lbf/hr
J52-P408A	11,200lb (49.82kN)	4.70 to 1	14.5:1	0.81lb/lbf/hr
F404-100D	11,000lb (48.93kN)	6.04 to 1	25.0:1	0.80lb/lbf/hr

TtW=Thrust to Weight
PR=Pressure Ratio
SFC=Specific Fuel Consumption.

preserved the pilot's night vision from the flash. The deflectors made useful steps for cockpit access, particularly when a ladder was not available. Singapore's A-4S and TA-4S models also received similar plates when they were upgraded to SU standard , although they differed in shape, having a curved leading edge. The starboard plate was mounted slightly above the refuelling probe, rather than directly on it as it was on US versions.

The intakes of the J52-engined models (and also the TA-4PTM) had a splitter plate and were stepped slightly outboard from the fuselage. The port intake had a small red light inset in its lip to illuminate the probe during night refuelling operations. The A-4M and other versions powered by the J52-P408, including the so-called A-4F 'Super Fox' had slightly enlarged intakes, although the difference in shape is quite subtle.

The aft fuselage was held on by only six bolts. Cannon plugs connected wiring bundles at the break point so that many systems could be disconnected with as little effort as possible. Quick disconnect fittings dealt with the control cables. The tail could

Accessibility of most important components was eased by the many access panels and the removeable rear fuselage as seen on this 'Avengers' A-4E.
Author's collection

An intimate view of the slats and their guides on an A-4N Author

be stored alongside the fuselage, minimising the deck space needed during maintenance. A reinforced section called a rebound strap protected the rear fuselage from the point of the tailhook. To keep the hook down, a hold-down cylinder of air (later nitrogen) compressed to 900psi was used.

Engines

Three different engines made the Skyhawk the success that it was. As related elsewhere, the Curtiss-Wright J65 was the only suitable engine available to Douglas in 1952, and the actual engines available were mostly Air Force surplus. Unlike some other contemporary designers, Ed Heinemann made provision for a 'growth engine' when he designed the A4D, and when the more powerful and lighter Pratt & Whitney J52 came along, it was a natural choice to power improved Skyhawk versions, although there was a false start with the unbuilt A4D-3 before it saw production use with the A4D-5/A-4E. The engine designations were assigned in numerical sequence separately by each service, so the Navy-sponsored J52 was in fact a later engine than the Air Force's J65, because there were fewer jets developed for naval use.

The Curtiss-Wright J65-W-16A was a turbojet with a thirteen-stage axial compressor, an annular combustor and a two-stage turbine. As well as the Skyhawk, the W-16A was used in the North American FJ-3 and -4 (F-1C/E) Fury fighters. Naval engines had even-numbered sub-type designations and Air Force ones were sequenced in odd numbers. The USAF often changed the sub-type depending on the aircraft to which it was fitted. The same engine was the W-3 when used in the USAF RF-84K Thunderflash, the W-5 in the B-57 and RB-57A, B, C, and E Canberra variants, and the W-7 in the F-84F and RF-84F. An afterburning J65 version was used as the W-18 in the Navy's Grumman F11F Tiger.

Due in part to their second-hand nature, the J65 gained a reputation for unreliability in the Skyhawk. In a 1957 letter to the CO of another A4D squadron, VA-72 skipper Commander Bob Hunt, under the heading 'J65 Precautions' wrote: 'On the J65 no precaution is too great'. Pre-oiling was essential, as was control of FOD (foreign object damage), by keeping ramp and runway areas clear of debris. After each flight the rundown time of the engine needed to be monitored for anomalies that might indicate an impending failure.

Pratt & Whitney J52

The J52 had its origins in the 7,850lb (34.9kN) thrust JT8A-1 civil turbojet, which was intended for the Douglas DC-9 and introduced in 1956. The USAF saw its high power and low weight had potential for use in the GAM-77/AGM-28 'Hound Dog' missile, designed for launch by the B-52 bomber. To this purpose it was militarized as the J52-P1 in 1958. As a missile motor, it required a working life of only fifty hours to

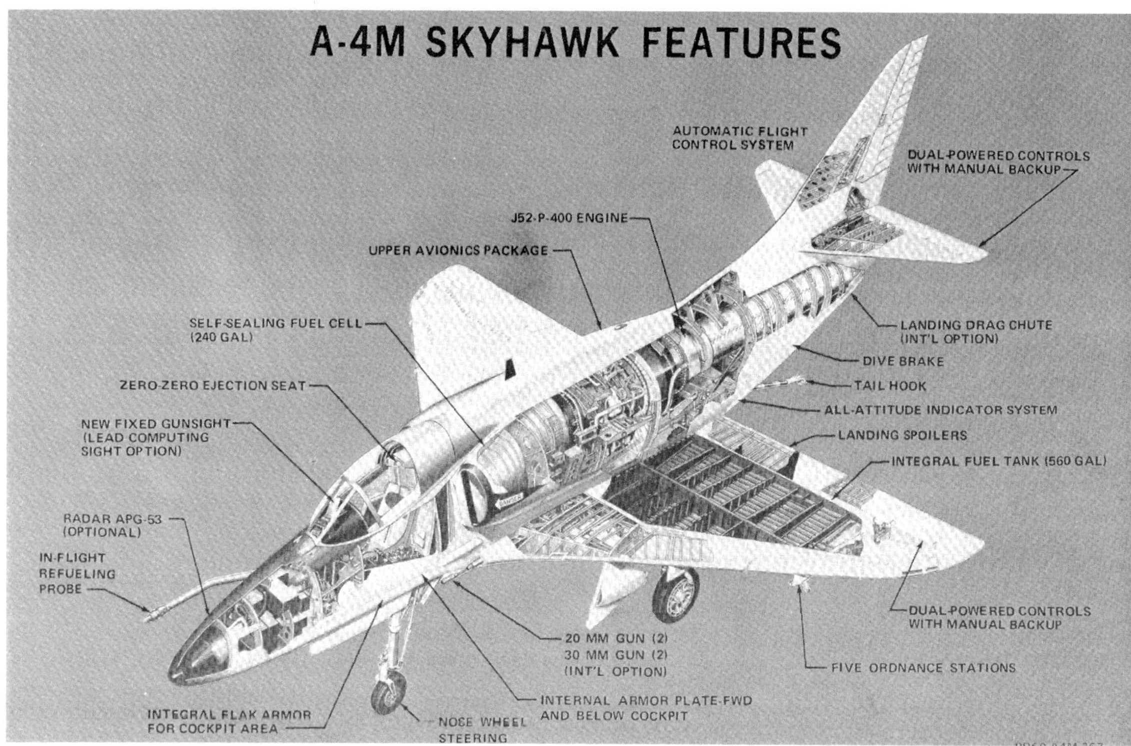

A cutaway of the A-4M shows the relevant features for potential export customers including the Pratt & Whitney J52-P-408 engine, referred to here as the 'P-400'. The J52 in different sub-variants powered 1,614 of the 2,960 Skyhawks or 55 per cent of new-built aircraft. McDonnell Douglas

include test running and a single one-way flight that would end in a nuclear fireball. This of course is not all that far removed from the Skyhawk's original mission.

In thirty-three years of production, more than 5,000 J52 engines were produced for the A-4, A-6 Intruder and EA-6B Prowler. The Prowler and the Skyhawk are the only aircraft still in service that use the J52.

F404 turbofan

The General Electric F404 has proved one of the most successful modern turbofans. In afterburning form, it is used in the F/A-18 Hornet and by several experimental aircraft, as well as in licence-built Volvo RM-12 form in the SAAB JAS 39 Gripen. A non-afterburning turbojet version powers the F-117 Nighthawk. The F404-GE-100D non-afterburning turbofan is only used in Singapore's Super Skyhawk. The F404 provides the Super Skyhawk with higher dash speed, better acceleration, improved turn performance and increased fuel efficiency.

The J65-W-16A's power-to-weight ratio was 2.80lb thrust per pound weight. In comparison it was 4.13 for the J52-P-6A. As well as being smaller and lighter, with ten per cent more thrust, the P&W engine had much better specific fuel consumption (SFC), as measured in thrust per weight of fuel used per operating hour. This is seen in the accompanying table. Oil consumption was far less for the J52 at 0.28lb (0.127kg) per hour versus 2.0lb (0.90kg) per hour for the J65. The air mass flow of each engine's compressor was the same, at 120lb (54kg) per second, but the J52-P6 had nearly twice

The automatic leading-edge slats were a feature of all Skyhawks except those few 'Blue Angels' and adversary A-4s which had them fixed shut. The slats greatly improved the low-speed handling and landing characteristics of the A-4. Accurate rigging of the slats was essential to prevent asymmetric operation and a possible departure from controlled flight. Author

the pressure ratio of the J65.

The two late-generation engines, the J52-P-408A/B (as used in the A-4M, N, KU, TA-4KU, the AF-1 and AF-1A, and some upgraded A-4Fs), and the General Electric F404-GE-100D of the A-4SU and TA-4SU bear a separate comparison. The -408A had a thrust-to-weight ratio of 4.83:1, and that of the F404-100D 6.04:1, with an airflow of 142lb (64kg) per second. The F404 turbofan has slightly lower thrust and very similar fuel consumption to the P408, but is 550lb (254kg) lighter.

The intake of the A-4N and other J52-P408-engined models was slightly widened, although the differences are subtle. The refuelling probe light can be seen on the lower left lip. Author

JATO system

All models of the A-4 from the C onwards had at least partial provisions for jet-assisted take-off or JATO. Full provisions included a firing button on the end of the catapult handgrip, two switches and a light on the flap control panel situated outboard of the throttle, three rocket attachment hooks (one thrust and two stabilisers) on the speedbrake, which had an interlock switch to prevent the brakes opening when the bottles were installed, and a hydraulic solenoid for jettisoning the empty bottles. Partial JATO provision, introduced during A-4E production, was just the installation of the basic wiring, allowing the rest of work to be completed with kits at squadron level. All A-4Ms were delivered with JATO provisions although it was little used after the early 1970s. The A-4 used a pair of Mk 7 Mod 0 rocket bottles, which weighed 200lbs (91kg) and were rated 5K4500, meaning they gave 4,500lbs (20kN) thrust for five seconds. When activated the JATO system gave double the thrust of the J52-P8 by itself.

Flight control system

The A4D as designed only had a single hydraulic system. After the loss of Jim Verdin in one of the YA4D-1s, a second hydraulic system was designed, and appeared during production of the A4D-2.

The hydraulics operated the landing gear, flaps, speedbrakes, wheel brakes, tailhook and the fuel jettison system. Warning lights would indicate loss of pressure in any of

In the confined space of a carrier deck, often massed manpower was needed to 'spot' an A-4.In September 1979 an A-4G was lost overboard from Melbourne *when the ship rolled unexpectedly while it was being manoeuvred with a tractor. The sailor working the brakes in the cockpit at the time was rescued.*
Author

these systems. If the hydraulics were damaged in combat, a mechanical system could be quickly engaged with a lever, although the control forces required became much greater. To overcome these, the joystick on the A-4A and B could be extended to give better leverage, but this feature was deleted from later models. The back-up manual system proved a life-saver to very many pilots in Vietnam, who were able to coax another hundred miles or more out of their crippled aircraft and reach the open sea where they stood a much greater chance of rescue. The undercarriage was lowered by releasing the mechanical uplocks and did not require hydraulics. Being forward retracting, the gear units would fall and lock into place with gravity and airflow pressure.

Unlike some contemporary combat aircraft, a two-speed rate of roll system was not installed. The ailerons were made large for good control authority at carrier approach

Where do we get such men? RAN maintenance troops take a break during an Integrated Air Defence System (IADS) exercise at Butterworth in Malaysia in late 1981.
Laurie Hillier

speeds but larger than needed for a bomber. Douglas decided to make the ailerons big and see how that worked in flight test. The result was very satisfactory and gave the Skyhawk excellent roll performance, which proved extremely useful as its role evolved to that of tactical bomber and fighter. The port aileron had a servo trim tab.

Electrical System

The engine powered a generator which was rated at 9KVA on the A-4A, B and C and 20 KVA on the A-4M. The Skyhawk had no battery, which was one of the first things omitted as part of Heinemann's weight saving drive. In the event of electrical failure (usually caused by failure of the engine's constant speed drive) a three-bladed Aeroproducts ram-air turbine (RAT) would drop from a hatch beside the starboard cannon muzzle to drive a 1.7kVA generator to provide electrical power. This was enough to power the flight instruments.

Refuelling

Most Skyhawks could be refuelled one of four ways. The exception were those aircraft (A-4As and some early A-4Bs) without IFR probes. The main wing tank could be gravity fuelled from a filler cap on the starboard wing, and also pressure refuelled through a receptacle behind the aft engine compartment hatch at the rear of the centre-section. 'Hot' refuelling on the ground could be achieved with the engine running and a fuel hose connected directly to the IFR probe. The height of the probe meant that the refueller needed to stand on a piece of ground support equipment to make the connection. The fuselage fuel tank (not found on two-seaters) had a filler cap behind the cockpit. The fuel system allowed up to thirty seconds of inverted flight, although 'Blue Angels' A-4s were modified to allow more prolonged inverted manoeuvres.

External fuel tanks were used during the vast majority of Skyhawk operations. The exceptions were mainly USMC use in Vietnam where the targets were often so close that all the pylons could be used for ordnance, and adversary missions, where the best air combat performance was achieved 'clean'. The initial fuel tank available for the A-4A/A4D-1 was of 150 gallon (534 litre) capacity, but this was replaced on the –2 by tanks containing

A worker at Lockheed Martin Aeronauticas Argentina, S.A. (LMAASA) connects a tailplane actuator during the rework programme that created the A-4AR Fightinghawk from the A-4M.
Lockheed Martin

The aft engine compartment (or 'hell-hole') contained a refuelling point at forward left. The access door mounted a bag for stowing landing gear safety pins. Author

300 gallons (1068 litres). The same tank could be used on the centreline station, but the tailcone with its horizontal fins needed to be removed to allow tailhook clearance. A 'bobtail' blunt tailcone could be fitted or no tailcone at all, exposing the rear pressure bulkhead of the fuel tank. A bobtail version of the 150-gallon tank was often used in later years and known as the 'peanut' tank. The later 400-gallon (1423-litre) fuel tank was shorter and had no fins. It could not be used on the wing pylons as it weighed 2000lb (1080kg) when full. It was also at the maximum moment for an

The buddy refuelling pod allowed the A-4 to top up most of the carrier's air wing and saved very many aircraft over the years. The receiver in this case appears to be an A-3 Skywarrior. via 'Aeroplane'

A-4G 877 saw the inside of many hangars in its long career. After combat in Vietnam with VA-155 it had at least two serious accidents with the US Navy and overturned on a wet runway shortly after transfer from the RAN to the RNZAF. Rebuilt to Kahu configuration, it is set to have a fourth career in civilian hands. Author

asymmetrical load, so if one tank failed to transfer, the excess weight compared to the other, emptying tank would make the aircraft impossible to handle, particularly on the approach. The same situation with the 300-gal tanks was 'a handful to land with' according to John Alger, an ex-Training Command instructor who once had to make such an asymmetric landing because of a forgotten rag jammed in the uptake, 'but it can be done – I'm still here!' he says.

An interesting characteristic of carrying three external fuel tanks, at least on the TA-4 with its reduced internal fuel capacity, was that during a longer flight their weight and to a lesser extent drag would cancel out the benefit of the extra fuel they carried. For this reason, TA-4s were rarely operated in 'triple bubble' configuration except when it was necessary to ferry the tanks themselves.

From the A4D-2/A-4B onwards, the Skyhawk was able to both receive and dispense fuel in the air. Receiver capability came through the fixed refuelling probe on the starboard side of the forward fuselage. Previous probe-and-drogue refuelling systems had generally relied on modified drop tanks (which could not transfer fuel to the main

A last-minute wheel change for a VC-8 Skyhawk before a mission in support of a carrier battle group's workups off the Virginia coast. The fuel tank is a 150-gallon 'peanut' tank. The big 400-gallon wing tanks were sometimes called 'Bob Marleys' Author

tanks), although some versions of a few earlier Navy aircraft (such as the F9F-8 Cougar) had fixed probes. In order to dispense fuel to other probe-equipped aircraft, a particularly important ability around the carrier when many aircraft were entering the pattern at once on return from a mission all short on gas, in 1955 Ed Heinemann developed the D-704 air refuelling store or 'buddy' tank. This was a modified Aero-1A series 300 gallon fuel tank shape with an airstream-driven propeller at the front. This powered a generator, which in turn supplied power to the hose reel within the pod, making the unit independent of the aircraft's own power. A governor controlled the precise blade angle and kept the RPM within a narrow range over a wide speed and altitude range. The generator extended the basket on a 43ft (13m) hose behind and below the tanker aircraft and retracted it when the receivers were done.

Although the amount of fuel available from an A-4 with a D-704 was not huge, a few hundred pounds of JP-4 could mean the difference between a safe trap and an ejection into the sea. Usually the available fuel was 1,300 US gallons (4,920 litres) if the A-4 was carrying two 300-gallon tanks. The A-4 tanker could offload about half of its total fuel load at a rate of 200 gallons (756 litres) per minute.

The buddy store was another of Ed Heinemann's lasting contributions to military aviation. It found wide application with other US naval aircraft such as the A-1, A-6, A-7 and S-3. British and Soviet manufacturers developed similar pods, allowing almost any tactical aircraft to act as a tanker, and most large tanker aircraft to increase their utility by simultaneous refuelling of multiple receivers.

Undercarriage

The stalky undercarriage and nose-up stance allowed the A-4 to land with an angle-of-attack 1.2 times the stalling value. One reason for the long legs was to give such a safe landing AOA with a delta wing. Other manufacturers such as Grumman were exploring swing-wings at the time to get around this problem.

The nosewheel strut varied considerably in length with the weight and centre of gravity of the aircraft and the fluid in the cylinder. In normal condition, the top of the canopy was 11ft (3.35m) above the deck and the tail was just under 15ft (4.57m) high. With the strut compressed, as under tension on the catapult with full fuel tanks, the nose dropped to 9.5ft (2.90m) and the tail rose to just over 16.5ft (5.03m). In this 'abnormal condition' as the manuals put it, ground clearance with a large store such as a buddy pod could be less than 10in (25.4cm). Many A-4s preserved in museums lose their nose-up stance, probably because of the draining of hydraulic fluid from the struts and the use of a short bracing clamp.

The nose leg was pre-shortened by a thin strut between the steering cylinder and well sidewall so as

A jacked-up TA-4 gives a good look at the jet pipe, 'sugar scoop' and other features such as the tailhook and liquid oxygen access bay to its left. Author

Details of the Skyhawk landing gear. Top left: the nosewheel leg of an A-4S shows details from its origins in the A-4B/C, including the carrier approach lights. Top right: the power steering unit on an A-4N nose leg. Up until A-4F production, the nosewheel castored freely. Bottom left: the mainwheel of a TA-4J with the later pattern hub. Bottom right: the mainwheel of a preserved A-4A shows the early pattern hub used on A-4As, Bs, Cs and at least some Es.

Author

to fit the wheel well as it retracted. Each main gear leg had a single Menasco strut, which rotated as the unit retracted forwards so the wheel could lie flat within the wells.

Cannon

Three types of cannon were fitted to Skyhawks over the years. All US and most export versions had the 20mm Colt Mk 12, which was a linear (rather than revolver) type gun also used on the F7U Crusader, F-8 Crusader and the A-7A and B Corsair II. Israeli Skyhawks (and those supplied by Israel to Indonesia) were fitted with the French 30mm DEFA 534 as used on the Mirage III and other French-built aircraft. Singapore's A-4S models were delivered with British 30mm ADEN cannons, but these were replaced by Mk 12s after refurbishment to A4S-1 standard. The basic specifications of these weapons are in the following table.

Colt Mk 12

As one former ordnanceman put it 'The Colt Mk 12 is a pneumatically charged, electrically fired, gas operated, bolt-action cannon and can deliver around 1,000 rounds of Mk100 series ammo per minute (in its dreams)'. The A-4A/B/C/E/ F and TA-4F/J used 100-round magazines with the ammo wound on a spool. The original can capacity was 100 rounds, but in reality would only hold ninety-five 'if you were lucky', and was often filled with only ninety rounds. Various 'shoehorn' ECM fits in Vietnam reduced the ammunition to as little as thirty-five rounds per gun. The A-4M, KU and TA-4KU used two layered magazines per gun (upper and lower) for a total of 200 rounds per gun.

Because of the narrow forward fuselage of the A-4, the cannons were staggered with the starboard one being mounted forward to allow the ammunition cans to be reached from the forward 'hell hole' access panel. Each can had an electric booster motor inside that would attempt to push the ammo down the feed chute and into the Mk 7 feed mechanism. The cannons were powered by compressed air, each using a bottle pressurized with 3,000psi of air. Nitrogen could also be used, and it gave a better seal and thus reliability. One of two regulators directed 1500psi to the charger that cocked the cannon.

The Mk 12 on most A-4s was charged before firing using switches on the weapons panel between the pilot's knees. On the A-4M this was done using push cubes at the upper left of the main instrument panel. The A-4M pilot could fire either the left or right gun one at a time, unlike earlier models.

The 'shoehorn' avionics modification reduced the ammunition capacity and required the ammunition to be loaded through a hatch normally used to access the LABS bombing system. Otherwise the belts were loaded from below. USMC

DEFA 534

The 30 MM DEFA 534 gun as fitted to Israeli A-4s from 1970 has a capacity of 125 rounds per gun and with a fire rate of 1,200 rounds per minute can put 8.1kg (17.8lb) of lead on target per second. The gun installation with 250 rounds of ammunition is 159kg (350lb) heavier than the MK 12 with 400 rounds. Indonesia's A-4Es and TA-4Hs also use this gun. Under project Halcón, begun in 1989, the Argentine Air Force fitted its surviving A-4Bs and Cs with the similar DEFA 553A-4 cannon.

Aden

The 30mm Aden Mk 4 cannon was widely used in various installations on British post-war aircraft from the Hunter to the Sea Harrier. It was a gas-operated single-barrel cannon derived from the wartime German Mauser MG213C revolver cannon. The Aden Mk 4 had a rate of fire of 1200 to 1400 rounds per minute and an effective range of 1510 metres. Singapore's early A-4S used the 30mm ADENs to simplify logistics as they were also used by the RSAF's Hunters. However the later A4S-1 and current A-4SU were refitted with the original Mk 12s.

Canopy and windscreens

The canopy on models up to the A-4E and F had fairly restricted rearward and downward vision, which was improved on the A-4M/N and KU as shown on an accompanying illustration. Malaysia's A-4PTMs also had a bulged canopy, but retained the original frame design. The rear canopy of the TA-4S/S-1/SU was also bulged to the sides. Most models had an oval central windscreen panel, but the TA-4F/J, A-4M and their derivatives had a windscreen with parallel frames.

Following several A-4 water landings, some of which the pilot did not escape, a pressure relief valve was added to the canopy to aid egress in a ditching situation. This valve allowed pressure to equalise as the aircraft sank so that the canopy could be released.

A single windscreen wiper, hinged at the lower right corner was fitted to many, but not all A-4Bs, and to Cs. On the E and later models, as well as factory-built two-seaters, this was replaced by an efficient air blower unit at the base of the windscreen. The A4D-1 had no rain removal equipment at all and flying into rain has been described as like driving a car in a thunderstorm with no wipers.

Radar

The A4D-2N (N standing for night) introduced radar in the form of a Stewart Warner AN/APG-53A set for terrain clearance and weapons aiming. The radar had quite a narrow beam and was of limited use in circumstances such as approaching a range of mountains. A crosswind (drift) component could cause the valley as displayed on the radar screen to become a peak by the time the A-4 arrived. The APG-53 was no use for

Skyhawk cannons compared

Type	Ammo size (weight)	Rate of fire	Muzzle velocity	Gun weight
Colt Mk 12 20mm	20 x 110mm (110g)	1000 rpm	1010fps (308m/s)	101lb (146kg)
DEFA 554 30mm	30 x 113mm (275g)	1800 rpm	820fps (250m/s)	176lb (80kg)
Aden Mk 4 30mm	30 x 113mm (220g)	1300 rpm	790fps (241m/s)	192lb (87kg)

Boots and all, an RNZAF airman buries himself in his work. Checking the health of the Constant Speed Drive (CSD) was an essential part of the pre-flight checks of the A-4. Robert Hewson

air-to-air combat, but did improve the bombing and navigation capabilities of the Skyhawk.

New Zealand's Kahu upgrade saw the installation of the F-16's Westinghouse APG-66 pulse Doppler X-Band multi-mode radar in a version designated APG-66(NZ). This had a cut-down dish to allow it to fit within the smaller radome of the A-4. An extra mode called the radar maritime target track mode enhanced the New Zealand Skyhawks' ability to detect and track surface targets for attack by AGM-65 Maverick missiles.

Both Argentina's A-4M (A-4AR) and OA-4M (TA-4AR) Skyhawks were modified with a downgraded version of the APG-66 with the local designation ARG-1. To fit the radar into the two-seater, a slightly enlarged nose cone needed to be designed. This features prominent lightning conductor strips along its length.

ECM

As built, the A-4A, B and C had no electronic counter-measures (ECM) or missile warning equipment. Ignorance certainly was bliss. In 1966, a programme was begun to fit ECM in the form of a ALQ-51 Deception Jammer and Track Breaker set in the A-4C. This was called the 'shoehorn' system, both because of the shape of the antennas under the wing roots and the need to squeeze the associated equipment into a very tight space. In some cases one cannon had to be removed altogether. There were four different shoehorn configurations, allowing space for one or two guns and as few as thirty-five rounds of ammunition per gun.

The A-4E had a little more room and was better able to accommodate the ALQ-51 as well as a rudimentary missile warning system. This gave an aural tone ('oodle, oodle, oodle') and a visual warning of a SAM launch in the form of a flashing red light marked 'SAM'. This was just about adequate in the days when there was only one type of SAM, the SA-2 'Guideline'. The nature of the particular threat – including gun-laying radars and later SAMs as they came along – could be determined with a practised ear depending on the sounds, particularly the raw pulse-repetition frequency (PRF) warble in the earphones.

ECM equipment fitted to many A-4Ms and retrofitted to some A-4Fs included the

Litton ALR-45 'Compass Tie' 2-18 GHz radar warning receiver, characterized by the 'hot dog' tailfin fairing, and the Raytheon ALR-50 Charger Blue L-band radar warning receiver, located in the avionics hump. The ALQ-162 Shadowbox/Compass Sail 6-8 and 10-20GHz continuous wave jammer was manufactured by Northrop for the A-4M. Infrared jammers included the Xerox ALQ-123 and the Sanders ALQ-132.

Maintaining the A-4

One reason for the Skyhawk's longevity was its comparative ease of maintenance. Generally speaking, the Skyhawk had its main systems well arranged for access. The tail section detached just aft of the main landing gear allowing access to most of the engine, while the forward fuselage and wing remained supported by the wheels. Other contemporary aircraft such as the F3H Demon required that the engine be slid out the back on a rail, a manoeuvre that was hard to accomplish on a crowded hangar deck, or on the flight deck without much of the engine protruding over the water.

The time to turn around a Skyhawk for another combat mission with a change of armament, refuelling, replenishment of oxygen and an external inspection was normally fifteen minutes. Under ideal conditions, with a crew of six personnel, this could be achieved in six minutes. The high position of the intakes allowed the crew to work around the aircraft with the engine idling with little danger.

The first J65-engined Skyhawks suffered from many troubles in early service, some of them because of the second-hand nature of the engines themselves. The J65 was also very noisy and 'sounded like it was coming unglued' much of the time remembers one pilot. A distinctive feature of the A-4A, B and C models was an oil breather outlet on the port fuselage side, which produced a dirty stain most of the time, defeating at least one effort at developing a high-altitude pale colour camouflage scheme. One pilot said the J65 was 'built around an oil leak'. This so-called 'total-loss' oil system consumed up to 0.4 gallons per hour, meaning the oil always had to be replenished after flight.

Otherwise the early A-4s were comparatively easy to maintain, with no folding wing joints to deal with, no nose wheel steering and no hydraulic accumulators to fret

To fit the nose of the RNZAF's Kahu Skyhawks, the dish of the APG-66 radar was cut down slightly. When the A-4 was developed, no radar of this power was available in compact size, but advances in electronics allowed New Zealand, Argentina (and probably in the future, Brazil) to give the Skyhawk a truly multi-role combat capability. Author

Splitting the fuselage allowed full access to the engine of the Skyhawk, as seen on this A-4K. The troublesome CSD was mounted on the forebody protruding from the front of the engine, covered here by a protective plate.. Author

with since they had a manual flight control system as backup if the primary system failed.

On the J52 engined Skyhawks, the most common maintenance headaches were caused by the constant speed drive or CSD, which was mounted between the engine and the generator, and which kept the generator at a constant speed, regardless of engine RPM. One 1970s Training Command pilot said that 'we went through them like Rolaids in Tijuana!'. Tom Bass, an engine mechanic on TA-4Js in the 1980s recalls that if a CSD lasted the first flight after being changed then most of the time it would last until its high time mark, but 'changing the CSD was a pain. If you had a small person to do it, then it wasn't too bad, but for a 6ft, 190lb man it was a pain'. G. C. Floyd, a very experienced A-4 mechanic adds: 'I suppose the most aggravating thing for the mechs was changing a CSD. You needed four arms...each six feet long and with two elbows'. Even if the ideal Skyhawk engine technician was a genetically-modified chimpanzee, normal men and women worked regular miracles to keep thousands of Skyhawks airworthy during the past half century.

The RNZAF replaced the original CSD with a Bendix Variable Speed Constant Frequency Generator (VSCFG) in the 1980s. This was more reliable, but even then rarely got more than 200 hours between failures, often averaging more like 50. RNZAF mechanic Les Stockley says that 'VSCFG failures were still happening in the RNZAF right to the end, they were the real weak point of the system'. When the CSD/VSCFG failed, thus cutting out the generator, a ram air turbine (RAT) dropped down into the airflow to provide power. 'In RNZAF service the RAT got lots of air time, so much so that we started recording their flight hours as we were wearing out the bearings in them!'

says engineer Don Simms.

Even with the odd serious failure, the Skyhawk would usually come home. In May 1980 a VT-25 TA-4J 'squirted out' its tailpipe on a low-level training flight west of San Antonio. The aircraft aborted the sortie and flew back to Chase Field near Beeville. The crew thought that they had only lost power on the engine. McDonnell Douglas said it should not have been able to generate enough thrust without the tailpipe to stay airborne, but they flew it back over one hundred miles. Heat had charred the paint aft of the wing, but the aircraft was repairable and served a further two decades.

As T E Bass said 'don't get me wrong though, the Skyhawk for it's age was a very good bird. I would never trade my time spent working on the Skyhawk and will always look back fondly on her'.

In common with other USN aircraft, the Skyhawk was designed for a three-level maintenance programme – unit, intermediate and depot. The highest degree of maintenance was Standard Depot Level Maintenance (SDLM, usually said as 'sidlim'), which was scheduled approximately every thirty-nine months.

Maintaining the cannon

The 20mm cannon used on most models of Skyhawk developed something of a reputation for poor reliability, a factor behind the rearming of all Israeli and some Argentine and Singaporean A-4s with 30mm weapons.

Marine armourer Dick Goldsberry remembers: 'The Mk 12 cannon didn't jam as much as it ran out of compressed air or had feeding problems. As with most automatic weapons, the feed mechanism is the weak spot, be it clips, magazines, or compressed air systems as the A-4 had. To narrow it down even further, it was the O-rings inside the Mk 7 feed mechanism that failed at a high rate, and the worst one was the 'T' O-ring on the valve stem. The Mk-12 cannon is a fine gun, it was the compressed air and feeding system that was weak. In the A-4 you really had to work at getting the whole gun system to function correctly. Every ordnance shop I was ever in had a designated 'gun crew".

'The RNZAF A-4 gun system had the same problems' recalls Des Sullivan. 'We used compressed nitrogen in our system. In an attempt to alleviate these problems the aircraft would not launch on a gunnery sortie with less than – from memory – 2000 psi of nitrogen in the reservoir. When we were not flying gunnery sorties a minimum pressure of 1200 – 1500 psi was maintained in the reservoir so that pressure was maintained on the O-rings. These measures provided some degree of success. The RNZAF also removed the spool from the magazine and layered the ammo belts in the magazines because we found that with the spool in place the ammo belts could twist in the magazine and cause a jam if the belts had insufficient tension or the pilot threw the aircraft around too much. I think we did refit some of the spools for air to air gunnery. The best stoppage rate that I can remember the RNZAF achieving was just over 4000 rounds fired from all aircraft without a single stoppage. This was in the early '80s and was quite an achievement at the time. From memory our cannons had to achieve a rate of fire of between 900 and 1100 rounds per minute during a post service butt test before they were released for fitment to an aircraft. If the rate of fire was outside these limits the weapon was returned to the servicing bay, 'tweaked', and retested'.'

A hand-held GPS unit mounted on the windscreen bow on this VC-8 TA-4J replaced several previous generations of navigation equipment. The Skyhawk pre-dated the first satellites by several years. Author

Maintenance challenges

Space precludes discussion of every system or component that presented a maintenance challenge over the years, but some examples from the first and last days of the Skyhawk may be of interest.

In March 1965, the US Navy was asked by the State Department's Director of Military Assistance to review its ability to provide initial and follow-on support for A-4A or B aircraft that might be supplied to 'various Latin American countries'. The A-4A by this time had gone from the inventory and the A-4B was being phased out as Vietnam operations increased. In recommending that the A-4A was unsuitable for supply to Latin America, the Deputy Chief of Naval Operations (DCNO) pointed out how the inventory of parts, particularly those unique to the A-4A was diminishing. He cited A-4A landing gear struts, of which eighty-four were required in the last year of operations with this version, and of which only eleven remained in store. A-4B parts that were in short supply, despite increased production, included the windshield, of which there were eighteen on hand and ninety-seven used in the previous year, bomb racks (three available and twenty-four used) and rudder assemblies, of which there were only four in the supply system but of which a staggering 299 had been expended. It is likely that some of these parts which were common to the A-4C and E had been needed to replace items on these models damaged in combat as well as for the few Bs in Vietnam. The A-4B was in fact supplied to Argentina from 1966, after refurbishment by Douglas' Tulsa plant. Presumably the manufacturer supplied many spare parts from its own inventory.

The last Skyhawk squadron in the US Navy service, VC-8 'Redtails' had its share of parts difficulties as the Skyhawk retired from Training Command and the spares inventory was wound down. One hard-to-get component was the aft engine access hatch. 'Redtails' maintenance crews on detachments to the mainland USA became adept at liberating items such as this 'hell hole' hatch from preserved aircraft or 'stick birds' on various bases. The original Douglas navigation package for the Skyhawk, a model of compactness for the 1950s was long gone, as were most of its successors. By the late 1990s VC-8 was relying largely on commercial Global Positioning System (GPS) satellite navigation units as used by private pilots. These $400 units were the most modern and sophisticated pieces of equipment in the last US military Skyhawks.

Private company Advanced Training Services International (ATSI) has brought the A-4 back to US skies in significant numbers. Two of ATSI's three TA-4Js are seen here at Pt. Mugu, California in August 2001.

CHAPTER EIGHT

Skyhawk Today – A-4s Forever

The military career of the Skyhawk still has some years to run, even though the basic design is a half-century-old and it is twenty-five years since the last A-4 rolled off the production line. Four nations still maintain the Skyhawk in their inventories in 2004, and it is not impossible that others will acquire surplus aircraft in the future. Increasing use of private contractors for military support tasks has seen a new lease of life for many Skyhawks, which offer high performance, relatively low running and maintenance costs and the ability to carry a wide range of external stores. One contractor is building up a fleet that will be larger than those of the four smallest export users. A small but growing number of Skyhawks have joined the US civil register as privately owned warbirds.

A-4s Forever

Argentina has confirmed the old maxim about another Douglas product, the immortal DC-3, proving that the only replacement for an A-4 is another A-4. When the fiftieth anniversary of the A-4 was celebrated in June 2004, a significant number of Skyhawks and Skyhawk pilots were still flying to mark the occasion.

Australia, Malaysia, Kuwait and New Zealand no longer operate A-4s. Australia's A-4Gs were passed to the RNZAF in 1984 and were used in New Zealand and at Nowra in Australia until 2001 when the New Zealand government disbanded the RNZAF's combat arm. The seventeen remaining A-4Ks and TA-4Ks are currently in storage at Ohakea awaiting delivery to a buyer.

Malaysia retired it's A-4PTMs in the mid-1990s and most are in open storage at Kuantan. Deterioration caused by the humid conditions mean that they are unlikely to be flown again. The additional aircraft procured by Malaysia and stored in Arizona have been put on the civil register, but seemed no more likely to fly until early 2004 when thirty-five were re-registered to companies in several US states, including one already operating tactical jets.

Singapore still operates up to seventy A-4S and TA-4S models with two squadrons in Singapore itself (Nos. 142 'Gryphon' and 145 'Hornet' Squadrons at Tengah) and an advanced jet training (AJT) detachment (No. 150 'Falcon' Squadron) at Cazaux in south-west France. The RSAF was expected decide on a replacement aircraft type in 2004.

Israel's remaining Skyhawks, all A-4Ns and TA-4Hs, plus a few TA-4Js supplied in the 1990s, serve with training and reserve units. Despite the large numbers of F-16 and F-15I bombers in IDF/AF service, the A-4s, flown by experienced instructor pilots and reservists would have a combat role in the event of a major conflict involving Israel. The Ayit will be replaced by the F-16I Sufa which began to enter service in 2004.

Indonesia's A-4s were largely supplanted by the BAe Hawk and the F-16 by 2003,

Many Skyhawks are stored at AMARC and elsewhere. This worn A-4A has been at China Lake since 1968.
Graham Robson

with small numbers in service with SkU.11 at Hasanuddin. The arrival of the first Sukhoi Flanker (of a rather eccentric initial purchase of two Su-27s and two Su-30s) in 2003 wearing SkU.11 markings spelt the end for the TNI-AU Skyhawks.

After years of efforts to get sanctions lifted, Argentina was allowed to purchase thirty-two surplus A-4Ms and four OA-4Ms in 1994, plus a further fifteen aircraft (eleven A-4Ms and four OA-4Ms) for spare parts recovery. Upgraded with a version of the APG-66 radar designated ARG-1, the aircraft are known as A-4AR and TA-4R Fightinghawks.

In 1997, the Brazilian navy (Marinha do Brasil) became the newest member of the

ATSI currently has eleven A-4N and TA-4J Skyhawks based in the US, one on lease in France and may acquire more in the future.
Graham Robson

Skyhawk club when they negotiated the purchase of twenty-three of the Kuwaiti aircraft. Delivered the following year, they became operational in 2001 aboard the Marinha's 'new' aircraft carrier, the São Paulo, formerly the French navy's Foch. In Brazilian service the A-4KU is known as the AF-1 and the TA-4KU as the AF-1A, and they serve with squadron VF-1 in the fighter role armed with four AIM-9 Sidewinders.

Further Skyhawk exports are still possible. The RNZAF aircraft were actively marketed to South-east Asian nations, some of whom (notably the Philippines) were said to have definitely been interested in their purchase. There was a plan to transfer some of Kuwait's A-4KUs to Bosnia, and another to supply six TA-4s (and six Sea King helicopters) to El Salvador. Salvadorian personnel were rumoured to have been undergoing training in Israel, but nothing appears to have come of such a proposal. Uruguay remains a possible customer when they can sort out their budget difficulties.

N260WL was one of ATSI's first A-4Ns. In a previous life it was IDF 322 with No. 116 Squadron.

Author

BAE Systems Flight Systems and Advanced Training Systems International (ATSI) are commercial firms that have each acquired former Israeli A-4s to offer a variety of services to military customers. Other contractors may purchase A-4s in the future. US law prohibits the sale of surplus military aircraft to private individuals, but permits the same type of aircraft to be imported from foreign surplus stocks.

The four BAE A-4Ns were delivered from Israel to Wittmund in September and November 2001 via a roundabout route. In order to receive FAA certification as civil aircraft, the A-4s had to 'set foot' on US soil, in this case Bangor, Maine. This required a transatlantic flight in each direction for each of two pairs of A-4s. The Skyhawks replaced F-100F Super Sabres as target tugs, towing the TDU-10 Dart target on gunnery training missions for Luftwaffe Phantoms, Tornadoes and 'Fulcrums'. Two or three times a year the A-4s travel to Decimomannu, Sardinia to take advantage of the good weather and the extensive instrumented air combat training ranges. Once the dart target has been shot away, the A-4s often take the opportunity to show why they have long been used for air combat training and in the fighter role by many air forces, by picking a fight with the Luftwaffe and engaging in some good old fashioned visual dogfighting.

ATSI

One of the largest private owners of tactical jet aircraft is Advanced Training Services International, based at Williams Gateway Airport (the former Williams AFB) near Phoenix, Arizona. The company is the brainchild of former Navy Captain Larry G

BAE Systems' A-4N N437FS was at one time IDF 432, delivered in November 1973. It no doubt saw action with No. 140 Squadron. Today its 'warload' is the TDU-10 dart target.

'Hoss' Pearson, who among other things, was the leader of the 'Blue Angels' demonstration team in 1985-6 when the team flew the A-4F. ATSI, which was founded in 1993 has been involved in some A-4 upgrading work in conjunction with Safe Air Engineering in New Zealand, but their main business is to operate a fleet of ex-Israeli Skyhawks on contract work for the US military and other agencies and to offer training to pilots of friendly foreign nations. In the past the US forces trained most of the air and ground crews for the aircraft America sold to its allies, but the increasingly stretched military needs to reserve most of its training capacity for its own personnel, leaving a gap for the commercial sector to step in.

US Federal laws forbid the sale of tactical jets to civilian operators, so to acquire suitable aircraft, ATSI looked farther afield to Israel, where large numbers of surplus A-4s were stored. A problem was that only three of the more useful two-seat TA-4Js were available, and to get all of those, ATSI had to buy ten single-seat A-4Ns.

The particular TA-4Js available had not flown at all since they were delivered to Israel in 1994 as part of a compensation package for staying out of the 1991 Gulf War. One of the 'T-birds' had in fact been on outdoor display at the Hatzerim base museum with a blue-tinted canopy. To bring these A-4s up to airworthy status, ATSI asked both Safe Air and Israel Aircraft Industries (IAI) to bid for the work. The Israelis were only prepared to restore the aircraft to IAF standards, whereas Safe Air was happy to work to USN standards as ATSI demanded. Additionally, they were cheaper, even taking into account the need to transport and house a team of engineers in Israel. From January 2001, the Safe team systematically stripped down, inspected and repaired the thirteen aircraft. On completion all but the last three aircraft, which were painted in a tactical grey colour scheme, were resprayed locally in the standard four-tone scheme of IAF Skyhawks. A series of ferry flights via Greenland or the Azores saw the aircraft delivered from the Israeli desert to the Arizona desert during 2001 and 2002. One of the earliest tasks for an ATSI A-4N was to portray an IAF Skyhawk in the film 'Sum of All Fears'; other work has included support of US Navy Joint Task Force Exercises (JTFX) and the 'Big Crow' electronic warfare programme for the Army. ATSI is reportedly providing training for United Arab Emirates pilots destined to fly the sophisticated F-16 Block 60. Sadly, one ATSI A-4N was lost with its pilot in Utah in May 2003 en route to support exercises in Canada.

Hoss Pearson has talked of acquiring up to forty aircraft, not necessarily all A-4s, for contract work, and may base some in a variety of locations for support of US and NATO training. ATSI has negotiated the purchase of the seventeen ex-RNZAF aircraft. At time of writing the sale had not gone through, reportedly held up by delays in getting US State Department approval.

One ATSI A-4N was leased to the French company AVDEF at Nîmes-Garons in southern France in late 2003 and placed on the French civil register. AVDEF operate a fleet of Mystère business jets on target facilities missions under contract to the French Navy. A former Aéronavale pilot flies the Skyhawk, which may be joined by another in the future.

Although the 'official retirement ceremony' for the US Navy A-4 was held at Pensacola, Florida in June 1999, one squadron continued to operate a half-dozen Skyhawks for a further four years. Fleet Composite Squadron Eight (VC-8) at NS Roosevelt Roads, Puerto Rico flew a mixed complement of TA-4Js and UH-3H Sea

A pair of BAE Systems' A-4Ns await a morning target towing mission at 'Deci', Sardinia. The A-37U tow reel pod is mounted on the port outboard pylon of the near aircraft and on the centreline of its partner.
Author

Kings until the squadron was disestablished in 2003. Four of the six Skyhawks were delivered to museums and two were put into desert storage alongside many others retired a decade or more earlier.

AMARC

Surplus US Skyhawks have been stored in the Arizona desert since the early 1960s at least. The Navy had its own storage facility at NAF (Naval Aviation Facility) Lichfield Park near Phoenix until it closed in 1967. From then on the Navy shared the Military Aircraft Storage and Disposal Center (MASDC) at Davis-Monthan AFB near Tucson with the other services. In 1985 MASDC was renamed the Aerospace Maintenance and Regeneration Center (AMARC). Over the years most of the A-4s that survived Navy service passed through either Litchfield Park or Davis-Monthan before sale to a foreign customer, reissuing to another unit (sometimes for spare parts use) or preservation.

The most recent available count of Skyhawks stored at AMARC lists four A-4Bs, nine A-4Es, twenty-two A-4Fs, fifty-three A-4Ms, eleven TA-4Fs and 166 TA-4Js for a total of 215 aircraft. The situation at AMARC is fluid – surplus A-4s are still available for export to friendly nations, such as the A-4Ms and OA-4Ms supplied to Argentina in the late 1990s. They are also available to US agencies. In 2001 four TA-4Js were transferred to the US Army for a currently unknown use associated with the 'Big Crow' electronic warfare programme. At least one has turned up with ATSI as a parts source. Others were delivered to VC-8 in Puerto Rico for spares recovery.

The latest and almost certainly last Skyhawks to arrive at AMARC were two VC-8 TA-4Js, BuNos 153486 and 153526, which arrived on 24 April 2003. One of the most recent to leave was 153524, released to the Collings Foundation in October 2001 to eventually join their Vietnam Memorial Flight. US military aircraft are not usually available for transfer to civilians, but in this case an act of Congress was passed as part of the Defense Authorization Act of 2001 to release one TA-4J aircraft for flight preservation to the Collings Foundation, a private group which operates a range of American ex-military aircraft from the B-17 to the F-4 Phantom. The Collings TA-4 was

This A-4B flew as N21NB in pseudo RAN colours from 1988. It suffered a landing accident in February 1998. Since then it has been restored for display at the Kalamazoo Air Zoo, Michigan. Graham Robson

Leading this lineup of VT-86 Scooters in June 1985 is 156925, later to become N75051J with Aeronautics Unlimited and (2004) with Airborne Tactical Advantage Co (ATAC). Author's collection

built as a TA-4F in 1968 and began its career with the Marines, later spending many years on test duties with the NATC at Patuxent River. The intention is to operate it in the markings of a TA-4F serving with H&MS-11 'Playboys' in Vietnam.

A number of other A-4s have been on the civil register at different times. The ability to some extent to 'mix and match' Skyhawk wings, tails and forward fuselages makes identifying the actual former identity of privately owned A-4s less than an exact science. Two A-4Bs were bailed back to McDonnell Douglas at Long Beach in the mid-1970s, apparently in conjunction with DC-10 testing. Flight Systems at Mojave operated two A-4Cs and an A-4L on contract work in that company's familiar white and blue colours. All three are now in museums, one masquerading as an A-4K in the RNZAF Museum. An A-4A was restored to flight, probably from parts, in 1986 but crashed the following year during filming of a car commercial. A couple of TA-4Js somehow found their way into private hands in the 1980s and have changed hands a few times. Air Capitol Warbirds in Wichita, Kansas have several airframes under restoration. Two TA-4Js have been registered and other Skyhawks in their workshop include an A-4A. An A-4B was flown for several years in pseudo RAN colours before suffering a landing accident. It is now being restored to static display condition at Kalamazoo, Michigan. The Combat Jets Flying Museum flew an A-4B from 1989 to 1992 in the colours of TR Swartz's MiG-killing A-4C, but this was retired to the Experimental Aviation Association's museum at Oshkosh. Jim Ritchie in Houston, Texas is working on an ex-Argentine Navy A-4Q, and no doubt other as yet unregistered projects will emerge in the future.

Thirty-four of the A-4Cs and Ls purchased by Malaysia, ostensibly for spare parts were reported to still be stored at the Dross Metals (DMI) scrapyard on the fringes of Davis-Monthan AFB in 2000. These aircraft have received US civil registrations ending in 'AT' as has one other not associated with the Malaysian purchase. In early 2004 the registrations of these aircraft were transferred from Aviation Technologies, a company registered in Sparks, Nevada to several other firms, including one based at the former NAS Cecil in Florida (eleven aircraft); one in Oregon (fourteen); an individual in Texas (two); another individual in Arizona (two); and six to the Airborne Tactical Advantage Company (ATAC) at Newport News, Virginia. ATAC already operate IAI Kfirs and Saab Drakens on contract work and has also acquired a TA-4J that has been registered for

A-4s on civil register 2004

Reg'n	BuNo	C/n	Model	Previous	Owner
N524CF	153524	13590	TA-4J		Collings Foundation
N82079	144989	12235	A-4Q	CANA 0662	Jim Ritchie, Houston, TX
N2262Z	145131	12377	A-4C		Donald Rounds, Manchester, TN.
N142AT	147671	12435	A-4C		Ace Aerospace, Jacksonville, FL
N144AT	147696	12460	A-4C		Ace Aerospace, Jacksonville, FL
N145AT	147754	12518	A-4L		Ace Aerospace, Jacksonville, FL
N153AT	147815	12579	A-4L		Ace Aerospace, Jacksonville, FL
N159AT	148500	12693	A-4C		Ace Aerospace, Jacksonville, FL
N204AT	148509	12702	A-4C		Ace Aerospace, Jacksonville, FL
N214AT	148597	12790	A-4C		Ace Aerospace, Jacksonville, FL
N224AT	149550	12875	A-4C		Ace Aerospace, Jacksonville, FL
N227AT	149581	12906	A-4C		Ace Aerospace, Jacksonville, FL
N229AT	149595	12920	A-4L		Ace Aerospace, Jacksonville, FL
N230AT	149636	12961	A-4C		Ace Aerospace, Jacksonville, FL
N128TA	158128	14165	TA-4J	N3203Z	Aero Group, Melbourne, FL
N7050J	158481	14286	TA-4J		Air Capitol Warbirds
N132AT	145128	12374	A-4L		ATAC, Newport News, VA
N143AT	147690	12454	A-4L		ATAC, Newport News, VA
N146AT	147761	12525	A-4L		ATAC, Newport News, VA
N147AT	147768	12532	A-4L		ATAC, Newport News, VA
N154AT	147836	12600	A-4L		ATAC, Newport News, VA
N207AT	148581	12774	A-4C		ATAC, Newport News, VA
N7051J	156925	14018	TA-4J		ATAC, Newport News, VA
N250WL	152853	13499	TA-4J	IDF 748	ATSI, Phoenix, AZ
N251WL	153500	13566	TA-4J	IDF 747	ATSI, Phoenix, AZ
N252WL	153672	13610	TA-4J	IDF 749	ATSI, Phoenix, AZ
N260WL	158730	14349	A-4N	IDF 321	ATSI, Phoenix, AZ
N261WL	159533	14453	A-4N	IDF 413	ATSI, Phoenix, AZ
N262WL	159545	14465	A-4N	IDF	ATSI, Phoenix, AZ
N264WL	159823	14522	A-4N	IDF	ATSI, Phoenix, AZ
N265WL	159544	14464	A-4N	IDF	ATSI, Phoenix, AZ
N266WL	159534	14454	A-4N	IDF	ATSI, Phoenix, AZ
N267WL	159051	14379	A-4N	IDF	ATSI, Phoenix, AZ
N268WL	159530	14450	A-4N	IDF	ATSI, Phoenix, AZ
N234LT	158141	14178	TA-4J		Aviation Enterprises, West Columbia, SC
N431FS	159805	14504	A-4N	IDF 335	BAE Systems, Germany
N432FS	159542	14462	A-4N	IDF 432	BAE Systems, Germany
N434FS	159815	14514	A-4N	IDF 373	BAE Systems, Germany
N437FS	159078	14384	A-4N	IDF 432	BAE Systems, Germany
N129AT	145076	12322	A-4L		Lonny Ferrin, Houston, TX
N219AT	149502	12827	A-4L		Lonny Ferrin, Houston, TX
N340DK	unknown	-	A-4B	N34DK	Richard Lavanture, Elkhart, IN
N130AT	148446	12639	A-4L		Merle Main Enterprises, Ontario, OR
N148AT	147793	12557	A-4L		Merle Main Enterprises, Ontario, OR
N156AT	148307	12617	A-4C		Merle Main Enterprises, Ontario, OR
N157AT	148316	12626	A-4L		Merle Main Enterprises, Ontario, OR
N203AT	148502	12695	A-4C		Merle Main Enterprises, Ontario, OR
N205AT	148573	12766	A-4C		Merle Main Enterprises, Ontario, OR
N215AT	148602	12795	A-4L		Merle Main Enterprises, Ontario, OR

Wearing a marking that indicates a successful intercept on a Soviet bomber, this A-4C of VSF-1 Det 10 aboard Yorktown *circa 1968-69 has since become N132AT and acquired by ATAC at Newport News, Virginia.*
Author's collection

Reg'n	BuNo	C/n	Model	Previous	Owner
N220AT	149540	12865	A-4C		Merle Main Enterprises, Ontario, OR
N225AT	149555	12880	A-4L		Merle Main Enterprises, Ontario, OR
N226AT	149575	12900	A-4C		Merle Main Enterprises, Ontario, OR
N228AT	149591	12916	A-4L		Merle Main Enterprises, Ontario, OR
N233AT	149620	12945	A-4L		Merle Main Enterprises, Ontario, OR
N235AT	150581	12992	A-4C		Merle Main Enterprises, Ontario, OR
N135AT	147669	12433	A-4L		David Vroom, Tuscon, AZ
N218AT	149500	12825	A-4L		David Vroom, Tuscon, AZ
F-ZVMD	159536	14456	A-4N	N269WL	AVDEF, Nimes, France

Note: the registrations N253WL to N259WL and N270WL are reserved for ATSI

some years to an owner in Wisconsin. The exact uses to which the single-seat aircraft, all J65-engined single-seaters, are to be put are unclear at time of writing.

Skyhawks on Display

The small size of the A-4 and the relative ease of moving them by road without disassembly means that they have been popular display items at museums, Veterans of Foreign Wars (VFW) posts, rest stops, high schools and public parks.

According to data gathered by the Skyhawk Association and the author, approximately 202 Skyhawks are displayed or under restoration for display around the world, sixty of them outside the United States. This is in addition to aircraft in indoor or outdoor storage, notably in Israel and Malaysia and at the time of writing, New Zealand. Thirty-six US states have one or more Skyhawks on display, comprising fourteen A-4As,

Previously registered A-4s

N-Reg	BuNo	C/n	Model	Registered to/notes
N3E	142112	11366	A-4B	Combat Jets Flying Museum, Houston, TX, Jan. 1987-92. Became N41CJ with EAA Aviation Foundation, Oshkosh, WI, 1992-2000.Retired to EAA Museum.
N53996	148571	12764	A-4C	Became N401FS
N401FS	148571	12764	A-4C	US Navy/Flight Systems Inc, Mojave, CA, 1977-1981. On display, Pima County Air and Space Museum
N402FS	149516	12841	A-4L	Flight Systems Inc, Mojave, CA. Static display, RNZAF Museum
N403FS	150586	12997	A-4L	US Navy/Flight Systems Inc, Mojave, CA, 1977-1986. Static Display, MCAS Yuma
N444AV	*		A-4A	Guy Neeley/Advanced Aero Enterprises Inc, Newport Beach, CA, 1986-1987. Crashed California City, CA 4 Jun 87
N5548	142166	11420	A-4A	George Baker Aviation School, Miami**
N900MD	unknown			A-4B US Navy, Long Beach, CA 1975 Reregistered N115MD
N116MD	142116	11370		US Navy, Long Beach, CA
N905MD	142905	11967	A-4B	Douglas, Long Beach, CA c.1977
N21NB	145011	12257	A-4B	Dave Strai ght/Sierra Hotel Inc, Addison, TX, 1988-1989 flew as RAN 011 Damaged 1998. On display Kalamazoo, MI
N2262Z	145131	12377	A-4C	Air Capitol Warbirds. BuNo in doubt. Nose at Kissimmee?
N91KD	unknown		TA-4J	John Dilley/Fort Wayne Air Service, Fort Wayne, IN, 1990-1992.
N263WL	159523	14443	A-4N	ATSI. Crashed Utah 10 May 2003

*The identity 14219 has been quoted for this aircraft, but this does not match any A-4 BuNo or c/n. The aircraft was most likely a composite airframe assembled from parts of several A-4s.
**Still on FAA register as of 2004 but has been static in a technical school since at least 1981

Delivered to Israel in the 1990s but probably never flown in that country, TA-4J 153500 was displayed at the Hatzerim museum but later sold to ATSI and refurbished as N251WL. Author's collection

Requiring some skilful work to represent an early A-4K, the RNZAF Museum's Skyhawk was formerly A-4L 149516 with the US Naval Reserve and N402FS with Flight Systems. It is painted to represent the first Skyhawk lost in New Zealand service in 1974. Author

twenty-four A-4Bs, twenty-seven A-4Cs, four A-4Ls, twenty-three A-4Es, ten A-4Fs, fourteen A-4Ms, two TA-4E/Fs and twenty-two TA-4Js.

A-4s of various models are still in use as ground instructional airframes at naval training schools such as that at Pensacola, Florida. A scrapyard in North Hollywood, Los Angeles has been found to contain a number of A-4Ms. Others are serving out their final duty as targets on bombing ranges in Arizona and for explosives testing in New Mexico.

Skyhawks are on display in all the customer nations except Indonesia and Brazil, plus Japan. In Israel there are at least twenty-six preserved, including some at technical schools. There are nineteen early models at air bases and museums in Argentina, six in Singapore, four in Malaysia, two in New Zealand, two in Kuwait, three ex-US examples in Japan (including an OA-4M), and one in Australia.

It is worth noting that the Australian and New Zealand examples never served xwith their respective air arms, The A-4G on display at Nowra and the A-4K at Wigram being earlier models supplied from the boneyard at Davis-Monthan AFB and converted to represent the appropriate types. The TA-4K at Ohakea, New Zealand is a composite of several airframes supplied to the RNZAF for spare parts, and so represents a 2,961st Skyhawk, although there are in fact several other such composite aircraft in existence.

The last of all the Skyhawks was displayed at El Toro but when that base closed it was moved to Miramar where it is displayed today, as is an A-4C. Author

Skyhawks on Display USA

Model	BuNo	C/n	Location and notes
A-4A	Unknown		Hickey Park, Lemoore, CA
A-4A	137813	10710	National Museum of Naval Aviation, NAS Pensacola, FL
A-4A	137814	10711	Naval Air Weapons Center, China Lake, CA
A-4A	137818	10715	Superior Valley Range, China Lake
A-4A	137826	10723	Estrella Warbirds Museum, Paso Robles, CA
A-4A	139929	11294	USS *Hornet* Museum, Alameda, CA. 'Blue Angels' colours
A-4A	139931	11296	Naval Air Warfare Training Systems Division, Orlando, FL. 'Blue Angels' colours as 154176
A-4A	139947	11312	Octave Chanute Air Museum, Rantoul, IL. 'Blue Angels' colours
A-4A	139956	11321	Naval Air Station Atlanta, GA. NMNA
A-4A	139969	11334	Naval Academy, Annapolis, MD. Marked as A-4B '142176'
A-4B	Unknown		Alameda Point, Alameda, CA
A-4B	Unknown		Planes of Fame, Chino, CA. 'Blue Angels' colours
A-4B	142094	11348	Naval Air Station, Lemoore, CA
A-4B	142100	11354	Naval Air Station, Fallon, NV
A-4B	142105	11359	Veterans of Foreign Wars Post 8076, Hartwell, GA
A-4B	142106	11360	Naval Air Engineering Station, Lakehurst, NJ. NMNA
A-4B	142112	11366	EAA Museum, Oshkosh, WI. Displayed as A-4C 148609
A-4B	142120	11374	Weapons Survivability Lab, China Lake, CA
A-4A	142166	11420	Baker Aviation School, Miami, FL
A-4A	142180	11434	NAS Wildwood Museum, Cape May County Airport, NJ. Folding wings, in 'Blue Angels' colours
A-4A	142219	11473	New England. Air Museum, Windsor Locks, CT
A-4A	142226	11480	Carolinas Historic Aviation Museum, Charlotte, NC
A-4A	142227	11481	Western Museum of Flight, Hawthorne, CA. 'Blue Angels' colours
A-4B	142892	11954	Yankee Air Museum, Chino, CA
A-4B	142928	11990	Pima Air & Space Museum, Tucson, AZ
A-4B	142940	12002	Shea Field Memorial Grove, Weymouth, MA
A-4B	142717	11779	Bee County Court House, Beeville, TX
A-4B	142741	11803	National Vietnam War Museum, Orlando, FL
A-4B	142761	11823	Selfridge ANG Base, Mt Clemens, MI
A-4B	142777	11839	FAA Facility, Nashua, NH

Model	BuNo	C/n	Location and notes
A-4B	142829	11891	Floyd Bennett Field, Brooklyn, NY
A-4B	142833	11895	Intrepid Sea-Air Museum, New York City
A-4B	142834	11896	Ropkey Armor Museum, Indianapolis, IN
A-4B	142848	11910	Veterans Memorial Park, Ewing Township, NJ. NMNA
A-4B	142905	11967	San Diego Aerospace Museum
A-4B	142922	11984	Naval Aviation Museum, Tillamook, OR. Marked '984'
A-4B	142929	11991	USS *Lexington* Museum on the Bay, Corpus Christi, TX. NMNA
A-4B	144930	12176	Proud Bird Restaurant, Aviation Blvd, Los Angeles CA. 'Blue Angels' colours
YA-4C	145067	12313	Plant 42 Heritage Airpark, Palmdale, CA
A-4C	145072	12318	Air Victory Museum, Medford, NJ. NMNA 'Blue Angels' colours
A-4C	145074	12320	Aerospace and Science Museum, Denver CO. NMNA
A-4C	145082	12328	Veterans Century of Sentries Park, Kenner, LA. NMNA
A-4C	145113	12359	Dick Kleberg Park, Kingsville, TX. NMNA
A-4C	145122	12368	Savannah State College, Savannah, GA. NMNA
A-4C	145133	12379	Marine Corps Air Ground Combat Center, 29 Palms, CA
A-4C	145135	12381	Northland Community College, Thief River Falls, MN
A-4C	147702	12466	Pueblo Historic Aircraft Society, Pueblo, CO
A-4L	147708	12472	Aviation Museum of Kentucky, Lexington, KY. NMNA 'Blue Angels' colours
A-4L	147727	12491	Municipal Airport, Porterville, CA
A-4C	147733	12497	Arkansas Air Museum, Fayetteville, AR. NMNA
A-4C	147750	12514	Joint Reserve Base, New Orleans, LA
A-4C	147772	12536	Marine Corps Air Station Beaufort, SC
A-4C	147787	12551	USS *Alabama* Battleship Memorial Park, Mobile, AL. NMNA
A-4C	147788	12552	Air Park, NAS Jacksonville, FL. NMNA
A-4C	148314	12624	National Air & Space Museum Washington, DC
A-4C	148316	12626	Yanks Air Museum, Chino, CA
A-4C	148463	12656	Naval Training Center, Great Lakes, IL
A-4C	148490	12683	I-10 rest stop, Santa Rosa County, FL. 'Blue Angels' colours
A-4C	148492	12685	Marine Corps Air Station Miramar, San Diego, CA
A-4C	Unknown		USS *Midway* museum, San Diego, CA. NMNA Marked as '148517'
A-4C	148571	12764	Pima Air & Space Museum, Tucson, AZ. Ex N401FS
A-4C	148572	12765	Cumberland County High School, Crossville, TN
A-4C	148586	12779	Naval Training Center, San Diego
A-4C	148610	12803	Encinal High School, Alameda, CA
A-4E	148613	12806	Oriskany Memorial Park, Village of Oriskany, NY. NMNA

There are two A-4Es displayed at NAS Key West,Florida in VF-45 markings. This one is 149977 ex VF-45 'Blackbirds', mounted beneath the control tower.

Author

Model	BuNo	C/n	Location and notes
A-4C	149508	12833	Municipal Airport, Covington, TN. Markings suspect
A-4C	149547	12872	Yanks Air Museum, Chino, CA
A-4C	Unknown		Freedom Park Naval Museum, Omaha, NE. Marked as '149618'
A-4L	149623	12948	Patriots Pt. Naval & Maritime Museum, Mt. Pleasant, SC
A-4L	149635	12960	Mid-America Air Museum, Liberal, KS. NMNA
A-4E	149656	12981	National Museum of Naval Aviation, NAS Pensacola, FL
A-4E	149977	13030	Naval Air Station Key West, FL
A-4E	150023	13076	Hawaii Museum of Flying, Kalaeloa Airport, Oahu, HI. NMNA
A-4E	150058	13111	Nauticus National Maritime Center, Norfolk, VA. NMNA 'Blue Angels' colours
A-4E	150076	13129	National Museum of Naval Aviation, NAS Pensacola, FL. 'Blue Angels' colours as A-4F 154180
A-4E	150110	13163	Herlong Airport, Jacksonville, FL
A-4E	150598	13009	New Century Air Center, Olathe, KS. NMNA
A-4E	152080	13468	Marine Corps Air Station, Cherry Point, NC
TA-4E	152102	13490	Armaments & Technology Museum, China Lake, CA.
A-4E	151033	13203	Naval Air Station Key West, FL
A-4E	151036	13206	Veterans Center Lihue, Kauai, HI
A-4E	151038	13208	Yanks Air Museum, Chino, CA
A-4E	151186	13356	Air Park, NAS Oceana, Virginia Beach, VA. NMNA
A-4E	151194	13364	Pacific Coast Air Museum, Santa Rosa, CA. NMNA
A-4E	152061	13449	Hawaii Museum of Flying, Kalaeola Airport, Oahu, HI. NMNA
A-4E	152071	13458	Evergreen Aviation Museum, McMinville, OR
TA-4J	152861	13507	Perryville, MO
TA-4J	152867	13513	Valiant Air Command, Titusville, FL. Ex VC-8 gate guard
TA-4J	153525	13552	Glenn Martin Aviation. Museum, Middle River, MD. VC-8 retired 2003
TA-4J	153678	13616	Air Classics Museum, Sugar Grove, IL
A-4F	154180	13637	Museum of Flight, Seattle, WA
A-4F	154200	13657	Army Airfield Museum, Millville, NJ
A-4F	154207	13664	AMARC, Davis-Monthan AFB, Tucson, AZ
A-4F	154217	13674	National Museum of Naval Aviation, NAS Pensacola, FL. 'Blue Angels' colours
TA-4J	154291	13679	Texas Air Museum, Rio Hondo, TX NMNA

The first Skyhawk built on the production line, 137814 has been displayed on this traffic circle at China Lake, where it spent most if not all of its career, since at least 1965.

Author

TA-4J 159798 was not a genuine 'Blue Angels' A-4, serving with VC-12 and VT-7. Today it is displayed at the 'Blues' winter training ground at El Centro, California.

Author

Model	BuNo	C/n	Location and notes
TA-4J	154332	13720	Western Aerospace Museum, Oakland, CA
TA-4J	154338	13726	NAS Kingsville, Texas
TA-4J	154342	13730	March Field Air Museum, Riverside, CA. VC-8 retired 2003
A-4F	154983	13799	National Museum of Naval Aviation, NAS Pensacola, FL. 'Blue Angels' colours
A-4F	155009	13825	Empire State Aerosciences Museum, Glenville, NY
A-4F	155025	13841	Air Park, Naval Air Station, Fallon, NV. NMNA
A-4F	155027	13843	Quonset Air Museum, North Kingston, RI. NMNA
A-4F	155033	13849	National Museum of Naval Aviation, NAS Pensacola, FL. 'Blue Angels' colours
A-4F	155036	13852	County Airport, Accomack, VA
A-4M	155049	13865	Patuxent Naval Air Museum, MD. Converted A-4F
TA-4J	155076	13892	Texas Air Museum, Rio Hondo, TX
TA-4J	156904	13997	Independent School District, Kingsville, TX
TA-4J	158073	14110	Joint Reserve Base, Fort Worth, TX
TA-4J	158087	14124	Naval Air Station, Corpus Christi, TX. NMNA
TA-4J	158120	14157	Marine Corps Air Station, Cherry Point, NC
TA-4J	158137	14174	USS *Hornet* Museum, Alameda Point, Alameda, CA.VC-8 retired 2003
TA-4J	158106	14143	Navy Test Pilot School, NAS Patuxent River, MD
TA-4F	154639	13757	Aviation High School, Long Island City, NY
TA-4J	154649	13767	Palm Springs Air Museum, Palm Springs,
A-4M	158148	14185	Quonset Air Museum, North Kingston, RI
A-4M	158182	14219	Delaware Valley Hist. Avia. Assn, Willow Grove, PA. NMNA
A-4M	158195	14232	Western Aerospace Museum, Oakland, CA. NMNA
A-4M	158430	14252	MAG-41, Joint Reserve Base, Ft. Worth, TX. NMNA
TA-4J	158490	14295	Mustin Beach Club, NAS Pensacola, FL. NMNA
TA-4J	158526	14331	Naval Air Station, Meridian, MS. NMNA
TA-4J	158716	14337	Combat Air Museum, Forbes Field, Topeka, KS. NMNA
TA-4J	158722	14343	USS *Lexington* Museum on the Bay, Corpus Christi, TX. NMNA
A-4M	159789	14488	Joint Reserve Base, Ft. Worth, TX. NMNA
TA-4J	159798	14497	Naval Air Facility, El Centro, CA. 'Blue Angels' colours
A-4M	160024	14526	Visitor Center, City of Havelock NC
A-4M	160031	14533	At Yanks Air Museum – for display Orange County Civic Center
A-4M	160036	14538	Prairie Aviation Museum, Bloomington, IL
A-4M	160255	14598	Grenada High School, Grenada, MS. NMNA 'Blue Angels' colours
A-4M	160264	14607	Flying Leatherneck Museum, MCAS Miramar, San Diego, CA. Last A-4 built

NMNA = loaned out by National Museum of Naval Aviation

Quite a collection of Skyhawks are or have been displayed (some might say stored) at the Israeli Air Force Museum at Hatzerim Since this picture was taken, A-4E 611 has been refurbished and is displayed at the main part of the museum.
Simon Watson

Skyhawks on display overseas

Derelict and stored aircraft not included

Model	BuNo	C/n	Location	Notes
Argentina				
A-4Q	144882	12128	Museo de la Aviación Naval Bahía Blanca	3-A-302/0655
A-4B	Unknown		Ground instructional BAN Bahía Blanca	Nose only, in USN colours
A-4B	144915	12161	CANA HQ Edificio Libertad, Buenos Aires	3-A-304/0657
A-4B	142757	11819	National Historical Museum, Buenos Aires	C-233
A-4P	142855	11917	Condor Building, Buenos Aires	C-240
A-4B	Unknown		Nose section	Ground trainer 'C-200'
A-4P	142688	11750	Museo Nacional de Aeronautica, Morón	C-207
A-4C	149514	12839	Museo Nacional de Aeronautica, Morón	C-322
A-4C	142803	11865	Ground Instructional, Córdoba	C-225
A-4C	142132	11386	Ezezia Airport	C-224
A-4Q	hybrid	-	Museo Naval de las Nacion, Tigre	'3-A-312'
A-4Q	144872	12118	Tech School, La Matanza, Buenos Aires	3-A-301/0654
A-4P	142749	12011	Grupo V HQ, Villa Reynolds	C-232
A-4C	149564	12889	BAM El Plumerillo, Mendoza	C-314
A-4P	142773	11835	Área de Material, Rio Cuarto	C-212, marked as 'C-204'
A-4P	142752	11814	Museo Tecnológico Aeroespacial, Rio Cuarto	C-222
A-4C	148438	12631	Museo Tecnológico Aeroespacial, Rio Cuarto	C-302
A-4F	composite		Museo Tecnológico Aeroespacial, Rio Cuarto	as A-4M 'C-937'
A-4P	142838	11900	Being restored IMPSA plant, Maipu, Mendoza	C-239,as'C-221'
Australia				
A-4B	142871	11933	Australia's Museum of Flight, Nowra, NSW	marked as A-4G 'N13-154906'
Israel				
A-4E	149964	13017	Israel Air Force Museum, Hatzerim	IDF 891
A-4E	151179	13347	Israel Air Force Museum, Hatzerim	IDF 885
A-4E	150092	13145	Israel Air Force Museum, Hatzerim	IDF 611
A-4H	155254	13949	Israel Air Force Museum, Hatzerim	IDF 222
A-4H	155271	13965	Israel Air Force Museum, Hatzerim	IDF 230
A-4H	155287	13981	Israel Air Force Museum, Hatzerim	IDF 261
A-4H	155289	13983	Israel Air Force Museum, Hatzerim	IDF 270
A-4E	151139	13309	Israel Air Force Museum, Hatzerim	IDF 814
A-4E	152099	13487	Israel Air Force Museum, Hatzerim	IDF 844
A-4E	152050	13438	Israel Air Force Museum, Hatzerim	IDF 854

Model	BuNo	C/n	Location	Notes
A-4N	159816	14515	Israel Air Force Museum, Hatzerim	IDF379
A-4N			Israel Air Force Museum, Hatzerim	IDF 393
A-4N			Israel Air Force Museum, Hatzerim	IDF 407
A-4E	152097	13485	IAF Museum, Hatzerim	IDF 884
A-4E	149994	13047	Haifa Airport collection	IDF 880
A-4H			Haifa Airport collection	IDF 215
A-4H			Haifa Airport collection	IDF 293
A-4E			Hatzor Air Base collection	IDF '01'
A-4N			Ramat David Air Base collection	IDF 328
A-4H			Tech school, Ramat David	IDF 241
A-4E	149984	13037	Holz Technical College	IDF 881
A-4E	149990	13043	Holz Technical College	IDF 887
A-4E	151184	13354	Holz Technical College	IDF 892
A-4E			Holz Technical College	IDF 894
A-4E	150127	13180	Holz Technical College	IDF 895
Japan				
A-4E	151095	13265	Penie Medical Center, Tokushima, Japan.	'Blue Angels' colours
A-4E	151074	13244	U.S. Naval Air Facility, Atsugi, Japan	
OA-4M	154638	13756	Marine Corps Station, Iwakuni, Japan	
Kuwait				
A-4KU	160184	14552	KAF Museum, Kuwait Airport	KAF 805
TA-4KU	160210	14578	KAF Museum, Kuwait Airport	KAF 881
TA-4KU	160211	14579	KAF Museum, Kuwait Airport	KAF 882 (composite using nose of 882)
Singapore				
TA-4S	145047	12293	Nose preserved, Paya Lebar	RSAF 651
TA-4S	144979	12225	SAFTECH, Jurong	RSAF 690
A-4S	142850	11912	Singapore Discovery Centre, Jurong	RSAF 600
A-4S	145013	12259	Singapore AF Museum, Paya Lebar	RSAF 607
A-4S			SAFTECH, Jurong	RSAF 622
A-4S	144956	12202	Tengah HQ as '28'	RSAF 657
A-4S	145059	12305	(AETI), Paya Lebar Air Base	RSAF 683
Malaysia				
TA-4PTM	145103	12349	AF Technical College, Alor Setar	M32-06
A-4PTM			AF Technical College, Alor Setar	
A-4PTM	145078	12898	TUDM Museum, Kuala Lumpur	M32-30
A-4PTM			Kuantan Air Base	
New Zealand				
A-4L	149516	12841	RNZAF Museum, Christchurch	'NZ6207'
TA-4K	-	-	Ohakea Museum, composite airframe	'NZ6257'

Guarding the HQ building at Tengah is A-4S 652 (marked as '28', an auspicious number to the Chinese), as A-4B 144937 it saw combat in Vietnam with VA-152.

Author

APPENDICES

Appendix I: A-4 Chronology

1952

January	Initial meetings between Douglas and BuAer
21 June	XA4D-1 contract awarded
26 July	Design work started
Summer-Fall	Douglas and Navy team visit Korean battlefronts
October	Design frozen. A4D-1 production go-ahead given
November	Prototype construction begins

1953

January	Tooling completed, production parts manufacture begins
February	Service pilots inspect mockup

1954

February	Roll-out of XA4D-1 (134812)
22 June	First flight of XA4D-1 at Edwards AFB
19 July	Construction of new factory at El Segundo begins
14 August	Second XA4D-1 (134813) flies
23 September	Third aircraft (134814) flies
November	New El Segundo factory opens

1955

September	Carrier qualifications conducted aboard USS *Ticonderoga*
29 September	First flight by Navy pilot
15 October	Lt Gordon Gray breaks Class C world 500-km closed-circuit record at 695.163 mph (1,118.7 km/h)
31 October	Weapons carriage trials begin.

1956

26 March	First flight of A4D-2 (A-4B)
9 September	First A4D-1s delivered to VA-72
October	First factory-to-fleet deliveries
October	Initial operating capability (IOC) achieved

1957

January	First Marine unit (VMA-224) operational
1 September	A4D-2 deliveries begin

1958

21 August	A4D-2N (A-4C) first flight

1958/59 Initial studies into a two-seat variant

1960

1 Feb	A4D-2N deliveries begin

1961

February	1,000th A-4 (an A4D-2N) delivered to USN/USMC (likely 148447)
12 July	First flight of A4D-5
December	Last delivery A4D-2N

1962

	IOC of A-4E
18 September	Redesignation of A4D-1 to A-4A, A4D-2 to A-4B, A4D-2N to A-4C and A4D-5 to A-4E.

1963

1 January	A-4E deliveries begin

1964

August	A-4s make first strikes on Vietnam

1965

30 June	First flight of TA-4E
December	First export contract (A-4P)

1966

31 August	A-4F first flight

1967

April	Douglas merges with McDonnell Aircraft Company
July	2,000th Skyhawk (a TA-4F) delivered
19 July	A-4G first flight
7 August	TA-4G first flight
27 October	A-4H first flight

1968

17 December	First flight TA-4J

1969

June	Service entry TA-4J
21 August	First flight A-4L conversion

1970

10 April	First flight A-4M

1971

16 April	First deliveries of A-4M to

	VMA-324 and VMA-331 at MCAS Beaufort, S.C.
	2,500th Skyhawk (A-4M 158156) delivered
1972	
8 June	First flight A-4N
1973	
27 January	USMC A-4E drops last US bomb in Vietnam War
14 June	2,700th Skyhawk (A-4M) delivered
14 July	First flight A-4S
October	Yom Kippur War, Operation Nickel Grass
1974	
	'Blue Angels' exchange F-4J for A-4F
1975	
12 December	Last regular USN attack A-4 squadrons (VA-55, VA-164 and VA-212) disestablished
1976	
20 July	First flight A-4KU
1979	
	Indonesia receives first A-4s
27 February	2,960th and last A-4 delivered (A-4M 160264)
1982	
March-June	Argentine A-4s saw action in South Atlantic
1984	
April	First flight of A-4PTM
July	RAN A-4s sold to RNZAF
1986	
	1,079 A-4s estimated in worldwide service
	Kahu update of RNZAF A-4s began
	'Blue Angels' exchange A-4F for F/A-18A
October	A-4S-1 first flight
1989	
	A-4SU Super Skyhawk enters service with RSAF
1990/91	
	Kuwaiti A-4s used in Gulf War
1993	
	Singapore retires original A-4S models
1994	
	Argentina orders A-4Ms and OA-4Ms
	Malaysia retires most T/A-4PTMs
August	US Marine Corps Reserve (VMA-131) retires A-4M
1997	
	Brazil agrees to purchase Kuwaiti Skyhawks
1998	
August	Argentina receives first refurbished A-4ARs
September	Brazil receives A-4KUs
1999	
	Malaysia retires remaining A-4PTMs
March	Argentine Air Force retires A-4P
July	Training Command A-4 Retirement Ceremony, Pensacola
30 September	Last VT-7 students carrier qualify on TA-4
October	VT-7 retires TA-4J from Training Command
2001	
May	ATSI receives first A-4s
September	BAE Systems receives first A-4Ns
13 December	RNZAF retires Skyhawks
2003	
	AvDef, France acquires first A-4N
2 April	VC-8 disestablishment announced
3 May	Last VC-8 TA-4J delivered to museum (154649 to Palm Springs)
23 August	A-4 retirement ceremony, Oceana
2004	
	Sale of A-4C/Ls stored in Arizona to civil owners

Appendix II: Dimensions and Weights

All A-4s have a span of 27ft 6in (8.38m) and a wing area of 260 sq ft (24.15 m^2)
Wing aspect ratio is 2.91, sweepback is 33 degrees at 25 per cent chord.
Wheel base 12ft (3.66m).
Wheel track 7ft 9.5in (2.37m).
Turning circle 12ft 4in (3.76m).

Model	Length	Height	Empty weight	Max Loaded
XA4D-1	38ft 5in (11.70m)	14ft 11in (4.54m)	8,136lb (3690kg)	14,600lb (6623kg)
A-4A	38ft 5in (11.70m)	14ft 11in (4.54m)	n/k n/k	20,578lb (9334kg)
A-4B/P/Q	38ft 5in (11.70m)	14ft 11in (4.54m)	9,146lb (4149kg)	22,500lb (10,206kg)
A-4C/S	39ft 2in (11.92m)	14ft 11in (4.54m)	9,728lb (4412kg)	22,500lb (10,206kg)
A-4E	40ft 3in (12.28m)	14ft 11in (4.54m)	9,853lb (4469kg)	24,500lb (11,113kg)
A-4F	40ft 3in (12.28m)	14ft 11in (4.54m)	10,448lb (4739kg)	24,500lb (11,113kg)
A-4G	40ft 3in (12.28m)	14ft 11in (4.54m)	10,100lb (4581kg)	27,420lb (12,438kg)
A-4H	40ft 3in (12.28m)	14ft 11in (4.54m)	n/k n/k	n/k n/k
A-4K	40ft 3in (12.28m)	14ft 11in (4.54m)	11,800lb (5352kg)	24,500lb (11,113kg)
A-4L	39ft 2in (11.92m)	14ft 11in (4.54m)	9,728lb (4412kg)	22,500lb (10,206kg)
A-4M	40ft 3in (12.28m)	14ft 11in (4.54m)	10,465lb (4747kg)	24,500lb (11,113kg)
A-4AR	40ft 3in (12.28m)	15ft 3in (4.65 m)	n/k n/k	n/k n/k
A-4N	40ft 3in (12.28m)	14ft 11in (4.54m)	n/k n/k	24,500lb (11113kg)
A-4KU/AF-1	40ft 3in (12.28m)	14ft 11in (4.54m)	n/k n/k	n/k n/k
A-4PTM	39ft 2in (11.92m)	14ft 11in (4.54m)	n/k n/k	n/k n/k
A-4SU	39ft 2in (11.92m)	14ft 11in (4.54m)	10,250lb (4650kg)	22,500lb (10,200kg)
TA-4F	42ft 7in (13.05m)	14ft 11in (4.54m)	10,602lb (4809kg)	24,500lb (11,113kg)
TA-4J	42ft 7in (13.05m)	14ft 11in (4.54m)	n/k n/k	n/k n/k
TA-4K	42ft 7in (13.05m)	14ft 11in (4.54m)	n/k n/k	n/k n/k
TA-4PTM	41ft 6in (12.65m)	14ft 11in (4.54m)	n/k n/k	n/k n/k
TA-4S	40ft 6in (12.34m)	14ft 11in (4.54m)	n/k n/k	n/k n/k
TA-4SU	41ft 8.5in (12.70m)	14ft 11in (4.54m)	n/k n/k	n/k n/k
OA-4M	42ft 7in (13.05m)	15ft 3in (4.65 m)	n/k n/k	n/k n/k
TA-4KU	42ft 7in (13.05m)	15ft 3in (4.65 m)	n/k n/k	n/k n/k

*estimate

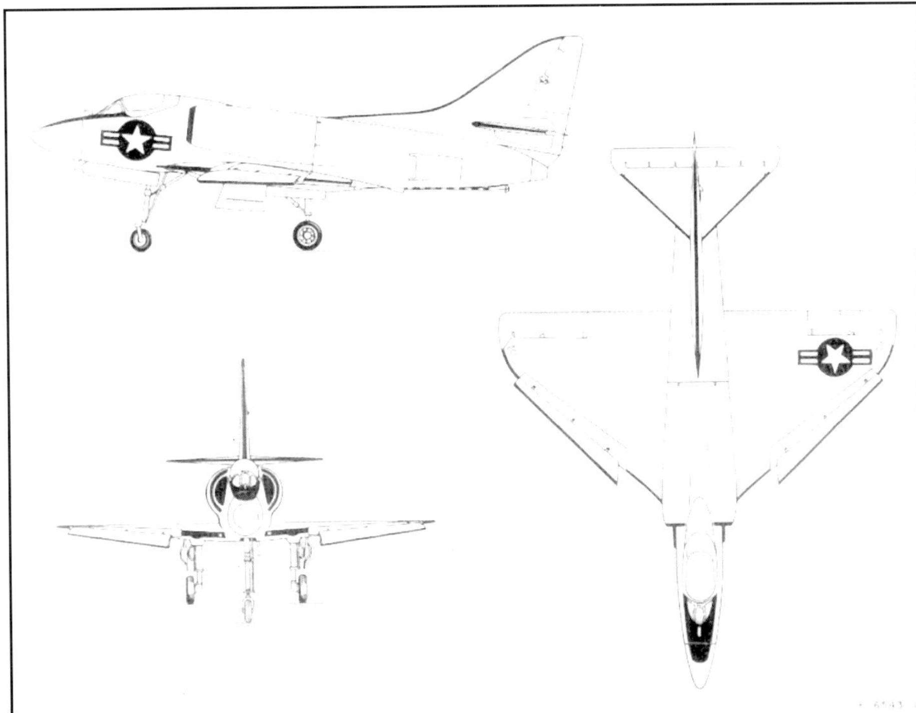

Appendix III: Performance

Note: Where accurate figures cannot be established they have been omitted
C-W = Curtiss-Wright
P&W = Pratt & Whitney
GE = General Electric

Model	Engine	Thrust	Max level speed	Range
XA4D-1	C-W J65-W-4B	7,000lb (31.14kN)	n/k	n/k
A-4A	C-W J65-W-16A	7,200lb (32.03kN)	664mph (1069km/h)	1,298 miles (2089km)
A-4B	C-W J65-W-16A	7,200lb (32.03kN)	661mph (1064km/h)	1,665 miles (2680km)
A-4C	C-W J65-W-16/20	7,700lb (34.25kN)	649mph (1045km/h)	1510 miles (2430km)
A-4E	P&W J52-P6A	8,500lb (37.81kN)	673mph (1083km/h)	n/k
A-4F	P&W J52-P8A/8B	8,500lb (37.81kN)	673mph (1083km/h)	1,995 miles (3211km)
A-4G	P&W J52-P8A	8,500lb (37.81kN)	675mph (1086 km/h)	n/k
A-4H	P&W J52-P8A/8B	8,500lb (37.81kN)	n/k	
A-4K	P&W J52-P8B	8,500lb (37.81kN)	n/k	2,013 miles (3241km)
A-4L	C-W J65-W-20	8,400lb (34.28kN)	649mph (1045km/h)	n/k
A-4M	P&W J52-P408	11,200lb (49.82kN)	673mph (1083km/h)	2057 miles (3310km)
A-4AR	P&W J52-P408	11,200lb (49.82kN)	673mph (1083km/h)	2057 miles (3310km)
A-4N	P&W J52-P408	11,200lb (49.82kN)	n/k	n/k
A-4KU	P&W J52-P408-A	11,200lb (49.82kN)	n/k	n/k
A-4P	C-W J65-W-20	8,400lb (34.28kN)	n/k	n/k
A-4PTM	C-W J65-W-20	8,400lb (34.28kN)	n/k	n/k
A-4Q	C-W J65-W-20	8,400lb (34.28kN)	n/k	n/k
A-4S	C-W J65-W-20	8,400lb (34.28kN)	n/k	n/k
A-4SU	GE F404-GE-100D	10,957lb (48.74kN)	700mph (1128km/h)	1,440miles (2880km)
TA-4F	P&W J52-P8A/8B	9,300lb (41.37kN)	675mph (1086km/h)	1,350 miles (2173km)
TA-4J	P&W J52-P6A	8,500lb (37.81kN)	660mph (1062km/h)	1,350 miles (2173km)
TA-4K	P&W J52-P8A/8B	9,300lb (41.37kN)	n/k	n/k
TA-4PTM	C-W J65-W-20	8,400lb (34.28kN)	n/k	n/k
TA-4S	C-W J65-W-20	8,400lb (34.28kN)	n/k	n/k
TA-4SU	GE F404-GE-100D	10,957lb (48.74kN)	n/k	n/k
OA-4M	P&W J52-P408	11,200lb (49.82kN)	n/k	n/k
TA-4KU	P&W J52-P408	11,200lb (49.82kN)	n/k	n/k

Climb rates

A-4A	9,350ft (2850m) per minute
A-4B	9,100ft (2774m) per minute
A-4C	8,200ft (2499m) per minute
A-4F	10,300ft (3139m) per minute
A-4M	13,500ft (4115m) per minute
A-4N	10,300ft (3139m) per minute
A-4SU	18,500ft (5400m) per minute, officially 10,900ft (3325m) per minute

Appendix IV: Further Reading

Skyhawk titles

- No.3	Douglas A-4 Skyhawk. Famous Airplanes of the World Bunrindo Co., Japan 1987 ISBN 4-89319-002-4
Benedetto, Fernando	A-4B/C in Argentine Air Force Service. Deyseg, Buenos Aires 2002 ISBN-987-20375-0-7
Chesneau, Roger	McDonnell Douglas A-4M Skyhawk Aeroguide 14 Linewrights Ltd, Chipping Ongar UK 1986, ISBN 0-946958-16-5
Dor, Amos	The A-4 Skyhawk 'Ayit'. The IAF Aircraft Series No.2 AD Graphics, Milan, 1999
Drendel, Lou	A-4 Skyhawk in Action. In Action series Squadron Signal, Carrolton, TX, 1973
Elward, Brad	McDonnell Douglas A-4 Skyhawk Crowood Publishing, Marlborough, UK 2000. ISBN 1-86126-340-6
Ewing, Ross	Topped Gun: Requiem for the Skyhawk Old Sausage Publishers, Christchurch, 2002. ISBN 0-473-08560-7
Gann, Harry	The Douglas A-4 Skyhawk Profile Publications Ltd. - Number 102
Gann, Harry S.	A-4 Skyhawk Variants Part 1 Wings of Fame Vol.4 Aerospace Publishing, London 1996
Gann, Harry S.	A-4 Skyhawk Variants Part 2 Wings of Fame Vol.5 Aerospace Publishing, London 1996
Ginter, Steve	Douglas A-4A/B Skyhawk in Navy Service. Naval Fighters Number Forty-Nine Steve Ginter 2001. ISBN 0-942612-49-3
Ginter, Steve	Douglas A-4E/F in Navy Service. Naval Fighters Number Fifty-One Steve Ginter 2001. ISBN 0-942612-51-5
Ginter, Steve	McDonnell Douglas A-4M Skyhawk. Naval Fighters Number Fifty-Five

Steve Ginter 2002. ISBN 0-942612-55-8

Ginter, Steve and Albright, Steven
Douglas A-4E/F in US Marine Service.
Naval Fighters Number Fifty-Two
Steve Ginter 2001.
ISBN 0-942612-52-3

Ginter, Steve and Albright, Steven
USMC/USMCR/USNR Douglas A-4A/B Skyhawk
Naval Fighters Number Fifty Steve Ginter 2002
ISBN 0-942612-50-7

Kilduff, Peter
Douglas A-4 Skyhawk
Osprey Publishing, London 1983.
ISBN 0-85045-529-4

Kinzey, Ray
A-4 Skyhawk in Detail & Scale. D&S Vol.32
TAB Books, California 1989
ISBN 0-85310-609-7

Kinzey, Ray
Colorful US Navy Skyhawks.Colors & Markings series
TAB Books, Blue Ridge Summit, PA 1990 I
SBN 1-85310-625-9

Mafé Huertas, Salvador
A-4 Skyhawk in the Falklands
Wings of Fame Vol. 12
Aerospace Publishing, London 1998

McDowell, Ernest R
McDonnell Douglas A-4A/L Skyhawk in USN, US Marine Corps, Royal Australian Navy & RNZAF Service,
Aircam Aviation Series Number 27
Osprey Publishing Ltd.,Berkshire UK 1971.

Munson, Kenneth
Skyhawk
War Data No.7 Eshel Dramit, Israel.
ISBN 965-256-015-3

Nunez Padin, Jorge F
McDonnell Douglas A-4P/C Skyhawk
Fuerza Aérea Argentina No.2,
Buenos Aires 1997

Peacock, Lindsay
McDonnell Douglas Skyhawk Variants
Warpaint Series No.3, Amersham UK 1978

Peacock, Lindsay
A-4 Skyhawk. Osprey Combat Aircraft Series
Osprey, London 1987.
ISBN 0-85045-817-X

Weiss, Ra'anan and Efrati, Yoav
McDonnell Douglas A-4 Skyhawk
Aircraft of the Israeli Air Force 3
Isradecal Publications, Israel 2001.
ISBN 965-7220-00-9

Wilson, Stewart
Phantom, Hornet and Skyhawk in Australian Service
Aerospace Publications Pty Ltd, Weston Creek, ACT, 1993
ISBN 1 875671 03 X

Other Titles

Burden, Rodney et al
Falklands: The Air War
British Aviation Research Group UK, 1986
ISBN 0-906339-05-7

Donald, David (Ed)
Carrier Aviation Air Power Directory
Airtime Publishing, Norwalk, CT 2001
ISBN 1-880588-42-0

Francillon René J,
McDonnell Douglas Aircraft Since 1920: Volume 1
Putnam, London, 1988.
ISBN 0-85177-827-5

Francillon, René
Tonkin Gulf Yacht Club: U.S. Carrier Operations off Vietnam
Naval Institute Press, Annapolis, 1988.
ISBN 1-85310-008-0

Foster, Captain Wynn F.
Captain Hook; A Pilot's Tragedy and Triumph in the Vietnam War
Naval Institute Press, Annapolis 1992.
ISBN 1-55750-256-0

Heinemann, Edward and Rausa, Rosario
Combat Aircraft Designer: The Ed Heinemann Story.
Macdonald and Jane's, London 1980.
ISBN 0-7106-0040-2

Hewson, Robert (Ed)
Jane's Air Launched Weapons 39th Ed.
Jane's Information Group, Coulsdon, UK 2001.
ISBN 0-7106-0866-7

Hobson, Chris
Vietnam Air Losses
Midland Publishing, Hinckley, UK 2001.
ISBN 1-85780-115-6

Kasulka, Duane — USN Aircraft Carrier Air Units Volume 2, 1957-1963
Squadron Signal, Carrolton, Texas, 1985
ISBN 0-89747-172-5

Kasulka, Duane — USN Aircraft Carrier Air Units Volume 3, 1964-1973
Squadron Signal, Carrolton, Texas, 1988

Levinson, Jeffrey L — Alpha Strike Vietnam: The Navy's Air War 1964 to 1973
Presidio Press, Novato, CA 1989.
ISBN 0-89141-338-3

Marden, Andy (compiler) — USA-Military Out of Service
Mach III Plus, UK 2000.
ISBN 1-898129-52-5

Marden, Andy (compiler) — World Military Out of Service
Mach III Plus, UK 2003.
ISBN 1-898129-84-3

Mersky, Peter — US Marine Corps Aviation
Nautical and Aviation Publishing Annapolis 1983.
ISBN 0-933-852-39-8

Nanson, Sid — Strikes: US Naval and Marine Corps Aviation Attrition 1962-85
Mach III Plus, UK 2003
ISBN 1-898129-85-1

Nichols, John B and Tillman, Barrett
On Yankee Station: The Naval Air War Over Vietnam
Naval Institute Press, Annapolis 1987
ISBN 1-85310-008-0

Norton, Bill — Air War on the Edge: A History of the Israel Air Force and its Aircraft
Midland Publishing, Hinckley, UK 2004.
ISBN 1-85780-088-5

Rahn, Bob with Rausa, Zip — Tempting Fate: An Experimental Test Pilot's Story
Specialty Press, North Branch, Minnesota 1997.
ISBN 0-933424-81-7

Van Waarde, Jan — US Crashes 1950-2002
Scramble Special Edition, 2004

Skyhawk Association Website: www.a4skyhawk@org

INDEX

Page numbers in *italics* refer to illustrations.